PREPARING TEACHERS TO EDUCATE WHOLE STUDENTS

AN INTERNATIONAL COMPARATIVE STUDY

Fernando M. Reimers
Connie K. Chung

EDITORS

HARVARD EDUCATION PRESS
CAMBRIDGE, MASSACHUSETTS

Paperback ISBN 978-1-68253-237-9
Library Edition ISBN 978-1-68253-238-6

Library of Congress Cataloging-in-Publication Data

Names: Reimers, Fernando, editor. | Chung, Connie K., editor.
Title: Preparing teachers to educate whole students : an international comparative study / Fernando M. Reimers, Connie K. Chung, editors.
Description: Cambridge, Massachusetts : Harvard Education Press, [2018] | Includes bibliographical references and index.
Identifiers: LCCN 2018033159| ISBN 9781682532379 (pbk.) | ISBN 9781682532386 (library edition)
Subjects: LCSH: Education and globalization. | Educational leadership. | Educational change. | Educational innovations. | Globalization. | World citizenship. | Education—Aims and objectives.
Classification: LCC LB41 .P7655 2018 | DDC 370.71/1—dc23 LC record available at https://lccn.loc.gov/2018033159

Published by Harvard Education Press,
an imprint of the Harvard Education Publishing Group

Harvard Education Press
8 Story Street
Cambridge, MA 02138

Cover Design: Ciano Design
The typefaces used in this book are Adobe Garamond Pro for text and Colaborate and Myriad Pro for display.

Contents

A Study in How Teachers Learn to Educate Whole Students and How Schools Build the Capacity to Support Them

Fernando M. Reimers
Global Education Innovation Initiative,
Harvard Graduate School of Education

Schools, a remarkable invention to develop human potential, face the challenge of continuously evolving so that they prepare students with the competencies necessary to participate and contribute civically and economically in their societies and, increasingly, across national boundaries. As societies and economies change, so do the competencies required to participate. For this reason, leaders of schools and school systems periodically question the purpose of education.

School leaders need to ask such a question of purpose because the very survival of humanity depends on helping students gain the competencies necessary to care for themselves, to improve their communities, and to address shared local and global challenges. The velocity at which the world is changing places growing demands on what people need to know to participate meaningfully in their communities. Technological developments have brought with them great opportunities to improve human well-being, but also challenges. One challenge is that those who do not have the skills to understand and use these technologies and who lack the competencies necessary for participation in the twenty-first century will be further excluded; another challenge is that those technologies can be used for destabilizing and destructive purposes, for example, eliminating jobs, disrupting politics, or allowing individuals or groups to harm others.[1]

The results are new opportunities, risks, and vulnerabilities, some significant, such as the social instability caused by exclusion and poverty, by the social and economic dislocations resulting from globalization, or by conflicts, environmental degradation, or terrorism. Whether we rise to address these challenges and whether we can advance more inclusive and sustainable progress are questions partly contingent on educational institutions' effectiveness in helping students learn how to act in ways that advance sustainability and well-being for all.

The Sustainable Development Goals, which the United Nations adopted at the Seventieth General Assembly in September 2015, are an aspirational and hopeful vision of a world in which humanity unites to create conditions that enable social progress, peace, and sustainability. The achievement of those goals is contingent on the capabilities and dispositions of most of humanity, as well as on the structures, systems, and processes that undergird the functioning of nation-states and organizations.

Schools *could* help all students develop the capabilities that will prepare them to successfully address these challenges. However, most schools don't do this effectively. To address these global challenges, students should develop an expanded range of cognitive as well as interpersonal and intrapersonal dispositions and competencies, including creative and critical thinking, collaboration, problem-solving and inquiry skills, competence to utilize versatile tools in learning and working, and ability to act in different contexts and to practice sustainable and responsible citizenship.

The Global Education Innovation Initiative (GEII) at the Harvard Graduate School of Education is a collaboration of institutions in several countries committed to supporting the necessary improvements in schools and school systems, particularly in public schools, so they help students develop the dispositions and competencies that will allow them to live good lives and contribute to sustainable development in their communities and the world.

In a previous research project, we synthesized existing knowledge on the competencies necessary for life and participation in the twenty-first century and used a taxonomy based on that synthesis to analyze the national curriculum frameworks of Chile, Colombia, India, Mexico, Singapore, and the United States.[2] We concluded that curricular aspirations had expanded in those countries. While cognitive purposes constituted the greatest focus of those aspirations, they included also the purposes to help students develop the capabilities to collaborate with others and to manage themselves—what some call interpersonal and intrapersonal skills, or social and emotional development.

Another conclusion of *Teaching and Learning for the Twenty-First Century*, the book that resulted from our earlier research, was that teacher professional development was critical to helping translate these curricular aspirations into new opportunities for learning and teaching in classrooms and in schools. We hypothesized that more robust forms of teacher professional development to advance *whole-child education* or *holistic education* would benefit from an integrated theory of the development of these various competencies, from a theory that articulated the nexus of such development of competency and the instructional practices supporting such development, and of how teachers gained the competencies to lead those practices.

To advance knowledge about how to support teachers in gaining the competencies to lead holistic education, we embarked on a new research project, the results of which we present here. In this project, we studied programs that aimed to support teachers in delivering a more holistic education to their students, which transcended the traditional focus on academic achievement to include the development of character and the capacities to collaborate with others. We set out to study how these programs developed the capacities of teachers, school leaders, and other staff to assist students in gaining cognitive, interpersonal, and intrapersonal skills, to educate them holistically. Our goal was to identify how those programs conceptualized the kind of organizational and instructional practices that supported holistic education, how they supported teachers in developing the competencies to engage in such practices, and what organizational conditions in schools and in systems made the programs possible.

We focused this study on programs in Chile, China, Colombia, India, Mexico, Singapore, and the United States. We chose these countries because they have large populations of schoolchildren, because education is an important priority of government, and because in those countries, governments and civil society organizations engage in innovation to increase education's relevance. In addition, we were able to find research partners in each country who were interested in exploring the questions with us, and who had the necessary capacity and resources. In each country, we consulted education leaders to identify potential programs to include in the study. We looked for programs that had a reputation for success, that had achieved a certain scale by reaching a number of schools, and that had been operating for a long time.

This approach and these criteria reflect an epistemological stance recognizing that we can best address important problems in educational practice by studying solutions already tested in practice and often developed by practitioners themselves. This stance drives our interest in finding existing innovative practices, which have already achieved some scale and success, to then study them to identify the underlying principles that account for success, so that further scale and impact are possible.

We see the global community of educational innovators as a rich laboratory for educational practices and design. Comparatively studying some of these innovative practices to understand their commonalities and differences recognizes in each an instantiation of fundamental principles. We can identify these fundamental principles for the benefit of the larger class of innovative practices and programs to which they belong, thereby advancing the reach and impact of efforts to educate students holistically.

In this chapter, we discuss why rethinking the goals and purposes of education requires that we rethink organizational practices as they pertain to professional development. We first review what we mean by twenty-first-century education and twenty-first-century competencies and skills for students. Then we turn to the topic of teacher development. We begin by reviewing what we know about teacher education and existing comparative evidence on the support teachers receive worldwide. We then examine this evidence in light of the aspirations to support students in gaining skills for the future, suggesting some key strands for how teacher professional development will have to evolve. We conclude by asking the questions that guide this study and foreshadowing our key findings.

SUPPORTING TEACHERS AND SCHOOLS FOR TWENTY-FIRST-CENTURY EDUCATION

Toward the end of the twentieth century, many education organizations and leaders reexamined the purposes of education for the new century. They were motivated, in part, by the transformations that technology was bringing to jobs and by the changing skill requirements for economic and social participation. They were motivated also by globalization; the rapid integration of each society with other societies resulting from trade, telecommunication, travel, and migration; and the impact that globalization had in national economies, civic life, and politics. Technological change, innovation, and globalization accelerating at exponential speed and the conclusion of the millennium itself were other causes to pause and consider the goals that education systems should pursue.

Jacques Delors of UNESCO led one such reexamination in a multiyear initiative (1990–1996) of the International Commission on Education for the 21st Century. As a result of roundtables and consultations in all major regions of the world, Delors and a commission of fifteen people from various backgrounds and countries called attention to the development of competencies in four domains: learning to know, learning to do, learning to be, and learning to live together. Their report expanded on the developmental drivers that motivate such an expanded vision for education: globalization, the arrival of the knowledge society, social cohesion, the challenges of inclusion and exclusion, the imperative of gender equality, and the democratic need for participation.

In 1997, the Organisation for Economic Co-operation and Development launched an international program to assess student competencies. The conceptual foundation of that work was a global consultation of experts known as the Definition and Selection of Key Competencies, the DESECO project. The project defined key competencies as using tools interactively, interacting in heterogeneous groups, and acting autonomously. The capacity to use tools interactively comprises using language, symbols, and texts; using knowledge and information; and using technology, all interactively. Interacting in heterogenous groups comprises relating well to others, cooperating, working in teams, and managing and resolving conflicts. The capacity to act autonomously requires forming and conducting life plans and personal projects, and defending and asserting rights, interests, limits, and needs.

In 2012, the National Research Council in the United States analyzed the capacities necessary for life and work and grouped them into three categories: cognitive skills, interpersonal skills, and intrapersonal skills.[3]

During the last two decades, others reported on the competencies necessary for meaningful participation in the twenty-first century, including an emerging interest in the development of socio-emotional competencies in schools and an interest in deep learning.

The World Economic Forum, for example, identified sixteen skills in three broad categories: foundational literacies, competencies, and character qualities. Foundational literacies include literacy, numeracy, scientific literacy, information and communications technology literacy, financial literacy, and cultural and civic literacy. Competencies are the capacity to approach complex challenges, such as critical thinking, creativity, communication, and collaboration. Character qualities include traits such as persistence and adaptability, curiosity and initiative, leadership, and cultural awareness.[4] A recent National Bureau of Economic Research study reports that, in the United States, there are growing returns to social skills, which have so far been unable to automate and therefore complement automation.[5]

According to educational change scholar Michael Fullan and his colleagues, deep learning "changes outcomes . . . the 6Cs of global competencies: character, citizenship, collaboration, communication, creativity, and critical thinking; and it changes learning by focusing on personally and collectively meaningful matters, and by delving into them in a way that alters forever the roles of students, teachers, families, and others."[6] A synthetic presentation of deep learning is what Dennis Shirley calls "achievement with integrity"; integrity refers to educating the whole person, igniting the intrinsic motivation of educators, and awakening the enthusiasm of students for learning.[7]

While there are differences in emphasis and in the number of competencies, these different authors and initiatives broadly agree that the competencies for the twenty-first century include knowledge, the capacity to use knowledge to solve problems, the capacity to collaborate with others, and self-knowledge and the capacity of self-management. Traditionally, the curriculum of public education systems has emphasized knowledge and the skills to use it to solve problems, with less emphasis on self-knowledge and social skills.

The expanded goals of education require rethinking of pedagogy and teaching, which in turn requires rethinking how to support teachers in gaining the competencies to help students master such a broad range of skills.

EXAMINING TEACHER PROFESSIONAL DEVELOPMENT FOR TWENTY-FIRST-CENTURY TEACHING AND LEARNING

Teacher Practice at the Core of Educational Opportunities

Teacher instructional practice provides the core of opportunity for student learning. Learning in schools essentially results from the actions students perform, following the design of sequences and pathways reflected in the curriculum, which their teachers lead or facilitate. An early model of opportunity to learn, which John B. Carroll developed in 1963, proposes that learning is fundamentally the result of interactions between students and teachers, which he termed "instructional quality." The model has generated much empirical research, and hundreds of studies have confirmed the role of the factors and relationships in the model.[8]

Decades of research on teacher quality and school effectiveness underscore that teachers are one of the most important contributors to student learning.[9] Three decades of school effectiveness and school improvement research confirm the importance of quality instructional practice and of teacher preparation and support to student learning. An often-quoted report states that "no education system can exceed the quality of their teachers."[10] In the words of two leading scholars of educational change, "The dynamos of educational change can and should be a system's thousands of teachers and its school leaders."[11] Increasingly, however, teacher quality is understood as the product of systemic supports to the practice of teaching and the profession and not merely as the result of individual attributes or skills of teachers.

Educators and policy makers alike now well understand the importance of quality teachers and teaching. The National Conference of State Legislatures in the United States, for example, drawing on a comparative study of high-performing education systems, has developed a seven-step protocol to build a world-class education system: build an inclusive team and set priorities, study and learn from top performers, create a shared statewide vision, benchmark policies, get started on one piece, work through "messiness," and invest the time.[12] The report identifies four elements of a world-class education system:

> Children come to school ready to learn, and extra support is given to struggling students so that all have the opportunity to achieve high standards . . .
>
> A world-class teaching profession supports a world-class instructional system, where every student has access to highly effective teachers and is expected to succeed . . .
>
> A highly effective, intellectually rigorous system of career and technical education is available to those preferring an applied education . . .
>
> Individual reforms are connected and aligned as parts of a clearly planned and carefully designed comprehensive system.[13]

The National Conference of State Legislatures report, in underscoring the importance of teacher quality, provides the following levers to influence teacher quality: selective teacher recruitment, rigorous initial preparation of licensure, thorough induction, career ladders, a professional work environment, high-quality school leaders, high compensation, and high standards. The report does not examine *how* teachers can improve their skills to be able to teach to a more ambitious and broader conception of instructional goals, such as twenty-first-century competencies.

Similarly, the National Center on Education and the Economy in the United States has synthesized nine building blocks for world-class education systems, drawing on a comparative study of high-performing education systems.[14] The building blocks also recognize the importance of teacher quality, including attention to in-service professional development and emphasis on incentives for continuous learning and school organization to support job-embedded learning. However, this framework also does not analyze in detail what forms of teacher professional development support capacities for twenty-first-century teaching and learning. The nine building blocks mentioned in the report are:

> 1. Provide strong support for children and their families before students arrive at school . . . 2. Provide more resources for at-risk students than for others . . . 3. Develop world-class, highly coherent instructional systems . . . . 4. Create clear gateways for students through the system, set to global standards, with no dead ends . . . 5. Assure an abundant supply of highly qualified teachers . . . 6. Redesign schools to be places in which teachers will be treated as professionals, with incentives and support to continuously improve their professional practice and the performance of their students . . . 7. Create an effective system of career and technical education and training . . . 8. Create a leadership development system that develops leaders at all levels to manage such systems effectively . . . 9. Institute a governance system that has the authority and legitimacy to develop coherent, powerful policies and is capable of implementing them at scale.[15]

Teacher Education, Preparation, and Development

From this recognition of the importance of instructional quality and of the quality of teachers' work follows an interest in teacher education, preparation, and development. Recent scholarship on teacher education highlights the importance of systems to support teachers and, to some extent, challenges the notion of "teacher effectiveness" as an individual attribute, in favor of teaching as a practice situated in a social context. Linda Darling-Hammond and Peter Youngs, for instance, argue that the notion of "highly qualified teachers" reflects a school accountability paradigm whose intention is to compare school and teacher performance.[16] Andy Hargreaves and Michael Fullan propose that education quality is the result of professional capital, which encompasses teachers' individual characteristics (human capital), relationships (social capital), and professional norms (decisional capital).[17] Other scholars challenge the notion of teacher effectiveness that equates instructional quality to students' performance on curriculum-based assessments.[18]

Since most of the empirical research on the effectiveness of teacher education assesses it in terms of its contributions to a limited range of domains in student achievement, typically language, mathematics, and science, some propose an alternative view of teacher quality that focuses on whether teachers have the capacities required to teach, including curriculum planning, teaching and assessment, and ensuring quality.[19] Still a third view of quality focuses on whether teachers practice according to professional standards.[20]

Scholarship on the effectiveness of teacher education and development programs has typically begun by defining the intended outcome of such preparation. Most studies start by defining teacher expertise, including the necessary knowledge, skills, and dispositions. Lee Shulman, for instance, identifies five key domains along which teachers need to develop:

Behavior—effectiveness is evidenced by teacher behavior and student learning outcomes.

Cognition—teachers as intelligent, thoughtful, sentient beings, characterized by intentions, strategies, decisions, and reflections.

Content—the nature and adequacy of teacher knowledge of the substance of the curriculum being taught.

Character—the teachers serve as moral agents, deploying a moral-pedagogical craft.

Knowledge of, and sensitivity to, the cultural, social, and political contexts and the environments of their students.[21]

A synthesis of research on teacher professional development identifies the following skills, knowledge, and dispositions that teachers must have to be effective:

- General pedagogical knowledge
- Subject-matter knowledge
- Pedagogical content knowledge
- Knowledge of student context and their families
- Repertoire of metaphors to bridge theory and practice
- External evaluation of learning
- Clinical training
- Strategies to create and sustain learning environments
- Knowledge, skills, and dispositions to work with students of diverse backgrounds
- Knowledge and attitudes that support social justice
- Knowledge and skills to use technology[22]

Teachers' development is a long-term process spanning their careers. Current research supports the notion that competencies are not fully developed in a single program of teacher education, but rather their development results from a series of structures and opportunities that constitute a continuum of development.[23] Initial teacher preparation, of high quality, is only the first step in a process of career development. This continuum includes how a teacher would be selected into the profession, incentives and respect afforded to the profession, initial preparation, career pathways, induction, and support all along their professional trajectory.[24]

The conceptualization of this continuum underscores the importance of ongoing in-service professional development for teachers. However, evidence also questions the effectiveness of many existing professional development programs. For example, a recent study in three large public school districts and a midsize charter school network in the United States challenges that we know how to help teachers improve. The findings, presented with the provocative title "The Mirage: Confronting the Hard Truth about Our Quest for Teacher Development," show that despite school districts' massive investments in teacher improvement, most teachers do not significantly improve on a range of outcomes, from year to year, and that when they do improve, their growth cannot be attributed to any development strategy.[25] Another recent synthesis of studies on teacher professional development concludes that "[t] here is currently too little robust evidence on the impact of different types of professional development for teachers."[26]

This, of course, does not mean that continuous professional development is irrelevant, only that we need more effective programs and fundamental rethinking about what kind of learning experiences lead to deep changes in teacher practice. Two reviews of the global research literature on teacher professional development concur that much of it is unrelated to the teachers' needs or to the challenges they experience in their current practice in the short term, and often lacks alignment with school curriculum or with intended development trajectories.[27]

A recent comparative study of teacher preparation and development in several high-performing countries characterizes teaching as the product of a system. Such a system results from mutually supportive policies in recruitment, teacher preparation, induction and mentoring, professional learning, teacher feedback and appraisal, and career and leadership development.[28] This study found a common goal in all countries to build a strong teaching profession.

> A professional approach suggests that policy is directed towards the development of a teacher workforce that is highly educated and empowered to make decisions about teaching for the best interests of their students, based on knowledge accumulated from their training and from what they learn about the wisdom of practice from their in-service experiences and sharing of expertise with colleagues.[29]

A recent review of the research literature on teacher professional development identifies ten features of effective professional learning, grouped into three domains: quality content, learning design and implementation, and support and scalability.[30] With respect to quality, effective programs are informed by evidence, focus on subject-specific and pedagogical content knowledge, focus on student outcomes, and offer a balance of teacher voice and system coherence. With respect to learning design and implementation, effective programs depend on active and variable learning, offer collaborative learning experiences, and provide opportunities for job-embedded learning. With respect to support and sustainability, effective programs are ongoing, have adequate resources, and have supportive and engaged leadership.[31] The same report notes an evolution in approaches to teachers' professional development, from learning from external experts to learning from professional reflection on teachers' own work, and concurrently an evolution in understanding schools as learning environments instead of only workplaces.[32]

Teacher Professional Development Today

Many opportunities for in-service professional development are currently available to most teachers. The Organisation for Economic Co-operation and Development (OECD) has conducted two cross-national studies, in 2008 and 2013. The Teaching and Learning International Survey (TALIS) examined teachers' descriptions of their working conditions and the professional support and development they receive.[33] The 2013 OECD report on the results of the TALIS survey, administered to representative samples of the teachers in lower secondary schools and leaders in mainstream schools in twenty-four nations that are members of the OECD and ten additional countries, describes teachers, their working conditions, and their opportunities for professional development. Some critics of the study argue that it has methodological limitations, particularly as a correlational study that does not allow establishment of causal inference; however, it remains one of the only cross-national surveys examining teacher and school leader practices in the world. The report describes the characteristics of teachers, their workplaces, the role of school principals, the kind of professional development activities that teachers participate in, the feedback teachers receive, how teachers spend their time, and what contributes to their job satisfaction. Four countries included in our current study—Chile, Mexico, Singapore, and the United States—also participated in the 2013 TALIS survey; in this chapter I will specifically mention data for those countries, as appropriate.

Given the velocity of social and technological change I described earlier, the demands on teachers will change during their careers. Those changes will require that they develop new skills. When we look at the ages, on average, of the teachers in the countries in the TALIS study, 59 percent are forty or older; 30 percent are over fifty. This suggests that many have been practicing for a long time since completing their initial education. On average, teachers have sixteen years of experience. Given the new demands on schools, such as those created by more ambitious curriculum standards, teachers would benefit from opportunities to develop competencies to construct learning opportunities for their students that can help achieve those aspirations. The age distribution of the teacher labor force in the countries in our study varies; Mexico and the United States have the largest percentages of teachers over age forty (58 percent and 56 percent), whereas in Chile, it is 51 percent, and in Singapore, only 30 percent. There is less variation in the years of teaching experience, suggesting that teachers' careers begin at different ages in these countries. On average, teachers have fifteen years of teaching experience in Chile, sixteen in Mexico, ten in Singapore, and fourteen in the United States. Singapore has distinctly younger teachers, suggesting that they are more likely to have been educated in programs reflecting more recent curricular priorities than teachers in the other countries.

The initial preparation teachers receive is generally at the tertiary level. Most teachers worldwide have completed a degree in a higher education institution; only 2 percent, on average, have not. In Mexico, however, 9 percent have less than a higher education degree, and at the primary level, 19 percent in Mexico have not completed a higher education degree. This suggests that the teachers in Mexico who are not graduates of a tertiary institution are likely to have less knowledge and fewer skills than those who have completed studies in higher education.

Most teachers—90 percent, on average—have completed a teacher education or a training program designed to prepare them to teach. The percentage who were specifically prepared to teach is much lower in Mexico, at 62 percent, compared with 86 percent in Chile, 99 percent in Singapore, or 95 percent in the United States. Not all teachers in lower secondary were prepared specifically to teach their current subjects. On average, 73 percent received subject-specific preparation in the subjects they are teaching, ranging from 61 percent in Chile, and 67 percent in Mexico, to 78 percent in Singapore and the United States. Not all teachers learned subject-specific pedagogy in their preparation program: only 70 percent did, on average, and even fewer participated in programs that included teaching practice, for an average of 67 percent. Most teachers feel prepared to teach the subjects they are teaching: 93 percent, on average, feel well or very well prepared, and although the feeling of preparedness is lower in Mexico at 76 percent, it is 86 percent in Singapore, 96 percent in the United States, and 97 percent in Chile.

Teachers vary also in the characteristics of the students they serve, which creates specific needs for preparation. On average, 21 percent in the TALIS survey work in schools where more than 10 percent of the students' first language differs from the language of instruction. This figure is the same as the OECD average for the United States (22 percent), but higher in Singapore (89 percent), and much lower in Chile (4 percent) or Mexico (3 percent). One in four teachers (26 percent) indicates that they work in schools with more than 10 percent of students with special needs. This figure is much higher in the United States (63 percent), than in Chile (28 percent), Mexico (7 percent), or Singapore (1 percent). The percentage of teachers who work in schools with more than 30 percent of students from disadvantaged homes also varies, with 20 percent on average, but 65 percent in the United States, 55 percent in Chile, 44 percent in Mexico, and 6 percent in Singapore.

While the majority of teachers report having received professional development, most have not received professional development specific to the subject they are teaching, with wide variations among countries, which shows that the professional development teachers received is decontextualized from their specific practice. Among language and literature teachers, the percentage who report they have received specific in-service professional development in the subject they teach averages 30 percent, ranging from 61 percent in the United States, to 12 percent in Chile, 27 percent in Mexico, and 50 percent in Singapore. Among mathematics teachers, 27 percent have received specific professional development, ranging from 43 percent in the United States, 46 percent in Singapore, to 12 percent in Chile, and 31 percent in Mexico. For science teachers, 26 percent have received specific professional development, ranging from 46 percent in Singapore, 36 percent in the United States, to 14 percent in Chile, and 25 percent in Mexico.

While teachers do have many professional development opportunities available, these don't help them address their needs of practice, suggested by the fact that principals identify inadequate teaching practice as a factor constraining the opportunity for students to learn in many areas. For example, the TALIS survey interviewed school principals about the factors that they considered were hindering the schools' capacity to offer quality instruction. Of all factors mentioned, the shortage of qualified or well-performing teachers and the shortage of teachers with competencies in teaching students with special needs were the most frequent. The percentage of principals who replied that the shortage of qualified teachers hindered school quality was 38 percent, on average, and ranged from 57 percent in Chile, 56 percent in Mexico, to 51 percent in Singapore, and 34 percent in the United States. The percentage who mentioned the shortage of teachers with competencies in teaching students with special needs, 48 percent on average, ranged from 52 percent in Chile to 58 percent in Mexico, 48 percent in Singapore, and 33 percent in the United States.

In summary, even though most teachers in the TALIS survey graduated from institutions of higher education and received some form of initial preparation, school principals indicate that one of the most important factors constraining the quality of instruction in their schools is the lack of well-qualified teachers. The explanation for this apparent contradiction is likely the varying quality of teacher preparation and higher education programs, the fact that many teachers are teaching outside the fields for which they were prepared, and the fact that professional development is, as established in the scholarly literature on teacher education, a long-term process where initial education needs support from continued opportunities for skill development; most professional development opportunities do not honor this continuum to build professional efficacy. Given the long-term nature of teachers' professional commitment, ongoing support to develop their skills is necessary.

Multiple forms of professional development are available to teachers, and most find the modalities they participate in valuable in terms of impact on their practice. Most teachers, 88 percent on average, participated in some professional development the year before their TALIS interview. This figure is 72 percent in Chile, 96 percent in Mexico, 98 percent in Singapore, and 95 percent in the United States. The most frequent forms of professional development are courses or workshops (71 percent had participated in one such course, on average), followed by conferences (44 percent). Less frequent are observation visits to schools (19 percent), observation visits to other organizations (13 percent), in-service courses in other organizations (14 percent), degree programs (18 percent), participating in professional development networks of teachers (37 percent), individual or collaborative research projects (31 percent), or mentoring, peer observation, or coaching (30 percent).

Table 1.1 summarizes the percentage of teachers who participate in various professional development programs in the countries we studied. Fewer teachers in Chile report participating in these various forms of professional development than teachers in other countries; proportionately more teachers in Singapore have access to the various modalities of professional development.

Teachers also have less frequent access to school-based professional development than courses or participation in conferences.

The content of professional development tends to focus on subject-matter knowledge and pedagogy, with relatively less attention to domains of practice that can help teachers personalize learning for students or cultivate holistic education. Table 1.2 summarizes the focus of the professional development teachers receive, and their appreciation of the impact such development had on their practice. Most teachers participate in professional development focusing on knowledge of subject matter (73 percent, on average) and pedagogical competencies to teach those subjects (68 percent, on average), and most value those opportunities as having a positive impact on their practice. Fewer teachers (56 percent, on average) participate in professional development covering knowledge of the curriculum. This figure is lower in Chile (55 percent) and the United States (66 percent) than in Mexico (90 percent) or Singapore (80 percent). For those who participate in such programs, this professional development is valuable. A little over half (57 percent) of the teachers participate in teacher professional development focused on student evaluation, and those who do consider it valuable. Even fewer teachers participate in classroom management programs (44 percent).

A much smaller percentage of teachers participate in programs that would prepare them to personalize learning, such as those covering approaches to individual learning (41 percent), use of technology in teaching (54 percent), teaching students with special needs (32 percent), and teaching in a multicultural setting (16 percent). Similarly, very few teachers participate in programs explicitly related to interdisciplinary teaching or teaching in ways that relate to future work or studies. In addition to the opportunities to gain knowledge, perspective, and skills afforded by conferences, visits to other schools or organizations, training courses, or collaborations with networks of teachers in other schools, teachers can learn on the job in ways that directly improve their practice. The results from the TALIS survey presented in table 1.2 show that most teachers have very few opportunities to be mentored in their school, with the exception of Singapore, where two-thirds are in schools where there is formal mentoring and coaching.

There is wide variation across countries in the percentage of teachers who have access to formal induction programs. On average, 49 percent report hav-

TABLE 1.1   Modalities of professional development available to teachers as reported in the TALIS survey (percentage of teachers who report that they have participated in each modality)

	Average	Chile	Mexico	Singapore	United States
Courses/workshops	71	55	90	93	84
Education conferences or seminars where teachers and/or researchers present their research results and discuss educational issues	44	30	39	61	49
Observation visits to other schools	19	9	11	24	13
Observation visits to business premises, public organizations, NGOs	13	9	12	21	7
In-service training courses in business premises, public organizations, NGOs	14	8	19	17	15
Qualification program (e.g., a degree program)	18	17	43	10	16
Participation in a network of teachers formed specifically for the professional development of teachers	37	22	41	53	47
Individual or collaborative research on a topic of interest to the teacher	31	33	49	45	41
Mentoring and/or peer observation and coaching, as part of a formal school arrangement	29	14	21	65	32

Source: Organisation for Economic Co-operation and Development, TALIS 2013 results: An international perspective on teaching and learning (Paris: OECD, 2014).

ing participated in an induction program. Singapore stands out for providing induction to most of its teachers (80 percent), in contrast to Chile, where only 37 percent participate in induction programs. In Mexico, only 57 percent do, and in the United States, only 59 percent do.

Mentoring, another process to support school-based professional development, is available to teachers in varying degrees. Some schools offer mentoring to some or all teachers, but just as many schools offer no mentoring. One in five teachers (26 percent), on average, is in a school where principals report no access to a mentoring system. Singapore consistently provides mentoring

Table 1.2   Participation in professional development opportunities to personalize learning (percentage of teachers who participate in each modality)

		Average	Chile	Mexico	Singapore	United States
Knowledge and under-standing of subject field(s)	Percentage of teachers	73	68	88	88	70
	Moderate or large positive impact	91	94	95	89	83
Pedagogical compe-tencies in teaching subject field(s)	Percentage of teachers	68	65	89	86	61
	Moderate or large positive impact	87	92	93	87	77
Knowledge of the curriculum	Percentage of teachers	56	55	90	80	66
	Moderate or large positive impact	84	86	91	87	78
Student evalua-tion and assessment practices	Percentage of teachers	57	52	81	70	72
	Moderate or large positive impact	83	87	88	84	72
Student behav-ior and classroom management	Percentage of teachers	44	41	67	45	38
	Moderate or large positive impact	81	91	88	79	67
Approaches to individ-ual learning	Percentage of teachers	41	33	54	39	58
	Moderate or large positive impact	80	89	82	75	69
ICT skills for teaching	Percentage of teachers	54	51	73	68	49
	Moderate or large positive impact	80	87	84	73	73
Teaching students with special needs[2]	Percentage of teachers	32	33	29	23	39
	Moderate or large positive impact	77	87	67	70	67
Teaching in a multi-cultural or multilingual setting	Percentage of teachers	16	18	27	19	24
	Moderate or large positive impact	77	84	77	75	61
Teaching cross-curricular skills (e.g., problem solving, learning-to-learn)	Percentage of teachers	38	46	67	36	50
	Moderate or large positive impact	80	92	85	75	64

		Average	Chile	Mexico	Singapore	United States
Approaches to developing cross-occupational competencies for future work or future studies	Percentage of teachers	21	29	39	17	17
	Moderate or large positive impact	79	91	83	74	69
New technologies in the workplace	Percentage of teachers	40	38	55	40	57
	Moderate or large positive impact	79	86	81	69	73
Student career guidance and counselling	Percentage of teachers	24	30	42	29	11
	Moderate or large positive impact	80	88	82	69	65
School management and administration	Percentage of teachers	18	26	36	33	16
	Moderate or large positive impact	76	85	75	72	64

Source: Organisation for Economic Co-operation and Development, *TALIS 2013 results: An international perspective on teaching and learning*, (Paris: OECD, 2014).

to most teachers, as only 1 percent are in schools with no mentoring, followed by the United States, where only 7 percent are in schools were mentoring is not available. Most teachers lack access to mentoring in Chile (74 percent) and Mexico (60 percent).

In the schools with available mentoring, it may only be for new teachers, for teachers new to the school, or for all teachers. On average, 27 percent of the teachers are in schools where mentoring is available only to those who are new to teaching; this figure is 2 percent in Chile, 8 percent in Mexico, 21 percent in Singapore, and 30 percent in the United States. On average, 22 percent are in schools where mentoring is available to all teachers who are new to the school, varying from 14 percent in Chile, 7 percent in Mexico, 47 percent in Singapore, and 45 percent in the United States. Finally, 25 percent, on average, are in schools where mentoring is available to all the teachers. This figure is 10 percent in Chile, 24 percent in Mexico, 32 percent in Singapore, and 18 percent in the United States. However, programs aren't always arranged so that the mentor teachers work in the same subject as the person they are mentoring. On average, only 68 percent report this is the case most of the time. This figure is 50 percent in Chile, 55 percent in Mexico, 86 percent in Singapore, and 71 percent in the United States.

Principals' survey responses document a wide variation in the extent to which teachers work in well-aligned and supportive school cultures. When asked whether teachers share common beliefs about schooling and learning, 87 percent of the principals agreed, on average, but this figure is much lower in Mexico (66 percent) than in Chile (91 percent), Singapore (97 percent), or the United States (98 percent). Other indicators of the professional climate in the school include whether there are open discussions among staff about difficulties, mutual respect for colleagues' ideas, a culture of sharing success, and cooperation between the school and the community. On average, 93 percent of the principals report open discussions about difficult issues, ranging from 96 percent in Chile, 96 percent in Singapore, 88 percent in Mexico, and 83 percent in the United States. Respect for the ideas of colleagues averages 93 percent, ranging from 90 percent in Chile, 92 percent in Mexico, 99 percent in Singapore, and 93 percent in the United States. The culture of sharing success averages 90 percent, ranging from 88 percent in Chile, 87 percent in Mexico, 97 percent in Singapore, and 89 percent in the United States. Cooperation with the community averages 75 percent, ranging from 71 percent in Chile, 70 percent in Mexico, 86 percent in Singapore, and 83 percent in the United States.

Most teachers take responsibility for developing students, as reflected in the percentage who indicate that most students in the school believe that students' well-being is important (97 percent, on average). Most teachers also respect their students, as most indicate that the majority in their school are interested in what students have to say (92 percent, on average) and most (91 percent) state that if a student needs extra assistance, the school provides it. Most teachers (95 percent) and principals (98 percent) report that relationships between students and teachers are good. In spite of the apparent priority teachers and principals give to the well-being of students, there is wide variation across countries in the percentage of students enrolled in schools where teachers agree that the socio-emotional development of students is their responsibility, as seen in figure 1.1.

School leaders can play a very important role creating conditions that foster organizational learning and teacher professional development. On aver-

FIGURE 1.1   Reporting percentage of students in schools where there is agreement in socio-emotional development as a priority for teachers

Percentage of students

Source: Organisation for Economic Co-operation and Development, *TALIS 2013 results: An international perspective on teaching and learning* (Paris: OECD, 2014).

age, principals report spending about 21 percent of their time in curriculum and teaching-related tasks and meetings, with the balance in administrative tasks (41 percent), student interactions (15 percent), interactions with parents (11 percent), and interactions with community members (7 percent). There are variations across countries and schools in how principals exercise their leadership, but the time they devote to instructional leadership is consistent across countries. On average, the percentage of time principals spend in curriculum and teaching-related tasks is 27 percent in Chile, 22 percent in Mexico, 22 percent in Singapore, and 25 percent in the United States.

Principals deploy a range of strategies for instructional leadership. Most collaborate with teachers in addressing disciplinary issues (68 percent on average). This figure is 80 percent in Chile, 75 percent in Mexico, 64 percent in Singapore, and 79 percent in the United States. Only one in two observe classroom instruction: this figure is 72 percent in Chile, 64 percent in Mexico, 59 percent in Singapore, and 79 percent in the United States. About two-thirds actively promote cooperation among teachers to develop new practices: this figure is 85 percent in Chile, 72 percent in Mexico, 65 percent in Singapore, and 75 percent in the United States. Over two-thirds (69 percent) encourage teachers to take responsibility for their own professional development: Chile, 88 percent; Mexico, 75 percent; Singapore, 84 percent; and United States, 78 percent. Three in four principals encourage teachers to take responsibility in regard to student learning outcomes; specifically, this figure is in Chile (93 percent), Mexico (86 percent), Singapore (91 percent), and United States (87 percent).

Most principals have a plan to achieve school goals and have created a professional development plan for the school. The percentage of principals who reported that they used student performance results to develop the school's goals and programs is 89 percent on average, and 86 percent in Chile, 96 percent in Mexico, 99 percent in Singapore, and 95 percent in the United States. The principals who worked on a professional development plan for the school is 79 percent on average, and 78 percent in Chile, 86 percent in Mexico, 99 percent in Singapore, and 94 percent in the United States.

Effective Teacher In-service Professional Development

Emerging research on teacher professional development underscores that teachers have different needs at various points of their professional trajectories and highlights the importance of understanding teachers' work as socially situated, and of the power of peers and school networks.[34] Teachers learn from their peers, and those with more supportive peers become more effective.[35] Novice teachers increase their effectiveness more rapidly when they have skilled colleagues teaching in the same grade or when they have opportunities to learn from colleagues in their schools.[36] This research also highlights the importance of networks of schools in supporting teacher improvement, and teachers who do their initial education practicums in schools with less developed support networks are less effective upon graduation.[37] Teacher development is also contingent on the conditions of the schools in which they teach, and teacher improvement is greater in more effective schools.[38] This scholarship on the socially situated nature of teaching underscores the significance of professional development that is tightly coupled with teacher practice and with the contexts in which they work. This scholarship builds on the idea that much adult learning takes place in contexts of practice; various studies confirm the effectiveness of communities of practice, teacher networks, and professional learning communities.[39]

The research highlights that professional development must respond to teachers' needs. Their needs are a function of the demands they must meet, as reflected in policy directives, for example, their students' requirements and their own gaps in knowledge and skills, which are a function of their prior education. The adequacy of professional development is context specific on those dimensions. The needs for development are different for teachers with varying levels of educational attainment and initial preparation, for those with varying years of professional experience, and for those serving different populations of students.

Emerging views of teacher professional development conceptualize quality not as an individual production, but as a team sport. Andy Hargreaves and Michael T. O'Connor define it as collaborative professionalism, which is "how teachers and other educators transform teaching and learning together to work with all students to develop fulfilling lives of meaning, purpose, and success."[40]

Paradoxically, the significant clarity regarding the importance of supporting teaching quality along a continuum of professional development and the knowledge of what policies can support it have not translated into adequate opportunities for students to develop the competencies they need to thrive in the twenty-first century. Far too many schools miss opportunities every day to empower students with the competencies necessary to become architects of their own lives and contributing members of their communities. The Organisation of Economic Co-operation and Development has, since 2000, worked with a growing number of countries assessing higher-order skills in language, mathematics, and science of fifteen-year-olds who are enrolled in school. The results of the Programme for International Student Assessment (PISA) show that many students fail to gain essential competencies to participate civically and economically, and document very wide disparities in the competencies students from different socioeconomic backgrounds demonstrate.[41]

Many of these missed opportunities are the direct result of inadequate and ineffective teaching. In many countries, teachers have not been well prepared and are inadequately supported. These limitations will be compounded as countries embrace more ambitious curriculum standards if the continuum of teacher professional development is not aligned with expanding aspirations. Advancing knowledge of how to design a professional development continuum, aligned with making education relevant and motivating, and empowering teachers and students to transform schools and classrooms into twenty-first-century learning institutions, is essential. The purpose of this book is to advance knowledge about the forms of preparation that support teachers in leading instructional practices in order to help students develop competencies, concurrently, in the cognitive, intrapersonal, and interpersonal domains.

OVERVIEW AND KEY THEMES

We conclude that teacher professional development is critical to translating curricular aspirations about twenty-first-century competencies into new teaching and learning practices in schools. We identify and study programs in various countries that have successfully transformed the culture of schools and instructional practices to advance multidimensional education, addressing cognitive, emotional, and social domains. The research team in each country participating in the consortium mapped the programs that they recognized as effective in advancing twenty-first-century education and selected one that had achieved sufficient scale, maturity, and stability for study. We developed research questions and instruments to conduct interviews and examine documents for an analysis of the program as the participants experienced it.

Our overarching goals are to understand the ways these programs support the development of teacher capacity to lead twenty-first-century pedagogies, advancing deeper learning and personalization. The following chapters focus on uncovering the theories of change in these organizations and on studying the operation of the programs in practice. Our main goal is to discern how support for teachers equips them with the skills and dispositions to translate curriculum into twenty-first-century pedagogy.

Importantly, we focus on analyzing the theory of change of each program, understanding how it plays out in its implementation and gaining a deep sense of the lived experience of the student and of the teacher, staff, and school or system leaders participating in the program. We provide information on evaluations of the results and outcomes of each program when available, but evaluating the fidelity of the implementation as each program has scaled and its effectiveness through rigorous experimental designs is beyond the scope of our study. While we believe that such analysis is valuable, our focus here remains on uncovering *how* organizations, schools, and teachers implement twenty-first-century education within programs that have already scaled; we think that rich and valuable information appears in this analysis.

Additionally, our unit of analysis remains at the program level. While we drew the programs examined from the full range of countries involved in the Global Education Innovation Initiative, even within these countries, there may be a variety of social, cultural, economic, and other diversity such that we cannot extrapolate the learnings from these programs to the country level. Rather, we consider that the most valuable lessons from our analysis will be in understanding how different *programs* in a variety of contexts can support teachers in bringing twenty-first-century education to life.

Given our belief that twenty-first-century competencies can be fostered in a variety of curricula and approaches, we intentionally did not set out to select programs that were similar in approaches (e.g., all science programs, or all civic education programs). As a result, the programs cover various approaches, such as an inquiry-based science program, a program to introduce technology to support deeper learning, a life skills curriculum, among others. The programs vary also in terms of whether they focus primarily on developing teacher or principal capacity or whether they are whole-school reform programs.

In chapter 2, "Providing Relevant Twenty-First-Century Science Education for All Students: A Case Study of the Chilean Inquiry-Based Science Education Program," Liliana Morawietz and Cristián Bellei analyze an inquiry-based science education program implemented in Chile since the early 2000s. The program advances a range of twenty-first-century competencies, as well as scientific literacy through a multidimensional intervention. The latter encompasses a highly structured, activity-based science curriculum supported with an intensive, immersive program of professional development for teachers and school administrators, frequent periodic coaching of teachers provided by a university-based consortium of scientists, in-school support of a master teacher, and professional communities across schools in a network supported by the program. In a context of abundant teacher professional development, but apparently too theoretical and disconnected from instructional practice, the chapter illustrates the benefits of a multidimensional strategy for professional development with clear guidance and support to teachers, aligned with the national curriculum, as well as the value of instructional materials aligned with the lesson plans. Existing evidence about the impact of this program shows that it is positive, although the intensity of resources required for support have subjected it to the vagaries of political change.

In chapter 3, "Building the Capacity for Twenty-First-Century Education: A Study of China's Qingyang School District," Xueqin Jiang and Zhijuan Ma analyze the experience of a district selected as an experimental zone by China's National Institute of Education Sciences. Qingyang District has more governance freedom than most districts in China, which it has used to advance system transformation to promote educational excellence and creativity among students, metacognitive skills, citizenship, and emotional regulation. The strategy to achieve these goals included professionalizing teaching and school leadership. The district relies on a Teacher Talent Center to build learning communities within the district, and to move high-performing teachers to low-performing schools and build professional teaching networks. The district also promotes to leadership positions those individuals who demonstrate excellence as classroom teachers and supports the professional development and growth mind-set of teachers and staff. Two key resources in advancing this strategy were multipronged, district-based, teacher professional development and ongoing student and school assessment to identify improvement targets. These efforts aim at valuing teachers as professionals, creating a risk-taking culture, and supporting continuous collaboration and learning together among teachers. The district supports professional development through various mechanisms, including clusters of schools that collaborate in pedagogy and teacher education, partnerships in which high-performing schools help turn around a low-performing school, and alliances in which schools share resources and expertise. This chapter highlights the powerful effects of transforming the culture of education in an entire district, and how to align this work with a compelling vision for economic and social development.

In chapter 4, "An Inclusive, Whole-School, and Sustainable Approach to Building Teachers' Capacity to Promote Twenty-First-Century Skills: Lessons Learned from the Public-Private Partnership of Escuela Activa Urbana in Manizales, Colombia," Silvia Diazgranados Ferráns, Luis Felipe Martínez, and María Figueroa discuss a whole-school reform program to develop twenty-first-century skills in high-poverty schools. The program promotes active learning, student participation, and autonomy through a series of strategies and instruments, including student-learning guides to enable personalized learning, flexible seating arrangements, project-based learning, self-assessment, and school and classroom student governments. The program also depends on school-based professional development provided by communities of learning in the school, which emphasizes supporting student-centered learning and personalization. The program benefits from a supportive policy framework that specifies the development of citizenship competencies as intended goals of the curriculum. Those include cognitive skills such as decision making, problem solving, and creativity; relational competencies such as leadership, teamwork, communication, and environmental responsibility; management skills including information management and technological management; and personal and socio-emotional skills such as empathy, appreciation for difference, and inclusion. A partnership between a nongovernmental organization (NGO), a foundation, and local government has implemented the program. A well-developed theory of change undergirds the program, which specifies how professional development will produce changes in the school culture and build capacities to support the development of twenty-first-century skills among students aligned with the societal goals of peace, inclusion, and democratic life.

In chapter 5, "Developing Life Skills in Children: A Study of India's Dream-a-Dream Program," Aditya Natraj and Monal Jayaram study an organization that supports the development of life skills of children from disadvantaged backgrounds and has reached approximately ten thousand children directly and around eighty thousand children indirectly. Dream-a-Dream offers an experiential teacher development program that cultivates teachers' mind-sets about the conditions in which their students can develop twenty-first-century learning, and the skills to become a facilitator of learning rather than "a sage in the stage." The program also fosters teachers' innovative capacities to develop solutions to the instructional challenges they face in personalizing instruction. The teacher development program is anchored in a creative community model that promotes using the arts to motivate learners to develop creativity, personal power, cross-cultural competency, and skills for leading purposeful lives, through methods like asking questions, reflecting on actions, and visioning.

In chapter 6, "Developing Twenty-First-Century Competencies in Mexico: How UNETE and School Communities Broaden the Goals of Education by Using Educational Technology," Sergio Cárdenas, Roberto Arriaga, and Francisco Cabrera analyze the professional development approach of UNETE, an NGO created in 1999 to introduce technology to students in public schools that evolved to support the development of twenty-first-century competencies. This model integrates a school-based approach to improvement that provides technology to teachers, professional development on using technology in the classroom, and access to professional development through technology. Coaches work in schools developing participatory school improvement plans, which align school-based coaching with improvement needs that teachers identify. The program aims to help students gain technological literacy and advanced cognitive skills and to develop their character and social skills. Its multidimensional strategy integrates providing technology to support students' engagement and motivation to learn, supporting teacher professional development through in-school and out-of-school coaches and professional learning communities, and providing technological resources for teachers to support personalized instruction. The chapter illustrates how a learning organizational culture can help adapt and refine an organization's theory of action to make it more relevant to the needs and conditions of the schools it serves.

In chapter 7, "Creating Cultures of Learning in the Twenty-First Century: A Study of EL Education in the United States," Connie K. Chung analyzes the multidimensional approach of EL in developing teachers' and principals' capacities that help students gain relevant, rigorous, and relational competencies. EL's longest established program involves working directly with a network of 152 schools in 30 different states. The organization has a multipronged approach to providing in-school and out-of-school professional development, building professional communities and networks, and reenvisioning roles to achieve those goals. A more recent program has developed a high-quality curriculum and videos of pedagogical practices to teach such a curriculum, aligned with the Common Core, delivered online free of charge. It explicitly seeks to cultivate cognitive as well as interpersonal skills and character traits among staff. Its theory of action involves a clear vision and mission communicated to the schools it works with, capacity building and construction of school cultures aligned with that vision, and support in the development of a culture of learning in the schools it works with.

In chapter 8, "Working in Times of Uncertainty to Prepare for the Future: A Study of Singapore's Leaders in Education Program," Oon-Seng Tan and Ee-Ling Low analyze one of Singapore's key programs to advance twenty-first-century education, an immersive program of professional development for school principals. The Leaders in Education Program is a six-month, intensive, cohort-based program that combines a range of learning opportunities to develop adaptive leadership capacities with a practicum in a placement site chosen to support the development of leadership without authority. It is delivered at the National Institute of Education, Singapore's sole institution of teacher and principal initial education and professional development. It aligns with the twenty-first-century competencies framework Singapore's Ministry of Education has adopted to educate students as confident persons, self-directed learners, concerned citizens, and active contributors. The program develops competencies in civic literacy, cross-cultural skills, critical and inventive thinking, communication, collaboration, and information skills. The development model for principals aims to prepare candidates for five roles: leading learning, leading culture, leading change, leading people, and leading nationally. These roles then translate into specific competencies that principal candidates are expected to develop, such as the capacity to formulate, communicate, and disseminate a clear mission and vision, the capacities to deploy various strategies of school development, and contextual and organizational awareness, among others. The program is based on a theory of change that balances the development of capacities in aligning an education philosophy to a model of practice. The capacities reflect on the results of implementing such models and refine them to make them contextually relevant and effective. This program of leadership development builds on the foundation established for human resource development of education professionals in Singapore, which provides each teacher ongoing development, feedback, and work experience in highly professional contexts. The candidates nominated for this program bring a strong foundation of teaching and instructional leadership, as well as demonstrated leadership potential.

The concluding chapter discusses the common themes emerging from each case study and relates them to the larger body of research discussed in this introductory chapter. The chapters underscore the following eleven key themes about promising practices in supporting the development of teachers' and leaders' capacities to advance twenty-first-century education:

- *The professional development programs reflect a conception of adult learning as socially situated and responding to current needs of teachers for learning.* This starkly contrasts with the kind of professional development programs available to most teachers, as we saw in the results of the TALIS study. The programs studieed here aim to develop teachers' capacities to address needs they have identified for themselves, and to influence not only individual capabilities, but the social context of schools by including many adults whose roles intersect, such as various teachers, school administrators, and occasionally administrators outside the school.

- *This form of professional development involves sustained, extensive opportunities for teachers to build capacities, during an entire school year or spanning multiple school years,* that contrasts with the more prevalent opportunities of short courses out of the school. None of the programs examined in this book are short courses or workshops, although short courses may be part of a larger portfolio of opportunities. The programs recognize that teachers' careers develop alongside trajectories and that professional development is a staged process through which individuals advance. These trajectories may or may not exist as formal structures in the systems where these programs operate.

- *The modalities of professional development examined in this book vary.* They include independent study of new material, discussion with peers and others, individual or group coaching, demonstrations of new practices, independent research projects, and opportunities for reflection.
- *The curriculum of the programs covers a blend of capacities, from a broad focus on helping students develop capacities to a highly granular identification of particular pedagogies and instructional practices that can help students gain those skills.* The programs aim to develop the autonomy and agency of teachers as professionals, their capacity for independent learning, their desire for continuous learning and increased effectiveness, and their intrinsic motivation to strive for excellent teaching. While the programs do not consistently rely on mastery of learning approaches, they all expect teachers to gain demonstrable competencies and see the process of gaining such competencies as gradual. The programs require repeated cycles of accessing new knowledge, enacting such knowledge in new practices, receiving feedback on such practices, reflecting on the new practice, and iterating in a cycle of increased mastery of the new instructional practices.
- *The curriculum of the various programs reflects a view of learning that includes cognitive skills in interaction with dispositions and socio-emotional skills.* The programs are seldom just approaches to developing instrumental techniques, but include opportunities for teachers to see the relationship between these new forms of teaching to values that are important to them and that align with broader social purposes for students and communities. In terms of social skills, the programs help teachers increase their capacity to communicate, collaborate, negotiate, and lead.
- *Professional development includes exposure to visible routines, protocols, and instructional practices, where teachers see new forms of instruction or assessment in practice.* The programs rely on protocols, toolkits, frameworks, videos with demonstration lessons or pedagogies that help scale the programs with fidelity across a range of contexts.
- *The programs rely on a mix of opportunities for learning situated in the context of the schools where teachers work.* These include coaching in the schools and professional development communities within the schools, with opportunities for teachers to talk with colleagues in different schools and who have different roles from classroom teaching.

- *To support the intensive and sustained activities of professional development that these various programs advance, the organizations in charge build a range of partnerships with institutions outside of schools that contribute various types of resources.* They all depend on new forms of engaging parents and communities at large on behalf of students' learning.
- *The programs see teacher practice as situated in specific organizations and social contexts and, in general, adopt a whole-school approach, rather than helping individual teachers increase their capacity.* As part of their goal to create conditions that sustain new and more ambitious teacher practices, they explicitly aim to change organizational culture and often school structures and roles, for instance, extending learning time, reorganizing learning opportunities in the disciplines, creating time within the school day for professional development, or extending learning opportunities outside the boundaries of the school. Efforts to develop a shared vision among all school staff about the broader goals they are trying to achieve for their students—for example, "all students will succeed," "we will all go to the top of the mountain"—are a common element of these processes.
- *The programs all develop capacities among teachers to advance pedagogies with the goal of developing competencies that are not formally assessed in the school or school system.* In this sense, the programs challenge the notion that "what gets measured gets done" and suggest that teachers can make decisions about what and how to teach that can transcend the formal accountability structures in the school.
- *The organizations that support the various programs all model a learning orientation.* They approach schools with an inquiry mind-set, engage in dialogue with school staff about their learning goals, use various forms of feedback to assess whether their work is achieving the intended results, and implement measures to course-correct and generate continuous improvement in their work.

CHAPTER TWO

Providing Relevant Twenty-First-Century Science Education for All Students

A Case Study of the Chilean Inquiry-Based Science Education Program

Liliana Morawietz and Cristián Bellei
Sociology Department and CIAE, Universidad de Chile

The Programa de Educación en Ciencias Basado en la Indagación, ECBI, a Chilean inquiry-based science education program, contributes to expanding education goals and learning opportunities within Chilean public education, especially for schools serving low-income students.[1] Since the early 2000s, ECBI has supported hundreds of primary schools across several Chilean cities to provide more challenging, engaging, and comprehensive science education to their students. The program is inspired by the belief that high-quality science education is important for all children. Inquiry-based science education not only expands children's understanding of the natural and material world, but also stimulates curiosity, introduces them to the practice of scientific inquiry and critical thinking, and prepares them for lifelong learning. In this regard, ECBI constitutes a concrete proposal to implement, in regular classrooms and schools, several of the key notions for teaching the twenty-first-century competencies promoted by the Chilean curriculum. Implementation has proven to be very difficult, partially because of the lack of practical knowledge in these settings for developing actual teaching practices that help students develop the competencies.[2]

We first briefly describe the study that provided the empirical material for this chapter; then, we address the relevance of our study by giving some context about both Chilean education and inquiry-based science education; and we then describe and analyze the main components of the ECBI program, including its philosophy, objectives, design, and implementation. We emphasize the actual experience of program participants instead of relying solely on official document descriptions. Additionally, we discuss several limitations and critical issues ECBI faces that have challenged its effectiveness and sustainability. Finally, we identify some relevant lessons for educators and policy makers aimed at implementing not only inquiry-based science education, but more broadly, school improvement programs focused on changing the prevalent notions of teaching and learning.

We based our findings on a case study about ECBI. We are intrinsically interested in ECBI because it represents a unique experience within the Chilean education system. In our qualitative case study, we collected evidence from several sources (see table 2.1). First, we conducted twenty-four semistructured interviews, using interview protocols and methods collectively designed by members of the GEII: six interviews with ECBI staff members and founders, one with a former staff member; fourteen individual and one group interview with teachers, principals, and academic coordinators of participating schools; and two interviews with science education experts who were not part of the program staff. We chose six schools to study: three schools currently implementing ECBI and three schools that previously participated in the program.

Second, we conducted five unstructured science class observations in the three schools currently participating in the program, in grades K (one observation), 4 (two observations), and 6 (two observations). We also observed four ECBI summer training sessions for teachers working in schools in the program. Third, we analyzed several related documents, including documents the ECBI team produced about the program (such as internal documents, public presentations, and academic research papers), program materials for students and teachers, three undergraduate and graduate theses about ECBI, two external evaluations, and documents by organizations devoted to science education that referred to ECBI. The empirical material was axial coded by the authors, using the common predefined list of codes. We based this chapter on the empirical material from these different sources, but emphasized the data we obtained from our interviews with program participants.

TABLE 2.1   Research activities

	Individual interviews	Collective interviews	Observations
ECBI founders	3		
ECBI staff	5		
Science education experts	2		
Schools currently participating in the program	9		5
Schools with participation in the program finished	4	1	
Training activities			3
Total	23	1	8

DEVELOPING TWENTY-FIRST-CENTURY COMPETENCIES IN CHILEAN CLASSROOMS

Since the early 1980s, the Chilean educational system has been highly decentralized. Forty percent of the students in the country are enrolled in public schools administered by hundreds of municipalities, 50 percent of the students are enrolled subsidized private schools, while the remaining 10 percent are in unsubsidized private schools. Both subsidized and unsubsidized private schools function autonomously. Moreover, market-oriented dynamics rule Chilean education: there is unrestricted school choice, and the government funds both private and public schools equally by using universal school vouchers, forcing all public and private schools to compete for family preferences. Thus, since the Ministry of Education has no direct link with the schools, it relies strongly on indirect policies like economic incentives and regulations like the national curriculum to promote changes oriented toward increasing quality and equity in education.[3]

Over the last two decades, several administrations of the national government have been very active in implementing various types of educational policies. In particular, the government progressively introduced an educational reform that included a curriculum reform starting in 1996. The new curriculum, adjusted in 2003 and 2009, incorporated several pedagogical principles and learning objectives as well as curricular content oriented toward helping Chilean students develop twenty-first-century competencies. The competencies were mainly cognitive and, to a lesser extent, interpersonal and intrapersonal, in the taxonomy developed in an expert report of the National Research Council.[4] A salient innovation of the new curriculum was the definition of learning objectives transversal to different subjects. Many of the twenty-first-century competencies introduced by the reform, such as citizenship, ethics, the relation between the individual and the environment, and self-evaluation, were connected to these crosscutting objectives.[5]

Although the reform extensively supported programs of in-service teacher education, increased school time (switching from a half to a full school day), and school improvement (including teaching materials and in-school professional development) to support the implementation of the new curriculum, studies showed uneven and heterogeneous changes in teaching practices, and an overall low impact on students' learning as a result.[6]

Many factors account for the observed low impact of the curriculum reform. A plausible explanation is that the gap between the skills available within the teaching force and the new, more complex, demanding teaching capacities was insufficiently addressed. In 1999, Trends in International Mathematics and Science Study (TIMSS) estimated that two out of three Chilean teachers felt a low level of confidence in their preparedness to teach science, while only 7 percent had a high level of confidence, one of the lowest proportions among participant countries.[7] The means used to support teachers' professional development in relation to the reform were mostly ineffective, and teachers found it difficult to translate the pedagogical aims of the reform into consistent daily classroom activities. Arguably, there is a lack of pedagogical know-how in Chile, including a lack of content and pedagogical knowledge among instructors in teacher preparation programs, school consultants, and supervisors in the Ministry of Education, to solve the practical challenges of implementing a twenty-first-century-oriented curriculum. In such conditions, it is difficult to organize innovative and effective pedagogical practices in regular classrooms.[8]

Additionally, the potential of the innovations introduced through the curriculum reform, such as crosscutting learning goals, proved limited in modifying actual practices: the traditional "grammar of schooling" that organizes teaching in pedagogical hours and by isolated subject matter. Together with traditional practices and insufficient implementation strategies, this challenge of the reform was additionally hindered by the increasing dominance of test-based accountability policies within the Chilean education system over the last decades. Since the midnineties, school rankings based on SIMCE (a compulsory National Evaluation System based on standardized testing) test scores have been broadly disseminated to inform parents' school choice, and economic incentives have been distributed among teachers working in high-performing schools. Also, starting in 2008, the Preferential Voucher Law mandated an ambitious set of goals measured by SIMCE language and mathematics scores that participating schools are to attain over a four-year period; schools failing to meet those goals are subjected to sanctions, including school restructuring and closure. Finally, in 2011, a compulsory quality assurance system was implemented: all Chilean schools are classified according to their performance (measured mostly in terms of SIMCE test scores), and chronically low-performing schools (also based on four-year cycles) are to be restructured and ultimately closed. The growing pressure to increase test scores has resulted in school environments that encourage test preparation and emphasize a "back to the basics" discourse (literacy and mathematics acquisition), setting other education goals aside, especially the most innovative aspects of the twenty-first-century-oriented curriculum reform, and narrowing the curriculum, all of which undermines the original goals of the reform.[9] Thus, twenty years later, Chilean education continues to center on teachers, is based on examinations, and focuses on rote learning and basic cognitive skills.

Science education has followed the same path. The curricular reform introduced several learning objectives aimed at twenty-first-century education goals, such as critical, abstract, and hypothetical thinking; problem solving; and analysis. However, the failure to communicate the reform to schools and teachers, and the lack of professional development support, along with the absence of pedagogical knowledge and teaching materials to implement the new approach at the classroom level, resulted in limited impact. Initial teacher preparation is comparatively weak in the science domain, and traditional teaching practices prevail in Chilean classrooms.[10] According to Hernán Cofré et al., when compared to developed countries, Chilean teachers' initial preparation programs lack scientific training on research, science history and constitution, and science didactics.[11] At the same time, in-school practice hours are scarce. Thus, it is not surprising that Chilean students have continued to perform comparatively low in international science evaluations, with at least a third of the students performing extremely low.[12]

In such a national context, ECBI, with its focus on inquiry-based science education, is an attempt to overcome the gap between the ambitious new goals of the Chilean curriculum and the students' opportunities to learn by changing classroom practices and accompanying teachers in addressing the required innovations. Moreover, based on its founders' conviction that all students have the right to access high-quality science education, ECBI has been primarily implemented in public schools serving low-income areas. While the low performance of disadvantaged students in standardized tests has resulted in authorities' emphasis on acquiring basic skills, thus reducing and narrowing curriculum ambitions for this group, ECBI has continued to argue for the relevance of broad educational goals. Although ECBI was partially designed to meet some of the new learning objectives that the reform defined, the program also introduced additional competencies into science education, going beyond the requirements of the curriculum. ECBI also proposed a pedagogical strategy to address the reform's goals and contents, for the national curriculum reform design did not include an official pedagogy to teach the new curriculum in the classroom. Notably, ECBI subsequently influenced the Ministry of Education to adjust the mandatory national curriculum to include an inquiry-based approach more explicitly in science education. All these factors make ECBI an even more interesting case for study.

ECBI'S GOALS AND PEDAGOGICAL APPROACH

A team of renowned scientists working at Universidad de Chile, the oldest higher education institution in the country, who belonged to the Chilean Academy of Sciences, created the ECBI program in 2002—the first year the new curriculum was fully implemented throughout schools. In the following years, ECBI addressed many of the issues that limited the national reform's full implementation in the science education area. In addition to these pedagogical goals, the program founders were inspired by the idea that all children should have the opportunity to experience high-quality science education, not just those who are more likely to pursue scientific careers, such as those with a higher socioeconomic status.

The program's vision is that effective science education will expand children's understanding of the natural and material world, introduce them to the practice of scientific inquiry and scientific attitudes, stimulate their curiosity, and prepare them to become lifelong learners. Furthermore, the program creators anticipated that effective science education would contribute to the full expression of children's creative potential, improving their quality of life and that of their communities.[13] According to ECBI's executive director,

> ECBI's vision is that children are happy in their science class, questioning themselves, sharing with others, observing, registering data, analyzing information, interpreting, writing their thoughts, giving their opinions, generating new questions; in other words, active children that hold opinions substantiated by evidence—and that they start to relate this ability they have of questioning the world and look for evidence and interpret it also in different scenarios.

Thus, ECBI seeks to develop among students many of the competencies and skills pertaining to a quality education in the twenty-first century.[14]

The program curriculum addresses communication skills; for example, students are encouraged to put their research process in writing, favoring metacognition, and to perform public lessons to disseminate their findings to their communities, developing their competencies in the cognitive domain.[15] By intensively using teamwork in the classroom, and requiring students to constantly review and discuss their ideas, ECBI aims to develop interpersonal skills such as collaboration, respect, and assertive communication. By promoting an active role for students in their learning processes, children will improve their self-esteem, self-confidence, motivation, and engagement with learning, all competencies pertaining to the intrapersonal domain.

Acquiring scientific literacy is also one of the main benefits of the program.[16] As opposed to the specialized deep knowledge of scientists, scientific literacy consists of grasping some basic or key ideas of and about science, its nature, limitations, and processes, and developing the capacity to use these ideas in making decisions as informed and concerned citizens.[17] Thus, ECBI aims to develop citizenship competencies, as a member of ECBI staff noted: "What we expect is to promote the development of the individual in a comprehensive way; contributing to develop critical thinking among students, who later become critical adults, who are active members of the society, hold opinions and are able to question themselves."

The program's capacity to achieve all these educational goals is underpinned mainly by its methodology, inquiry-based science education (IBSE). This methodology is based on the premise that the learning process for students should be similar to that which scientists use to study the natural and material world in their search for new knowledge. They are guided by their own curiosity and passion to understand defined phenomena. The approach has been defined as "a cluster of learning and teaching approaches in which students' inquiry or research drives the learning experience."[18]

This notion has been at the center of science education reform over the last decades; classrooms worldwide have adopted it.[19] In 1996, the US National Science Education Standards characterized IBSE as "making observations; posing questions; examining books and other sources of information to see what is already known; planning investigations; reviewing available knowledge in light of experimental evidence; using tools to gather, analyze, and interpret data; proposing answers, explanations, and predictions; and communicating the results."[20] Thus, in addition to learning scientific concepts, children are encouraged to develop scientific thinking, monitor their own learning process, and develop critical thinking through IBSE.[21]

Inquiry-based methodologies combine the focus of a hands-on approach and competency development, with the progressive acquisition of concepts, considering both scientific ideas and scientific principles.[22] Teachers become the key players in implementing IBSE pedagogies in regular school classrooms.[23] The methodology has an impact on their practices by providing a basis for introducing creative contributions and innovations, since it challenges teachers to establish conditions in which "students' inquiries are stimulated and can flourish, and in which they are supported effectively in developing relevant inquiry competencies and other process skills."[24] Consequently, when compared to traditional science classes, IBSE methodology implies changes not only in the curricular contents, but also in the ways teachers interact with students.

Therefore, adequate professional development for teachers has been identified as critical to the adoption of the approach. Ideally, high-quality teachers' professional development focuses on what the students are to learn, models what is expected in the classroom, is continuous and embedded in the daily work of teachers, recognizes the different needs of teachers with different experiences, supports systemic change, and involves all team members.[25] It creates a professional learning community "that focuses on student work and changes teaching," as a means for school improvement.[26]

The issue of increasing teachers' capacity to teach more effectively has become central not only for inquiry-based education programs, but in discussions about implementing twenty-first-century curriculum reforms.

ECBI'S DESIGN TO EXPAND SCIENCE LEARNING AT SCHOOLS

ECBI creators conceive the process of inquiry as the cornerstone of science education, since it links the science taught in schools with the actual work of scientists, making the learning process not only more motivating for students, but also more authentic to the work of scientists. A program founder connected scientific skills with broader ones: "I believe that science is useful for non-scientists too, because it is a way of thinking with a certain rigor and with a searching attitude, about things like how far does the evidence go, how certain the evidence is. Therefore, in some way, it'll teach you how to face problems."

To achieve the program's goals, science lessons shift from lectures to learning units that enable students to experience the scientific processes of knowledge creation. Following the inquiry-based pedagogical approach, children play the leading role in the learning process.

As a program, ECBI has two additional purposes. First, it connects the field of science with the educational system, engaging scientists and science graduates in regular collaboration with science teachers. ECBI founders were concerned with the wide social distances between students, especially those in low-income communities, and scientists, because they perceived it would ultimately jeopardize the generational renewal of scientists and the future of Chilean science. Second, the program aims to improve the quality of science education in schools, particularly in those institutions serving low socioeconomic status (SES) students. Overall, because the inquiry-based approach to science education addresses science as the result of social processes subjected to continuous revision and change, students will perceive science as a tool related to their life, not just a set of concepts and definitions disconnected from reality. These secondary goals feed ECBI's main objective: ECBI designers expect that with exposure to the logic and processes of actual science and real scientists, students from disadvantaged areas will expand their sense of the meaning of citizenship.

Despite its innovative goals, its leaders designed ECBI for implementation in public schools during regular science lessons and not as an extracurricular, voluntary activity for only a few motivated students. This feature prompted school adherence to the program, as one staff member noted, "We have a national curriculum that is compulsory; so, one of our advantages is that when we arrive at the schools we are not proposing an extracurricular program."

Certainly, to run a high-quality IBSE program is very challenging; implementing it as part of the official curriculum in regular public schools located in poor areas is far more challenging. That endeavor was the vision of ECBI's leaders.

History of ECBI

The Chilean scientists who created ECBI were inspired by the work of the US National Academy of Sciences and the Smithsonian Institution in the area of science education. They obtained support from the Chilean National Academy of Sciences and funding from the Ministry of Education and the Andes Foundation, a nonprofit private organization, and assembled a team of scientists and educators. They launched a pilot program in 2003 and implemented it in six participating public schools located in a low-income municipality in Santiago de Chile, with a thousand students in grades six and seven. The next year, the number of schools participating increased to twenty-six and covered grades 5–8.

In 2005, the Ministry of Education incorporated ECBI into its national educational improvement strategy (previously focused only on mathematics and reading). To reach more schools, it worked in alliance with the University of Chile and collaborated with twelve other Chilean universities located in different cities. The Ministry of Education funded the production of teaching materials and guides, teaching training sessions, and ECBI advisers to work at the school level. The program's coverage increased rapidly: participating schools (mainly public) scaled up to 250, located in both urban and rural areas across the country, and about 90,000 children benefited from the program.[27]

As a result of this collaboration, "scientific thinking skills" were incorporated as an axis of the national science curriculum from grades 1 to 8 when the Ministry of Education adjusted it in 2009, introducing the IBSE approach more explicitly into the official curriculum.[28] Thus, these competencies became a mandatory goal for science education in the country.

However, in 2010, the partnership between the Ministry of Education and the ECBI program ceased, concluding its implementation at the national level. A change in the government's political coalition and educational priorities were the main reason. Consequently, the emergent national network of collaborating universities implementing the program ended, participating schools decreased to thirty-eight, and the number of children served fell to about 3,320. The ECBI program was relocated to the University of Chile, and its staff significantly reduced.

In the new context, the work of ECBI continued with the support of the University of Chile and of Fundación Allende-Connelly, a small nonprofit foundation created by one of the ECBI founders. The ECBI program began operating as one among more than a thousand external technical support providers available to local school administrators and private school owners, who could make direct contracts by allocating a recently created public voucher targeted to schools serving low-income students.[29] In other words, ECBI went from a national school improvement program supported by the Ministry of Education to an individual provider competing in the educational services market. To complicate matters, national authorities prompted local authorities and school administrators to increasingly allocate available resources to improvement programs focused on raising performance in standardized tests, where mathematics and language are prioritized.

This arrangement proved extraordinarily challenging for ECBI's survival, and the program's continuity was challenged on multiple occasions. Thus, during the last few years, private sources of funding have been relevant to support program operation. For example, two private companies funded ECBI's implementation in some public schools located in their operation zones by using corporate social responsibility tax laws, and more recently, ECBI signed a contract with the Siemens Foundation for the implementation of its Experiment program in Chile.

Overall, the collaborative partnership forged between scientists and educators, and the prestigious status of the scientists leading ECBI and their networks clearly helped the program to obtain political and financial support from the Ministry of Education and to influence national curriculum decisions. However, the close relationship with the Ministry of Education also made ECBI vulnerable to changes in the political agenda, as the person who was in charge of the program's implementation at the ministry and one of its funders noted:

> I had to talk with seven ministers of education in a very short period of time, trying to convince them each time that we need to keep ECBI, that it was something interesting—because each minister had come with their own new idea and it could be that science education was not part of their new idea. (Ministry of Education counterpart)

> In politics there is the haste of results, because the next election will come, so there is the need to show the effects now, right, and this is about education, which demands much more on having signals which are more or less clear about how things are going. So, that's a complexity. (Program founder)

Despite those difficulties, ECBI highly values its relationship with the Ministry of Education, as it has enabled it to scale and benefit hundreds of teachers and schools, and allowed it to influence the national curricula. Thus, having a strong link with the Ministry of Education is seen as a necessary way to affect the educational system as a whole, argued one of its founders. "Sooner or later you have to somehow interact with the Ministry of Education, because otherwise the program becomes too isolated, as a pilot project. The scaling has to be done by the authorities, who have the possibility to make it happen."

The introduction of the IBSE approach to the curriculum recently opened the door to new collaborations between the program and the government. In 2015, the ministry called for the design of certified courses on IBSE methodologies for science teachers in different regions of the country, and it commissioned ECBI to implement the course in the Santiago Metropolitan area. The course, which combines in-person and online participation, is expected to train teachers up to the expert level. Also, former members of ECBI have become involved in teacher training programs in other universities, incorporating IBSE as the approach for science education.

The collaboration with national and international networks of scientists and science academies has been a constant feature of the ECBI program. Along with the support of the US National Academy of Sciences and the Smithsonian Institution, it has received the cooperation of people and institutions executing similar projects in France, Mexico, Brazil, and Colombia. Together with these collaborations, the program leaders have specified that "this help has come in many different forms that include training of the leadership team, the right to use high quality materials; the sharing of translated material, collaboration in strategic planning workshops and the participation and organization of international conferences."[30]

At the same time, the Chilean Academy of Sciences (in which ECBI leaders are strongly involved) has been coordinating the science education program of the Inter Academy Panel and the Inter-American Network of Academies of Sciences since 2004, and through the organization of strategic planning workshops, the ECBI program has stimulated the establishment of similar programs in Venezuela, Peru, Bolivia, and Panama.

ECBI Staff: Focus on Expert Knowledge, Interpersonal Skills, and Collaboration

ECBI's leadership comprises the program's executive director and the scientists who founded the program. The executive director focuses on the relationship between the program and schools, the promotion and agreements of the program with new schools, the generation of academic and collaborative networks, and fund-raising.

Broadly, ECBI's efforts focus on two main components: the implementation of IBSE within schools and the development of teachers' professional capacities. In order to achieve its goals, ECBI organized a multidisciplinary staff comprising science teachers, science graduates, and scientists. They work mainly as advisers at the school level, supporting teachers in planning and conducting science lessons.

Since ECBI's implementation depends on the quality of its relationship with participating schools, attracting appropriate human resources is critical for program success. ECBI's advisers possess the pedagogical knowledge and competencies that are scarce among Chilean primary teachers: knowledge about the scientific method, processes, and concepts, as well as an understanding of the inquiry-based approach. They are expected to have interpersonal competencies that allow them to work closely and respectfully with participating teachers and school staff, enhancing their understanding and appreciation of the program's methodology.

Although motivating children to pursue scientific careers is not a direct goal of ECBI, having scientists who visit the schools as members of the staff is a way to engage the students with science. As one program founder, an acclaimed scientist himself, noted, "Notice that out of the 150 students who have performed these [ECBI] experiments, 85 percent reported that they'd never seen a scientist or a postgraduate science student in their lives. So, how can they imagine a scientific career for themselves if they don't know anyone in their environment that is following that path?"

Additionally, ECBI staff members—including some school-level advisers—designed and implemented teacher professional development activities, and developed a certified program about the IBSE approach for teachers. ECBI staff also developed the teaching materials that the program provides to teachers to structure science lessons. In developing those materials, scientists, school advisers, and some participating teachers work as a team, discussing and piloting proposed activities in actual science lessons at schools.

Program participants perceive the collaborative work of classroom teachers, science graduates, and scientists as a key feature of ECBI, because it blurs the frontiers and hierarchies among different levels of the educational system, which are very strong in Chile. As a school teacher implementing ECBI noted:

> To me, the collaborative work with the monitor was very good, because they learned, and we also learned; they were specialists in something, like chemists, biologists, or physicists, therefore, they had a level of knowledge that was much deeper than the one I had in science, but they did not know how to transfer that knowledge to the classroom. Because you need to translate the knowledge, manage a group of children, relate the topics to the children; they learned all that from us. So, it was something mutual and good alliances were established there.

Moreover, since some classroom teachers have later become ECBI advisers, and in turn, some advisers have become responsible for teacher training programs, ECBI has opened a valuable and rare path to professional development for science educators.

ECBI IN THE SCHOOLS

ECBI, implemented at the school level, is a multidimensional system that ultimately supports science teaching practices. It comprises five components:

professional development, curriculum, teaching materials, community support, and evaluation. The program has been tailored to Chilean local context mainly through the creation of learning units adjusted to the national curriculum, and by the incorporation of school advisers: members of the organization's staff who work in schools supporting the program's implementation.

Professional Development Activities

The ECBI program provides teachers with needed support to enhance the implementation of a new approach to science education. The program aims at increasing teachers' understanding of science, improving their pedagogical and social skills, and "building capacities to sustain the systemic model for science education."[31] Hence, once a school joins the program, future participating teachers attend a two-week professional development program. Usually, participating schools' principals or academic coordinators also attend.

ECBI's professional development activities for participant schools' staff are mainly oriented toward the acquisition of IBSE methodology. They are exposed to some of the learning units the program created to use with students in classrooms:

> It was a very practical training, because it was as if we were students: we worked in groups, I mean, everything we teach the children, the steps we follow with them, we did it . . . It was very encouraging and motivating . . . when working with very simple materials, for instance the topic of light, I could imagine the faces of my students when they see the reflection, when they see the lights, and I never thought about working with a laser, with a mirror. Thus, these simple things that we experienced in situ, doing them later with the children in practice—great, great! Yes, it was good, it was good because it was very practical, applied. It wasn't like sitting to write down notes, and being told what to do and what not to do. (Teacher)

Following their hands-on approach, ECBI leaders stated that teachers have to learn the way they need to teach. Thus, the training is mostly practical. The ECBI staff members (mainly advisers who work with schools) lead the experience and expose participants to the scientific learning cycle those units recreate. In an interview, one adviser recounted a conversation:

> *Interviewer:* Thinking about teachers, what are the main skills or abilities that you aim to develop in them?

Staff member: The same as we want for children. Ability to state questions, for-mulate predictions, to design activities that allow them to obtain data, analyze the data, register observations, elaborate the evidence they have for their case and then to communicate . . . And they realize that it is pro-ductive, because no one is giving them the recipe; they discover and are amazed.

ECBI expects that through these activities, participants will become famil-iar with inquiry-based methodology, based on experiencing the learning pro-cess rather than being lectured to, become familiar with both the lesson plans and the teaching materials they will subsequently use in their classrooms, and learn how to guide the process when teaching their students. There is also time to discuss and reflect on the contents and more general issues of the ECBI proposal. During training sessions, teachers also become familiar with the role advisers play in classrooms.

We found that teachers highly value the applied, hands-on, and school-based approach to teacher training, which is in direct contrast with the more theoretically oriented, university-based courses predominant in the educa-tional field. For example, a school academic coordinator described the process:

First, it was having the same classes that we were going to teach to the children, the same modules . . . There was an exploration model where you first state pre-dictions, generate hypotheses, questions, and then you have your experiment, there was a moment to reflect on the experiment, it had data collection, then it had another phase where you have to arrive at some conclusions and regis-ter them, how to register them also, and then communicate . . . so teachers enjoyed it so much . . . and that vision allows us to say "yes, we actually want this." (School academic coordinator)

School leaders also value the contribution of ECBI to increase teachers' capacities:

Teacher preparation is very criticized, mainly the initial teacher preparation, but I think that if we want to move forward, we have to deal with that criti-cism, but not only the training institutions have to deal with it . . . but also the schools . . . How do we overcome the barriers with those teachers? How do we improve with those colleagues? So we have to address the issue of how to manage professional development and we think that ECBI was a good oppor-tunity for the colleagues to have professional development. (School academic coordinator)

Since professional development activities are expected to help teachers develop the same competencies ECBI intends students to develop, another focus of the professional development activities is to bring participants together to discuss the social implications of contemporary processes related to scientific knowledge, such as the food industry, medical advances, or climate change. ECBI staff members also lead the discussions, and their organization also uses IBSE methodology in gathering previous knowledge and distinguishing evidence from assumptions. They will eventually sensitize teachers to the relevance of scientific literacy in enabling more critical and robust citizenship. Teachers are to replicate the discussions with their students.

In the professional development sessions, there are three levels of participants: beginner, intermediate, and competent. Teachers and principals of schools who join the program participate in training sessions before initiating the program implementation. As *beginners*, their sessions consist mainly of exposure to IBSE methodology and some of the lesson plans they are to teach the next year; the sessions detail, analyze, and discuss inquiry-based process components. The sessions also include planning training for each of the IBSE learning cycle stages. Most of the school principals and school academic coordinators also attend the summer training program. The objective is to introduce them to the methodology so they understand the complexities (e.g., ECBI classrooms will be noisier than usual) and new requirements teachers will have in their schools (e.g., storing teaching materials, organizing the work with the adviser), and give them organizational support. The participation of school principals and academic coordinators in these sessions is crucial to ensure program implementation and sustainability. Finally, ECBI also organizes strategic planning workshops for leadership teams responsible for launching ECBI in schools entering the program.

At the end of the first year of program implementation, participating teachers reach the *intermediate* level. In those training sessions, they spend half their time experiencing lesson plans and move on to analyze the learning process that takes place through IBSE, and prepare a lesson plan themselves. More recently, they have been introduced to the appropriate methods to evaluate students' learning in the IBSE approach.

Teachers participating in the program for two years or more join the *competent* team during training sessions. Competent teachers discuss how to transfer IBSE methodology to the school as a whole, including other subjects and teachers' professional activities. Some principals of schools implementing ECBI for several years also voluntarily participate in these sessions.

In addition, ECBI often organizes supplementary educational experiences for participants, like workshops, seminars, conferences, and short courses. Often, these activities fulfill emergent local needs and demands.

Overall, for various teachers, ECBI has opened a rich path of professional development in the field of science education:

> I wanted to continue studying because I noticed I had many gaps, so I said, "OK, I have to study" and I went to study, and I obtained the science specialization and also I even continued my training with ECBI. (Teacher)

> I think that it's been something that has marked my life a bit. (Teacher/current school coordinator)

> It was a wonderful experience for me. In fact, ECBI developed my appreciation for science, because I didn't have the specialization when the project started. Since then I trained myself, I studied the science specialization, so I've grown a lot professionally from this project. (Teacher)

ECBI Throughout the School Year

Schools implement ECBI in regular science classes from grades K to 8. Implementation starts at the beginning of the academic year. In most cases, the local educational authority responsible for managing public schools suggests ECBI to schools. Once a school joins ECBI, the program assigns a school adviser who will support both teachers and school leaders in the program's implementation.

Program coordinators and monitors discuss and negotiate with local school authorities and school principals some conditions necessary to implement the program at the school level, such as time allotted for teachers to participate in weekly planning and training sessions. According to ECBI members, the emphasis of the program is to focus its intervention at the school and classroom levels, based on evidence about the low effectiveness of improvement programs that rely solely on offsite teacher training courses or in the distribution of teaching materials.[32]

Certainly, the primary direct goal of ECBI is to modify science classroom practices by introducing an inquiry-based pedagogical approach. Each science lesson ECBI implements addresses one of the content units the program provides.

During the first years of program implementation, ECBI used lesson plans created by the US National Science Resources Center; however, as the program evolved, ECBI developed its own lesson plans for grades K–8, better aligned with the Chilean curriculum. These units guide teachers during their science lessons. Each follows a precise "learning cycle" with the students that emulates that of scientists: (1) activate previous knowledge: teachers and advisers motivate children to express their previous knowledge and beliefs on the contents of the lesson; (2) exploration: experimental materials and tools are introduced, and students are free to manipulate them, make predictions about their functions and what will happen, and propose hypotheses; (3) experiment: students conduct an actual scientific experiment; (4) analysis: students compare their knowledge, beliefs, and hypotheses with the experiment results; and (5) application: children discuss the broader consequences and implications of what they have experienced.

Next, teachers and program advisers spend most of the class time interacting with the students. Teachers guide them through the planned sequence, asking questions, providing instructions, inviting them to make predictions and to manipulate the materials, organizing experiments and other forms of hypothesis testing. They guide students in collecting new information, lead discussions, ask students to present their ideas, and help them draw some conclusions and formalize the new knowledge.

During ECBI classes, students work in teams—in contrast to most Chilean classrooms, where desks are organized in rows, with students working in isolation—and conversation and discussion are not only accepted, but encouraged. Each student plays a role within his or her group during the session, especially in the experimentation stage, participating as team leader, secretary, materials handler, and so on. At the end of the class period, each student puts his or her thinking in writing.

The program incorporated this final stage of the proposed lesson plans, known as "scientific writing," in 2010.[33] Students register not only observations and outcomes, but also their thinking process. Although ECBI puts less emphasis on the acquisition of the specific content knowledge taught in each unit than on the thinking and learning process involved, by encouraging students to do scientific writing, the program ensures they will formalize the knowledge and basic concepts discussed in the class. As one program founder explained, this stage is intended to somewhat balance the hands-on approach that was all-encompassing during the first years of the program, and to strengthen the program's contributions to students' communication skills: "'Activism' is always a risk to all hands-on programs . . . We are tackling this, today with all the work that is being done on scientific argument, scientific writing . . . ; systematizing, writing using data—of course, not only from imagination—and argumentation . . . But that requires well-trained teachers." Thus, ECBI has evolved over time by continually evaluating its effects among schools, teachers, and students.

Although detailed, ECBI lesson plans still require teachers to adapt them to the particular characteristics of their classes. For example, teachers need to adjust the level of difficulty, select appropriate examples, link content to previous classes, and organize class activities and materials for students. To make these kinds of thoughtful adjustments, teachers require school time outside the classroom. In Chile, teachers' contracts stipulate that at least 25 percent of paid teacher time be allocated to nonteaching professional activities, and participating schools are expected to commit to assigning teachers one hour of this time per week to science lesson planning for each grade they teach. During this time, teachers work with the assigned ECBI adviser to organize the next science lesson in detail, reviewing contents, activities, and the methodology of the class. Although we found that in some schools, planning time was limited, many program participants viewed this time to work collaboratively as an enriching opportunity for professional development. One teacher we interviewed described the process: "The monitor came once a week, we met, planned the activities, analyzed feedback, discussed: 'How did it work for you?' . . . We made changes to better implement the activities. So for me it was also a good source of continuous learning."

With such a reliance on teachers, school advisers are critical for ECBI in implementing IBSE. While Chilean primary teachers are prepared to teach all first- through eighth-grade subject matter in the curriculum, with emphasis on literacy and numeracy, they have little specific knowledge about sciences. Thus, ECBI designers created the role of school advisers to support teachers in the program's implementation. Advisers clarify scientific concepts and guide teachers in following the IBSE method. Schools advisers also meet regularly—ideally every week—with each participating teacher planning science lessons and discussing pedagogical or curricular issues raised during previous class sessions. According to a school adviser we interviewed: "[We] first do an initial training for the teachers, and after that we accompany them in the classroom, on the one hand planning the class, and on the other hand accompanying them in the class, and then we evaluate the class and we plan again, and we accompany them again."

School advisers accompany teachers in the classroom during science lessons to support them by collaborating on different tasks, such as organizing teaching materials and supervising students' work. They may pose questions to students, clarify scientific concepts, and occasionally lead the class while conducting an experiment, or model for teachers their pedagogical role within the inquiry-based methodology. They are assistants and do not conduct the lessons. A school adviser described her role: "We are going to collaborate, not to evaluate with an instrument, but to be there working in the field, modeling . . . The teachers have an experience that is valid and we consider that."

By observing teachers conducting a science lesson, ECBI advisers are also able to give feedback to improve their competencies. Since teachers and advisers plan the science lesson together, they coordinate and agree on in advance the kind of interventions advisers are to perform in front of the students. As we observed, these interactions varied according to the quality of the teacher-adviser relationship that developed.

After the lesson (immediately or in the next weekly meeting), the ECBI adviser provides feedback to teachers and discusses relevant issues raised during the class. Thus, although the aim is to provide in situ coaching to teachers, this can easily be perceived as supervision or evaluation of the teacher's performance. Certainly, the role of the ECBI adviser is both critical and very delicate, and its success strongly depends on the personal trust and professional respect between advisers and teachers. As a teacher noted, "She was always there as a complement or a support . . . Very respectful of my role as a teacher, she always came to accompany me." A former ECBI staff member agreed, "I think that it is key that the monitor is slightly more of an expert in something, it is not that they're an expert in everything, but a counterpart, they're still my partner, my coworker."

Because of the expertise required, ECBI's school advisers are science teachers—some former program participants—with graduate degrees in science and work in schools as coaches to ensure the program's adequate implementation and provide in-school professional development. As Rosa Devés and Pilar Reyes state, "[T]heir main function [is] to support the teachers in the development of effective learning experiences."[34] Schools advisers are trained in seminars and participate in the program's internal evaluation sessions. They work in teams, providing feedback to each other and with the program's managers. In the program's theory of change, advisers are seen as key agents.

In addition to the advisers, ECBI also gives participant schools all the materials required to ensure the program's full implementation. The program staff members have developed curricular materials such as handbooks for teachers and students, which include all the lesson plans for the semester. ECBI also provides all the required pedagogical resources and supplies for conducting the suggested experiments and generally all activities included in the lesson plans. Schools receive these materials at the beginning of the academic year and ideally create a small resources center. For example, in a lesson about electricity, the resources consisted mainly of small pieces of materials such as aluminum, plastic, cotton fabric, and wood. During the class, the students created a small electric circuit, with the batteries and wire also provided, and tested which materials were electricity conductors. In later sessions, they illuminated a house mock-up. ECBI also provided the materials for that lesson.

Thus, school administrators and teachers do not have to search for the materials or resources to buy them. This is very relevant since teachers and students make intense use of different materials during ECBI class sessions, which students value highly. According to an ECBI teacher: "The child gets motivated working with the materials . . . because when we conduct a frontal class, although it's true that we can obtain results, I feel, according to my preparation, and what I have experienced, that it is not the same compared to when they handle, observe, and investigate."

Indeed, the key contribution of the ECBI program is not the financial aspect, because ECBI materials are comparatively simple and cheap, but the coherence between the materials and the planned pedagogical activities, which shows teachers an interesting way to engage students in active learning. According to our interviews, ECBI teaching materials are one of the most valued components of the program. This illustrates the point that changes in curricular content imply a need to change not just pedagogy but also pedagogical materials, something linked to school improvement more broadly.[35]

Engaging schools' communities is also an ECBI goal. Thus, it holds public lessons yearly at the end of the school year. During the public lessons, students recreate the learning process followed in ECBI science classes, this time with the students leading and their parents and families playing the role of learners. Students select a lesson according to their interests, prepare it, and perform it in front of parents, teachers, and peers. They pose questions and ask their families to explain what they know about scientific phenomena and then invite them to test their knowledge by participating in the experiments.

Public lessons are a strong feature of the program. The program's staff and schools value them as evidence of the program's engaging methodology and efficacy in empowering children.[36] An ECBI school principal noted: "Parents were also surprised to see how their children were able to express themselves and the personality they acquired in doing that, because even the shyest children were able to show what they'd learned."

According to our interviewees, public science lessons not only are a moving symbolic ritual and a very unusual activity in Chilean schools, but are also a true instance in which students demonstrate the kind of competencies and knowledge they have acquired during the school year. An ECBI teacher described her experience: "It was a novelty for them, at the beginning, they'd never seen a public lesson in the schools . . . also the students were the creators, the main authors of these classes, because they prepared them, they usually prepared for two weeks for the class, also for them it was a debut as a teacher, and they felt delighted in teaching what they'd learned, and also they felt proud."

Participating teachers reported that parents and students were extremely positive about public science lessons and considered the activities a significant innovation of ECBI, not only for science classes, but also for the entire school culture:

> *Teacher:* When we were told that we had to do the open class in January, . . . at that point we had to demonstrate what the children had learned, and not only to the school teachers but also to the educational community, parents, guardians—it was hard . . . Because the children made an impression; I felt that it was like "wow, they learned!"
>
> *Interviewer:* And which children participated?
>
> *T:* All of them.

I: Did you feel happy with that class?

T: Yes, very moved.

I: Had you done something like that before?

T: Never in my life . . . never, I would have never thought of doing something like that.

Evaluation

Program members and participants see the public lessons as evidence of its effects on students. The program also considers other forms of evaluation: the assessment of student learning outcomes and its implementation at the school level, and evaluation of the function of the ECBI program as a whole.[37] National standardized tests on science also measure students' learning outcomes in relation to the national curriculum. All these inform the program's continuous adjustments.

As IBSE has expanded, student assessment has gained relevance—it plays a key role in informing innovation effectiveness and in guiding educational change planning, thus expanding or restraining the possibility of scaling or institutionalizing the use of this methodology—but assessment techniques specific to inquiry-based methodologies are not yet fully developed.[38]

In the ECBI program teachers test student learning about science content and thinking before and after each learning unit, and evaluate students' notebooks in order to assess their performance in scientific writing. Without evaluation tools aligned with its methodology, teachers assess their students using mostly traditional methodologies, like summative evaluations that measure content and conceptual learning in relation to the national curricula, not the additional competencies the program seeks to develop in students. Both ECBI teachers and the program's team see this as a limitation of the program. A teacher noted that "[t]here is a little imbalance, because I haven't found yet the best way to assess this kind of learning . . . I know who learned mainly based on what I observe and hear, but the system asks me to have a more formal written assessment instrument."

Consequently, in recent years, the program has incorporated formative assessment as part of its summer training sessions. A program founder said, "The evaluation is a topic that we need to develop more, I think. It is complex, because large-scale tests, in general, are not very informative, if they use multiple choice questions . . . It is difficult, but somehow we have the expression of the teachers and the children, and the enthusiasm they have . . . the appreciation of science."

Program participants emphasized the key role of teaching materials in increasing teachers' acceptance and adherence to the program. However, because of the standards-based policies being implemented (which include strong test-based accountability), Chilean teachers are heavily pressed to cover the entire mandatory curriculum. One teacher commented, "We are evaluated through the SIMCE . . . last year we had a good result . . . then, the issue of curriculum coverage, according to this test, is achieved. However, I work not only with ECBI but also with the text book; I try to be flexible with the methods. One has to have a responsibility as a teacher: if I think that ECBI does not fulfill a goal, I try to do it through another activity."

In order to persuade teachers to implement inquiry-based methodologies in their classrooms, ECBI demonstrates that its students will have the opportunity to learn the mandatory curriculum and perform well on the SIMCE. The person in charge of the program's implementation at a national level at the Ministry of Education noted:

> At the end of the day, everyone wants SIMCE to improve. We tried for this not to be the focus here, because we knew that we were not going to have immediate impact on SIMCE, because SIMCE was very centered only on conceptual knowledge. We tried to propose that increases in the SIMCE scores were going to take some time, but that children were going to have real opportunities to learn science, to develop scientific thinking skills, and therefore all that would influence their learning, so children would receive a more well-rounded education, that was what we could commit to.

The tension between the achievement of program goals and test results is also felt within the organization. Some schools have made their participation in ECBI conditional on the performance of their students on standardized tests. Regarding the program's implementation at a particular school, the program's executive director asserted: "They are a school of academic excellence and they've always had good SIMCE results, and they felt that the program was taking too much time developing high-level intellectual skills."

Until 2015, SIMCE evaluated science in fourth and eighth grades on alternate years, but it has recently removed that test, and will now evaluate science in sixth and tenth grades, in alternate years. SIMCE tests evaluate curriculum contents expressed in performance standards. Starting in 2004, when standards were introduced, students' competencies have been evaluated, including scientific inquiry. This was strengthened in 2009 by the aforementioned curriculum adjustment. Notwithstanding, a 2013 study commissioned by the Australian Council for Educational Research included the improvement in evaluation of scientific thinking skills on SIMCE science tests among its recommendations.[39]

PROGRAM EFFECTS AND SUSTAINABILITY

External evaluations that ECBI has commissioned and academic research—based on classroom observations and students' reports—have found the program's effects consistent with its design at the classroom level.[40] Research has also found that teachers value the main components of ECBI, in particular, the careful implementation design, which adapts to their needs, including lesson plans and teaching materials, and the contribution the program advisers make to the class development.[41] Previous research found that students highly valued the program's classroom activities, as participant teachers and students have reported, and teachers also reported on ECBI's impact on enhancing students' motivation and engagement in science classes.[42] However, an impact evaluation found no program effect on the official standardized science test.[43] Our findings are consistent with previous research on those and additional dimensions.

Based on our interviews and observations, we found that ECBI successfully supports IBSE classroom practices and increases the motivation and confidence of primary teachers to teach science. Teachers feel supported in the implementation of IBSE and state that many challenges they face when trying to innovate classroom practice—such as the lack of conceptual knowledge, teaching materials, class organization and management, planning time—are solved by the program's design.

ECBI showed teachers a practical way of implementing some pedagogical concepts that Chilean reform has promoted since the 1990s, such as active learning, learning by experience, learning by discovering, and peer learning, but that had proven very difficult to adopt within regular classroom practices. Some teachers said ECBI changed their approach to teaching, inspiring them to innovate and expand the inquiry-based approach to teaching other subject matter. A school principal argued: "Seeing how the students learn and how they were able to communicate those learnings, I mean, they teach them because they know them, they've really mastered them, and they developed the vocabulary, regulated their relations within the classroom, worked as a team, they learned how to listen, to state questions, to realize what they've learned. This has made me want to stay always in the program."

School authorities also reported that ECBI contributed to developing students' key competencies such as creativity, self-confidence, teamwork, and communication. Teachers strongly value the program's effect on motivating children to participate in science lessons and expanding their interest in their environment. Teachers perceived that all of their students benefited from participating in ECBI, in terms of their individual skills, abilities, or behavior; thus, teachers particularly value the fact that ECBI activities motivated low-performing students. Teachers sense that students value ECBI lessons because they feel they are learning real science, acquiring knowledge and competencies valued in real life; thus, they acquire knowledge that is socially valued. Teachers, school authorities, and program advisers especially value students' public science lessons, not only as a learning instance for students but also as an indicator that students have acquired relevant science knowledge and competencies (including the capacity to make an oral public presentation).

Perceptions about ECBI's impact are consistent among former and current teachers and school leaders participating in the program, and they emphasize the program's effects on students. According to them, students participating in ECBI have increased their motivation and developed key competencies. Program participants described the following:

> Now students like to do science, not in the past, that was boring. They like the fact that you have to experiment . . . , they are paying attention to what you are going to do, there is more interest for the science class now. (Teacher)

> I felt rewarded by the children, I mean, the spark when a child realizes, you see the face that something lights up in their head, like when literally the light bulb is turned on, you can see it, you see that, and just a few times you can experience that in the classroom. (School academic coordinator)

The competencies teachers perceive that students acquire by participating in ECBI are in the cognitive, interpersonal, and intrapersonal domains. Curiosity is among the most mentioned abilities; communication skills are also stressed, mostly in connection with students' self-esteem:

Well, curiosity is one of the first things that is regained, the sense of wonder, that the child thinks that something is going to happen and something different occurs, and then s/he thinks "well, why did that happen?" So that's the base, to discover things. So the classes are no longer predictable. (School academic coordinator)

There is a capacity to develop inference, to develop synthesis, because they have to communicate, you experiment and you have to say what you've discovered, so you have to develop communicational skills also, you have to be able to translate data, to see a table and understand that it means something. (School academic coordinator)

We realized that children have lowered their ability to observe, but as we did more experimentation, the ability increased, they were able to look at details, they could see patterns, and were able to distinguish what was different in a phenomenon. (School academic coordinator)

No, they don't learn the same, they learn more with this method [than with the traditional] . . . now they are the ones who have to discover that there is an energy transfer, now there is a reason; before it was just like "this is because it is, because the book said so." (Teacher)

Teachers and principals also identified significant ECBI effects on teachers' motivation; some teachers reported that participating in ECBI made them recover their passion for their teaching practices, as described in the following interview quotes:

That was how ECBI started to be implemented, the teachers loved—as I did— to see how you could develop the potential from the children, a potential that was lost for so much time, because everyone had to follow the book, because everyone was taught in an abstract way. (School principal)

When this project appeared I became reenchanted with my profession, because to have contact with real scientists, having training with them, it was wonderful for us. (Teacher)

Nevertheless, the sustainability of ECBI teaching practices after program participation has proved very difficult. Once the program leaves the school, the lack of teaching and pedagogical materials, planning time, and classroom support has hindered schools' adherence to the inquiry-based methodology, in a context of limited time and resources. Thus, ECBI support devices are central to program adherence, challenging the sustainability of the new practices when absent. ECBI's executive director commented: "An important mistake we made [in the pilot schools] was that all the implementation load was on us. If the adviser did not go, the teacher did not do ECBI . . . We did not develop, we did not transfer the skills there. We have to develop local capacities."

More broadly, in the early years, ECBI lacked a sustainability strategy at the school and local levels. To tackle this issue during the last two years, the program created networks of teachers both within schools and at the municipal level in order to enhance the program's sustainability once ECBI leaves. ECBI is also preparing school teachers to act as advisers to their peers. The idea is that isolated teachers cannot develop IBSE. Hence, currently, ECBI training and ECBI advisers have to help develop teachers' autonomy in continuing to use IBSE methods after program participation. However, once ECBI's direct work with a school ceases, the program cannot ensure the continuity of teachers' time and the provision of teaching materials. Some external observers have found significant the issue of potential teachers' dependence on both ECBI advisers and ECBI lesson plans. ECBI designers expect that through these new networks, participating teachers will also become increasingly autonomous in adapting and creating lesson plans.

> The exit [from the program] has to do with the strengthening of the community, with the community work. Surely there will be occasional visits . . . We think that that teacher will always require support, s/he will always need his/her peers, dialogue, interaction to grow. Therefore, what you need to install . . . is a teacher who is in a community that shares and assumes that common task . . . It is like the replacement of the adviser for the construction of this community. Then, I don't think that there is another long-term solution . . . : to incorporate as advisers, teachers of the school, that is key. (Program founder)

Regarding program implementation, one of the organizational learnings that ECBI members stress was the relevance of addressing local needs and tailoring the program strategy to the characteristics of the schools, teachers, and students. This became relevant in order to ensure schools' commitment to the program, and resulted in many forms of support, described by a staff member: "We considered all the variables, because we are with the teacher, planning and implementing hopefully in 100 percent of his/her classes. We adapt, there is not a fixed way of working, it is not that we have only one strategy to operate at the school; the strategy is generated taking into account the needs, the commitment, and the disposition of that school . . . But the trust develops with time."

To increase program sustainability at the school level, in recent years ECBI has been promoting the creation of collaborative work among participant teachers within schools, and the creation of networks among teachers implementing ECBI in different schools in the same geographic region, mainly municipalities. The purpose is to promote school involvement in decision making and autonomy, preventing an excessive dependency on ECBI advisers for program implementation. These collaborative networks—led by school teachers—are expected to create learning communities and to reinforce the competencies of participant teachers to use inquiry-based methodologies.[44]

In addition to schools directly participating in the program, ECBI has also contributed to building capacity within the Chilean educational system to develop twenty-first-century competencies, among both students and teachers. ECBI's additional contributions to Chilean education include connecting the educational system with the field of science; preparing many professionals (both scientists and educators) in science education; influencing the 2009 curriculum change to incorporate the IBSE approach to the national official curriculum; promoting the adoption of the IBSE approach to some initial teacher preparation and teacher training programs; and implementing a certified course.

At the same time, through the successful adaption of international science education programs and teaching materials to the Chilean context and curriculum framework, ECBI has accumulated valuable experience in the transferability of educational initiatives focused on twenty-first-century competencies. As mentioned, the ECBI team has been an active member of many international initiatives promoting IBSE in educational systems, and bringing scientists and educators together. The ECBI team has in turn played a relevant role in expanding IBSE to other Latin American countries, providing technical assistance.

Limitations, Challenges, and Critical Issues

The analysis of ECBI has allowed us to identify some weaknesses that may have limited program implementation and impact in participating schools, some challenges that have been very difficult for the program to overcome, and critical issues relevant to designing and implementing a high-quality, twenty-first-century-oriented school improvement program.

Teachers' professional development and capacity building

One of the aspects of ECBI that program participants most value is that it provides teachers with all the materials and support required for its implementation. Teachers define the educational impact produced by students' manipulation of ECBI materials as an achievement in itself. Teachers perceive the pedagogical guidelines of the program as workable opportunities to break the routine of traditional practices. In fact, motivating teachers in their own work has been a goal of the program over time. One teacher remarked: "For instance, an experiment we did to see how sound rebounded . . . I would have never thought of it . . . because sometimes you get so absorbed by monotonous things; I've been teaching for thirteen years, but suddenly they show you another way of illustrating things that you wouldn't have thought of, due to the daily activities, the monotony, the routine of work, the house, your personal life."

For many teachers, ECBI's methodology is innovative and motivating. Implementing ECBI in the classroom changes the teachers' role in relation to students in a way that can be summed up as "from answering to asking questions." Thus, various ECBI teachers noted:

> If not for this inquiring method, the class would have been more linear, more like transferring knowledge from the teacher to the student, and also working with the book, questioning and answering . . . The children would have had to copy the information that I write down on the board. (Teacher)
>
> I was traditional . . . but here everything changes, from the design of the class to the way you think . . . I mean, you guide them [the students] until they understand the concept of density, but in order to do that you have to change, and it is not something that happens overnight, it is a slow process and also gradual. It was difficult. Because the traditional teacher tends to give answers . . . In the program, the inquiry starts picking up what the child already knows, because within the traditional teaching, the teacher is not interested in what the child knows or doesn't know, the teacher transmits information, because the words are wonderful, but the child does not resonate with what s/he is hearing . . . you always start with what the child thinks, and you question him/her. I mean, the challenge is: "you believe this thing, so then how would you do

it?" They design by themselves the prediction or hypothesis, and after that they design whatever activity can provide relevant data . . . Our target is the child, but if the teacher doesn't change, we cannot expect changes in the child. (Staff member, former ECBI teacher)

However, critics have questioned the perceived prescriptive nature of the learning cycle of ECBI's methodology and the use of teaching materials. Since ECBI provides detailed lesson plans, trains teachers in a structured inquiry-based approach, and more importantly, incorporates an adviser for every teacher, some critics have asked whether ECBI might de-professionalize participating teachers, for they are left with a passive role. For example, the critics argue that the program could limit teachers' ability to choose different pedagogical strategies in relation to their students' activities.

The critics also state that in the program's implementation, materials and the learning cycle become more relevant than the inquiry processes, where the teacher's role is key. A science education expert said, "I think it is OK to have materials, but it is important to make very explicit that the materials are not a straitjacket. Being flexible . . . , distancing yourself from this rigid 'learning cycle,' because at the end of the day the issue is not the structure, but . . . that the child makes questions and is able to answer them."

The structured nature of ECBI's lessons has also been criticized. The program proposes lesson plans that are addressed during one class session (lasting ninety minutes); nevertheless, almost all interviewed teachers reported being unable to go through all of the units' steps during the class period. This has been made more difficult in light of ECBI's recent emphasis on scientific writing. Although this difficulty may indicate the lack of both teachers' capacity and autonomy, it may also reflect some rigidity in the way teachers perceive the program.

In turn, the program's staff and participants stressed the relevance of teachers' involvement in ECBI implementation, beyond a mechanical application of lesson plans: for each curriculum unit, teachers have to evaluate whether the program's proposal fits the required learning goals, deciding whether to use inquiry-based or a more traditional methodology, and to create their own contents:

Teachers are creative, because they don't follow only the ECBI book, or the worksheet, instead, they enrich it with their own material. (School principal)

Sometimes you have to try before what is being proposed by ECBI to see whether it's going to work or not. Sometimes the learning objectives require us to follow the curriculum, then you have to look and balance what is worth or useful studying. (Teacher)

According to ECBI's theory of action, the tools the program provides are intended to ensure the essential support for teachers with highly heterogeneous professional capacities in science education, and more competent and experienced teachers are expected to use them more flexibly. Additionally, the program has attempted to address these concerns by creating networks that explicitly promote teacher autonomy.

Teachers and ECBI members agree that the role of teachers in the program's implementation evolves over time: as teachers become more familiar with the program, they are increasingly more able to adapt contents to their contexts and to create their own. Experience in developing the modules with the students is critical for gaining expertise and autonomy from prescribed contents; staff members and teachers agree:

We trust teachers; we give them confidence to adapt the program to the context, what s/he has available . . . so the teacher starts realizing that s/he could think about how to make his/her practice different. And, that is generated over time. (School adviser)

I've become a little more of an expert in ECBI . . . now, I'm kind of in a reflexive stage, because before I was more like just experimenting. I feel that I've learned more through the interaction with students and their questions; I know how to get along better. . . . I handle myself with the ECBI manual, and now I have created a lesson based on what we are studying about the ecosystem. (Teacher)

The national curriculum

The existence of a national compulsory curriculum opened the opportunity to implement IBSE methodologies in regular education (i.e., not as an after-school complementary workshop), but it also implied a very important constraint because teachers are required to expose students to fixed content units, teach specific subjects, and attain defined learning objectives. In Chile, those curriculum elements are defined for each K–12 grade subject matter, including science. Thus, in order to increase the alignment between ECBI lessons and the national curriculum, the program developed teaching units for each science learning objective mandated by the official curriculum for kindergarten and primary grades. Moreover, those teaching units are organized in course guides (specific for each grade) that provide teachers with detailed lesson plans for the entire school year. In other words, ECBI has translated the national science curriculum framework into curriculum materials that are ready to implement at the classroom level, using IBSE methodologies and generating twenty-first-century competencies. As mentioned, the development of those teaching units has also been a very important instance of collaboration between program staff and school teachers.

This has not always been the case. As explained, during the early years, ECBI provided teachers teaching units developed by the US National Science Resource Center. Although translated to Spanish and slightly adapted to the Chilean context, those units were not aligned with national curriculum, a factor that prevented program implementation at the classroom level.

Although ECBI course guides currently cover the entire official curriculum and include lesson plans for every class session, we found that participating teachers frequently alternate ECBI classes with traditional classes. Teachers explained that they consider ECBI an excellent method to develop competencies and skills, but when teaching science content to students, ECBI does not seem an efficient method to attain all of the learning goals defined in the official curriculum. In this sense, teachers decide which methodology to use by mainly considering the agenda of internal and external evaluations.

Certainly, since inquiry-based objectives and methodologies were incorporated as guidelines into the official curriculum in 2009, schools working with ECBI are familiar with them. A school principal said, "Now this inquiring method is part of the science curriculum, so these new curricular guidelines start with an inquiry method, thus we are a little bit ahead in relation to what is being promoted now."

Teachers generally agreed that ECBI is a slower teaching method, because the need to debate, discover, and go in depth takes more time for students. Consequently, teachers also use traditional pedagogical methods, such as lecturing to students and reading textbooks, to ensure students learn the required science content knowledge, which the national test later evaluates. Two teachers explained their hybrid approach:

One has to fulfill the minimum contents, and in real time it is very hard to achieve that, especially with a method that is only experimenting and inquiring . . . ECBI leaves aside what is related to subject contents, and one gets evaluated with SIMCE which is all about contents . . . So what happens to me (and we have shared this with some colleagues) is that we have to take hours from other subjects to use in teaching science contents, which is complicated.

The students experiment and experiment, but you don't have much time to work on the concepts; and basically there are just concepts in science [SIMCE], therefore the results are not very good, despite the fact that I think the program is very good.

The ECBI team acknowledges the need for combining ECBI and traditional methodologies in order to cover the entire curriculum and stressed its impact on higher-order cognitive abilities. One of the program founders argued that "[t]his doesn't mean that all the classes have to be experimental; maybe there are pauses where you can reinforce with more traditional methods, maybe texts, writing, and essays."

Pedagogical emphases

ECBI bases its proposal on a strong conceptual framework for the superiority of the inquiry-based approach when compared to the traditional pedagogical approach for teaching sciences. This may have postponed interest in evaluating whether participating students actually learned more and better science and acquired the expected competencies. This lack of emphasis on evaluating the additional competencies that ECBI promotes has also affected classroom teachers, since ECBI has provided them little training and support, and few guidelines to incorporate classroom student assessment practices coherent with the IBSE approach. ECBI has only recently tackled this limitation, incorporating student assessment as a relevant unit in the summer training program.

Additionally, ECBI's strong emphasis on activities and experiments in the pedagogical dimension, and on skills and competencies in the curricular dimension, may have limited the opportunities for students to learn some fundamental scientific concepts and knowledge, and to develop other higher-order competencies like analysis and reasoning. For some critics, active learning to increase students' engagement can easily turn into pedagogical activism without clear focus on learning. Despite the incorporation of scientific writing, there is still a perceived trade-off between content and competencies; this is a major issue among participating teachers, increasingly pressed by high-stakes testing.

Program sustainability and scalability

Program sustainability at the school level has been a critical issue, primarily related to the development of autonomous teacher professional capacities. It is also linked to the program institutionalization at schools, that is, the adoption of ECBI practices as regular organizational practices, at least in reference to science teaching. It depends on the capacity of school managers to provide teachers and students the conditions, such as time, materials, and support, needed to continue working with the program's approach. We observed that sustainability of IBSE practices heavily depended on the program's presence in schools; certainly, after program participation, some teachers continue to partially use these methods, but this was an individual idiosyncratic feature, not an institutional characteristic. Only recently has ECBI addressed the issue of sustainability at the school level by training teachers to be internal advisers or leaders among colleagues, and creating local networks of teachers.

ECBI program sustainability and scalability depend heavily on national and local education policy. Local public school authorities and private school owners decide on key inputs that might constrain ECBI implementation at the school level; for example, we found that in most of the schools, authorities only partially provided required teachers' planning time, because teachers used it for other tasks, which limited program impact on their capacity building. Given current funding methods, scaling is limited by schools' and school districts' interest in implementing the program. Nevertheless, some participants think that given the current emphasis placed on school's performance on official standardized tests, the program's ability to show impact on learning achievements became critical, since it determines schools' interest in investing resources in its implementation.

The relationship with the national educational authorities has also played a critical role in the evolution of the ECBI program. ECBI's experience shows the complexity of this collaboration. Moreover, national educational policies have affected ECBI in different and somehow contrasting ways: while ECBI has been able to influence the national curriculum, test-based accountability has made it difficult for teachers to fully adopt the ECBI pedagogical proposal. Also, an open question is whether ECBI affected initial teacher education programs: although ECBI initially created a large network of partner universities to implement the program across the country, this later disbanded with the withdrawal of the Ministry of Education's support.

CONCLUSION

The ECBI program has designed a powerful school-level intervention, which supports teachers in providing a relevant education for the twenty-first century. The program addresses most of the dimensions pertaining to an education that is relevant in our century, both in the international domain and for the Chilean context.[45] ECBI has developed a curriculum that is both innovating and twenty-first-century oriented; the program provides concrete teaching materials that are relevant for schools' and students' contexts, and enhances teachers' work by providing organized pedagogical guidelines and very concrete pedagogical ideas. The ECBI program also supports teachers' work by providing in-class professional development opportunities that model what the classes it is proposing should look like. At the same time, the program provides institutional support at the school level. Thus, ECBI's vision of a more comprehensive and relevant twenty-first-century education is materialized through an action program that can be implemented in regular Chilean public schools.

ECBI's program strength also comes from the fact that its design considers other dimensions that have not been emphasized in related programs but enhance its chances of success, such as an intervention strategy at the school level that is sustained over time, a focus on linking scientists in the academy with school teachers, supporting schools and teachers in their everyday work, and offering continuous professional development opportunities. Even more, the ECBI program has been designed to meet the requirements of schools located in low SES areas and has been successful in addressing this equity goal.

Innovation in education hardly affects the traditional grammar of schooling, rarely scales up to impact a significant proportion of the school system, and seldom remains as part of regular schooling practices for a long time.[46] There are many factors that account for this lack of success and sustainability of educational change. Recent evidence on school improvement programs in Chile showed that in order to be effective, comprehensive, and sustainable over time, they need to implement multidimensional strategies that tackle pedagogical-curricular issues as well as the school management dimension, focus clearly on developing teachers' capacities, affect school culture, and reinforce teachers' professional culture and horizontal accountability.[47] This case study found that the ECBI program has made significant progress on that track in Chilean education.

ECBI has accumulated valuable experience on how to initiate relevant improvement processes in low-performing and socially disadvantaged schools. Certainly, we also identified both internal and external challenges and constraints that jeopardize ECBI innovation. Nevertheless, ECBI's experience demonstrates how finely tuned implementation devices and continuous support for teachers, as well as an approach that addresses practical teachers' needs in a collaborative way, are extremely important for school improvement. Thus, good educational ideas need well-designed and sustained efforts to travel their long way to the actual classrooms in ordinary schools.

Still, two issues are critical for ECBI program's successful implementation: the sustainability of its interventions over time, and the relevance given by educational policies to the goals it supports. The program has addressed the challenge of sustainability mainly by collaborating with relevant actors: with the Ministry of Education, influencing the national science curriculum; developing networks with national universities; creating local capacities; maintaining connections with science academies at the international level.

However, the second challenge is harder to address by ECBI program alone. Often, the program's goal of supporting teachers in helping their students develop diverse and complex competencies has been at odds with national educational policies focused on standardized evaluations that address mainly rote content and a limited number of cognitive skills. The pressure for achievement is very high among schools, and simply rejecting standardization will not change the current context. The development of professional capacities both at a systemic level and among teachers so these new competencies can be adequately evaluated is still an underdeveloped area, which will continue to challenge the success of these types of programs.

CHAPTER THREE

Building the Capacity for Twenty-First-Century Education

A Study of China's Qingyang School District

Xueqin Jiang and Zhijuan Ma
21st Century Education Research Institute, China

C hengdu, the capital of Sichuan province, was once a sleepy inland city of two million. The city has focused on urbanization and economic growth for the past twenty years; today, its land area has tripled, and its population has quintupled to over ten million. From the onset, provincial and city leaders had an overarching vision that the development of human capital leads to a more prosperous economy, a more vibrant culture, and a better governed society. Thanks in part to its focus on its education system, Chengdu is now one of China's top-performing economies.[1]

Qingyang is one of Chengdu's ten districts and the best example of how Chengdu used its best education resources to ensure a whole-child education for all. Chengdu's city center is enclosed by the Third Ring Road. In the early nineties, Qingyang District was Chengdu's western city center, where the provincial and city governments, many universities, and multinationals were located. It was also home to the province's two best elementary schools. Then the city merged the district with the western suburbs and rural farmlands outside the Third Ring Road, requiring Qingyang to use its education resources to turn around low-performing rural schools. Qingyang District has made efforts not just to integrate rural children with its own schoolchildren, but also with the children of migrant workers and those with special needs.

Today, Qingyang has a population of 640,000 permanent residents, 840,000 long-term nonresidents, as well as an undisclosed number of migrant workers. The district manages 34 primary schools, 10 junior high schools, 4 high schools, and 1 vocational school. Here, we focus only on the primary school level, which has 40,000 students and 4,105 teachers.

To increase test scores that measured students' cognitive abilities, Qingyang District believed that it had to focus on teaching its children twenty-first-century core competencies, which it defines as the following:[2]

- *Meta-learning skills*—Willingness to ask questions in class, ability to synthesize material and prepare for tests, careful and critical reading skills, and positive attitude toward learning
- *Creativity*—Openness and curiosity, willingness to take risks, courage to take on challenges (Qingyang's understanding of "creativity" is more aligned with Carol Dweck's idea of growth mind-set.[3] Throughout this chapter, we use the two terms interchangeably.)
- *Citizenship*—Respect for school rules and environment, empathy for others, ability to collaborate, sense of civic responsibility
- *Emotional regulation*—Self-control

Ample evidence suggests that Qingyang's focus on a whole-child education has translated into a more equitable school system in which students develop mastery of basic cognitive skills. In 2014, Qingyang District commissioned the Beijing-based Public Education Research Center to assess all its fourth graders for math and Chinese language aptitude. Figure 3.1 shows that the district's thirty-four schools performed equally well, with some exceptions.

Moreover, although 30 percent of Qingyang's students are the children of migrant workers, 100 percent of its elementary school students will graduate to junior high school, and 97 percent will move to senior high school. Qingyang's 2014 internal assessment, "Diversify Assessment, Deepen Equity," reported that its thirty-four primary schools had instilled a "growth mind-set" in students, and that 84 percent of students enjoyed school.[4]

In 2014, Chengdu gave Qingyang a rating of 99 percent for equity and quality in its school system, and 97 percent for parental satisfaction (as a city, Chengdu averaged 90 and 82, respectively).[5] The district has received many awards from China's Ministry of Education, and the educational leaders from the provinces of Guangdong, Shandong, Jiangsu, Jilin, and Hubei have studied and emulated Qingyang's education policies and practices.

FIGURE 3.1   Equity and excellence in Qingyang schools

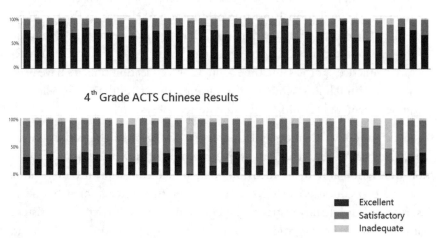

4th Grade ACTS Math Results

4th Grade ACTS Chinese Results

- Excellent
- Satisfactory
- Inadequate

Qingyang District has produced these results because:

- It has a broad and compelling narrative of how a focus on equity and curriculum experimentation in its schools will help build a more democratic society and a more prosperous economy.
- It believes that a whole-child education requires a whole-school approach, and reforming an organizational culture means shifting the mind-set of teachers. It believes that continuous and targeted professional development can help shift the teachers' mind-set, and that formative assessment can identify problems and scale solutions. To this end, it has created a "learning ecosystem," and the three main institutions of this learning ecosystem are a John Dewey–inspired laboratory elementary school that has trained many of the district's top administrators and teachers, the district's Teacher Talent Service Center that aligns professional development with professional mobility, and the Qingyang Institute of Education Sciences, a district-based research center that oversees in-service teacher education and conducts formative assessment.
- As a public school system, the district must align its actions with the larger policy environment. China's "Go West" directive focused on developing the human capital of its western provinces, and its "One Road, One Belt"

initiative links Chengdu via railway to Central Asia and beyond. As such, Qingyang's mandate became to educate globally conscious, creative professionals. Qingyang's efforts were assisted when it became an experimental zone under the National Institute of Education Sciences (NIES), China's national Ministry of Education think tank, which permitted Qingyang the freedom and flexibility to experiment with curriculum and instructional practice. At the same time, Qingyang's education policies have been aligned with China's Ministry of Education directives that have called for student-centered learning and equity in school systems.

As Fernando M. Reimers and Connie K. Chung highlight in the conclusion, Qingyang District is yet another example of how the Global Education Innovation Initiative's focus on comparative education research shows that effective education practices transcend culture and national boundaries. Many of the characteristics of the Qingyang school district are consistent with those of other case studies featured in this book. Its administrators and teachers have a sense of mission and believe their reforms in the classroom will lead to a more democratic, creative, and prosperous society. It believes that the end goal of teacher professional development is to ensure a whole-child education, which means innovating instructional practice to be child-centered. It believes that pedagogical experimentation must be teacher-led so that teachers feel empowered and intrinsically motivated, and that creative school leadership, district institutional support, and formative assessment can help guide this process.

Figure 3.2 provides a visual representation of how the school district achieves its priorities—experimentation within institutions (creativity), effective allocation of resources (equity), and democratic governance (sustainability). We argue that this theory of change succeeds because it is clearly aligned and structured around the district's main narrative and core values, and because it rewards the mobility of people, information, and ideas.

- *Mobility of people.* Created in 2005, the district's Teacher Talent Service Center provides incentives and promotional opportunities for talented teachers to move from high-performing to low-performing schools. The Qingyang Institute of Education Sciences (QIES) provides continuous and targeted professional development for teachers and formative assessment to schools. The mobility of people leads to a more efficient alloca-

FIGURE 3.2   How Qingyang School District achieves its priorities

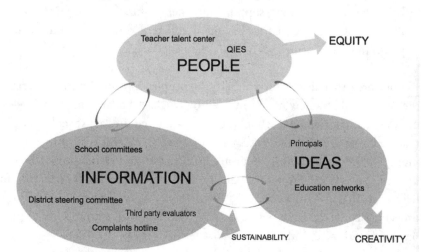

tion of talent and greater capacity building, which in turn leads to a more equitable school system.

- *Mobility of information.* The district has an array of mechanisms, institutions, and procedures that gather various educational data from a wide range of stakeholders and shares information with them to ensure openness and transparency and to provide formative feedback to teachers and school principals. Parent and faculty committees offer guidance and feedback to school principals. The district permits parents and teachers to make complaints either by mail, by phone, or in person. The district also contracts third-party evaluators to assess the district's performance as a whole; evaluators test students, survey parents, and inspect teachers and provide this information to district authorities and school principals. Mobility of information leads to stronger governance, higher performance, more engaged stakeholders, and ultimately sustainability.
- *Mobility of ideas.* The district has a variety of policies to support pedagogical innovation and diffusion of good practices. District officials task school principals with innovating curriculum and pedagogy to achieve whole-child education in schools, and they actively seek to hire principals most willing to innovate. School principals are empowered with the autonomy

to define their own school mission and make their own mistakes while being given appropriate support and mentorship. To ensure that good ideas are scaled, the district has many different forms of education networks to permit principals to share their experiences with each other.

The force that drives the mobility of people, information, and ideas is the "push-pull" framework formulated by Michael Fullan and Alan Boyle.[6] They argue that successful school transformation requires a district leadership that sets high expectations and goals (the push), are able to "create a commonly owned strategy, develop professional power, and attend to sustainability" (the pull). We believe that Fullan and Boyle's push-pull framework can help explain Qingyang's success. We will explain how district officials' high expectations are the push, while capacity building through mobility of people, information, and ideas is the pull.

We first explain our research methodology and provide background and context on the district. Then we describe how Qingyang District's capacity-building policies and practices work together as a coherent system of actions that support continuous improvement toward achieving an ambitious vision for education. To illustrate how the district implements a whole-child education at the school level, we provide two examples near the end of the chapter. We conclude by discussing the school district's challenges and limitations.

RESEARCH METHODOLOGY

Our organization, 21st Century Education Research Institute, has studied local school systems throughout China since 2003. Based on our research, we believe the Qingyang school district is a strong example of a successful school system transformation. Our organization's close working relationship with the district allowed us the access to examine and analyze the factors that account for its success.

In December 2015, we conducted extended observations and interviews in Tonghui Primary School, considered Qingyang's most creative school. The school leadership granted us open and free access, and over the course of three weeks, we sat in on school meetings, audited classes, observed student clubs, and interviewed school leaders and teachers. We also interviewed parents, conducted focus groups with students, and surveyed students about their growth mind-set.[7] In our observations, we focused on school culture and staff capacity building. We determined that much of Tonghui's success was the result of the policies and practices of the Qingyang school district, which supported the professional development of teachers and principals, and gave space and support for school leaders to create Tonghui's distinctive school culture.

In late June 2016, we returned to Qingyang for a week to conduct additional interviews for the GEII to help us understand the role of district policies in the improvement of the system. We interviewed Xu Jiangyong, vice superintendent of the school district since 2005, who has personally overseen many of the district's reforms and innovations. He provided us access to district officials and school principals (for a full list of our interviewees, see the chapter appendix). We interviewed each for thirty to sixty minutes, according to the interview protocols of the GEII.

In addition, we collected government reports and data gathered from a variety of sources to inform our analysis. In 2009, Qingyang had become an NIES experimental education zone. In 2014, NIES published a report, "Work Report on Development of Qingyang Education Experimental Zone (2009–2013)," which highlighted Qingyang's achievements to date. In the fall of 2014, the Qingyang school district and QIES evaluated their performance in a report system called "Diversify Assessment, Deepen Equity." Zhang Yong of the Beijing-based, private think tank Public Education Research Center has been testing students in Qingyang schools since 2014 on measures of cognitive ability. He gave us complete access to his test data for Qingyang schools, and we were able to see each school's individual performance in math, English, and Chinese language competencies. QIES, which provides a range of teacher professional development services, gave us their teacher training protocols and standards. In March 2017, we conducted a follow-up interview with Xu Jiangyong to ensure our data and research findings were up to date.

BACKGROUND AND CONTEXT

Qingyang District has a large segment of Chengdu's teaching talent because the district is home to Sichuan's two top primary schools, as well as universities, multinational headquarters, and provincial and city government departments. Such a large cluster of talent means that parents and teachers are forward-looking and willing to experiment in the pursuit of excellence. When interviewed, Li Bo, director of the school district's steering committee, explained the three distinct conditions for Qingyang's education success:

> Qingyang's teachers and principals have a sense of mission, and want to innovate in order to pursue excellence. This sense of mission comes from an organizational culture that has democracy, openness, and pursuit of excellence as its core principles. This culture respects teachers, and grants them autonomy to experiment in the classroom. It also provides assessment to identify problems, and scale out classroom innovations. What's most important to us is that we're always seeking to learn and innovate. Our district allocates one million yuan for research, and we collaborate closely with education research institutes at the district, city, provincial, and national level. Schools have their own budgets for research and experimentation.

To innovate, Qingyang believes in rapid prototyping of solutions that practitioners have identified. Qingyang's laboratory for curriculum and pedagogical innovation is Chengdu Experimental Primary School, considered the best primary school in Sichuan province. Founded in 1918, it has a mandate to modernize the instructional practice of all of Sichuan province through research and experimentation; the school has adhered to this mandate to this day. Its most influential principal was Hu Yanli, who became the school's second principal in 1935 and shaped the culture of the school. He had studied under John Dewey and, as dean of academics for Nanjing Teachers' College, did much to bring experiential learning to China. When interviewed, Xia Ying, party secretary of Chengdu Experimental Primary School, described the school's culture that Hu Yanli had built:

> We recruit the best talent in the province, and our culture is to encourage this talent to pursue excellence. We want our teachers to publish papers, innovate and share their new ideas with everyone, and to always look for opportunities to develop themselves, even if it means leaving the school. Our culture means that innovation is always bottom-up, driven by the teachers themselves. What makes our culture so cohesive and what drives everyone to work so hard is that everyone is conscious of our history and our sense of mission. We don't purposefully train our teachers to be principals, but it just happens that our culture is very good at producing principals who are self-motivated and willing to experiment. Every semester, two thousand teachers and principals will come to our school for different types of training. We have principals who come here

for a whole year just to shadow our administrators, and when they return to run their own school they tell us they're less conscious about test scores, and more conscious about creating an open and innovative school culture.

Because of its culture, Chengdu Experimental Primary School has become an incubator for the school district's top talent, and many of its teachers and midlevel administrators have gone on to positions of power, influence, and authority across the district. Since 1996, seventy-six of the school's teachers have been promoted either to positions of principals running their own schools or to administrative positions at the school district.[8] District vice head Xu Jiangyong, Tonghui principal Li Yong, Tonghui vice principal Qu Xi, Qingyang Special Education School principal Bian Rong, and Wanchun Primary School principal Chen Shaoguang all started their teaching careers at the school. The school maintains its culture and cohesiveness because its top administrators stay for a long time; since 1935, the school has only had four principals.

CAPACITY-BUILDING POLICIES AND PRACTICES

The 4,105 Qingyang teachers are young and dynamic. Over half of the district's teachers are less than thirty-five years old, and 1,300 are between the ages of thirty-six and forty-five. There are 395 teachers between the ages of forty-six and fifty-five; sixty-nine are older than fifty-six and are about to retire.

When Qingyang District began its systemic school transformation drive in 2003, it launched many bold initiatives to build capacity in low-performing schools. District leaders sent young ambitious teachers to start their own schools and to transform school cultures. In 2004, former district vice head Yao Ming was in her midtwenties when she was sent to transform a rural school; Caotang Primary School principal Lan Jihong was in her midthirties when she was asked to turn around Caotang Primary School (both had no previous management experience). Also, the top-performing schools were asked to partner with and transform low-performing schools. The district head mandated each school to create its own distinctive school culture.

The early years of Qingyang District's systemwide overhaul were marked by innovation, flux, and volatility. The district responded to problems and challenges rather than implement a specific set of reform directives ("First do, then fix"). This worked in large part because the district decided that capacity building would be a systemwide effort and collective responsibility; rather than assign blame and hold principals accountable, district officials supported school leaders with funding, policies, and mentorship.

Beginning in 2007, district officials took the lessons learned and developed formal mechanisms and strategies to make the school system more equitable in the academic performance achieved by students attending different schools. Today, these mechanisms and strategies constitute Qingyang District's theory of change.

Qingyang's professional development programs are effective because they're continuous, concerted, and collaborative with clearly defined goals and outcomes. In the next two sections we list the district's expectations for its schools, principals, and teachers (the push), and then we explain how the different mechanisms and strategies in Qingyang's theory of change help develop capacity by mobilizing people, information, and ideas (the pull).

The Push Factor: District's Expectations of Schools, Principals, and Teachers

Schools

Qingyang District officials expect their primary schools to have three distinct qualities:

- A culture of collaboration so that all help each other to improve.
- A democratic governance structure so that parents and teachers are involved in major school decisions.
- A spirit of experimentation and innovation so that schools develop their own distinctive approaches to solve education challenges that they can share with the wider education community. The innovation approach involves encouraging rapid prototyping of practitioner-generated solutions, evaluation, replication, and further dissemination.

Principals

District officials expect their principals to have the following attributes:

- They are proven effective classroom teachers with a deep understanding of curriculum and pedagogy. In this way, they have the authority to lead the school and know how to best use district resources to fully develop faculty.

- They can manage teams by creating a culture of collaboration and mutual respect. In this way, they can motivate the faculty and parents.
- They must have the imagination and intellectual ability to adapt to ever-shifting circumstances. Each school situation is distinct, so ultimately, they must rely on their own judgment and learning ability to navigate the uncertainty and complexity of school leadership.

Teachers

District officials expect teachers to have the following attributes:

- Genuine passion to use education to improve society
- Love of students for who they are and who they can be
- Ability to inspire students to be open and curious lifelong learners
- Ability to maintain a positive attitude and be an exemplary role model to everyone in the school community
- Passion for learning and self-improvement
- Deep understanding of curriculum and pedagogy

Pull Strategy #1: Mobility of People

Teacher Talent Service Center

District officials and principals that we interviewed told us that a main constraint of school transformation was the conservative, closed, and inward-looking culture of rural and/or low-performing schools. The district realized that teacher mobility was key to breaking this mind-set and introducing new talent and ideas. In 2007, the district created the Qingyang Teacher Talent Service Center to formalize mechanisms of professional mobility. Experienced teachers and administrators had to be moved into a different position or transferred to a new school after six years in their current positions. The district formalized incentives to attract teachers to move outside the Third Ring Road, including fast-track promotion, bonus pay (300–400 yuan per month), housing subsidies, and more training opportunities. In 2013, the district formally introduced policies and mechanisms to end employment contracts for teachers; since then, fifteen teachers have had their employment contract terminated. When interviewed, district officials explained that teachers proactively want to move to schools outside the Third Ring Road because housing is cheaper, and school facilities are better.

The Qingyang Institute of Education Sciences (QIES)

QIES is the district's think tank responsible for in-service teacher professional development and assessment. It has fifty to sixty experts on staff who have proved themselves effective classroom teachers. They are responsible for training the district's four thousand teachers. The ratio of roughly one expert to eighty teachers means that QIES has a good sense of the needs and abilities of every district teacher.

The district divides teachers into four grades: qualified, core, elite, and expert. QIES has created guidelines and standards for each grade, and it expects all its teachers to undergo continuous training. The district plans to categorize 38 percent of its teachers as qualified, 50 percent as core, 10 percent as elite, and 2 percent as expert. Currently, the district has 1,166 core teachers (making up 31 percent of all teachers).

Teachers are motivated to participate in training because of opportunities for career advancement, which lead to higher pay (elite teachers get a 300 yuan a month bonus; expert teachers get a bonus of 600 yuan a month) and more prestige. Since 2007, the district has promoted 750 teachers.

The QIES offers targeted training to new teachers. First, for a half year, new hires are apprenticed to an expert teacher; they shadow the expert teacher's every movement from class preparation to homework grading. Then new hires undergo a QIES orientation program, focused on developing their ability to work on a team. When they're assigned a school, they work directly with an experienced teacher who provides curriculum and pedagogical guidance and feedback. The new teachers immerse themselves in the school's own training regimen, while over the next two to three years, QIES provides follow-up training. After three years, new teachers are assessed by a third-party. If they perform at levels that do not meet the criteria expected, then they return to the QIES for training, and the district conducts an investigation at the school. Schools therefore have a direct interest in ensuring that new teachers pass the evaluation. There is collective responsibility to help all new teachers gain the competencies necessary to demonstrate proficiency as expected for the stage in their career.

Research has demonstrated a correlation between a focus on teacher development and student learning outcomes. Scholars agree that "professional learning communities" lead to greater capacity building in schools.[9] They also agree that professional development leads to effective outcomes when it is targeted, embedded, and provided with contextual coaching and mentoring.[10] Research has also shown that collaboration also leads to higher morale and motivation among teachers.[11] Since third-party evaluation came into effect, 370 new teachers became qualified after three years; only four new teachers were returned for retraining.

A distinctive feature of Qingyang's teacher development program is that, even though QIES has classified teachers into four different grades (qualified, core, elite, and expert) and even though the Teacher Talent Service Center has an incentives and promotion program, the Qingyang school district's capacity-building framework is neither rigid nor bureaucratic. As district officials explained to us, there is a rigorous evaluation process for new teachers to become qualified, in order to maintain quality control. A select provincial committee controls the process of moving from elite to expert because becoming an expert teacher is a prestigious honor. But in between, teachers can choose a variety of strategies to move from one grade to the next, including administrative sponsorship, peer recognition, publication of papers, and student and parent satisfaction surveys.

The district also runs teaching competitions and talent searches. In this way, teachers who feel they do not get enough recognition at the school can come to the attention of the district itself. In promoting their teachers, the district emphasizes talent and expertise over credentials and seniority.

Pull Mechanism #2: Mobility of Information

What makes the district's approach to capacity building work is that individuals who have proven themselves to be effective classroom teachers lead the various institutions involved, and information flow is free, open, and fast. The district fosters the flow of information through various formative feedback mechanisms that ensure that teachers, principals, and district administrators are continuously learning and improving.

District steering committee and the QIES

The Qingyang school district steering committee conducts site visits to each school every semester. The committee consists of the heads of the district's organization and the personnel, finance, human resources, and education departments. The goal of the visits is to identify a school's needs and problems. If the steering committee believes a school is not meeting the district's expectations, it will not assign blame. Rather, it will devote strategic resources—such as more funding for facilities and teacher training—to help the school improve. In most instances, the committee will ask QIES to intervene and send in experts for one week per semester. The attitude of the QIES is that it is there not to criticize the school, but to help it grow a culture of collaboration and camaraderie. The QIES mandate is: "Provide continuous support rather than quick solutions, help faculty develop their own curriculum rather than implement a top-down one, make teaching a collective effort rather than an individual pursuit, shift the focus from nitpicking about problems to envisioning a healthy school culture, and develop preventive healthcare rather than provide medicine." By understanding individual school transformation as a systemwide responsibility and effort, the district steering committee and QIES ensure that staff in individual schools are open and cooperative in providing the information necessary to implement solutions.

School committees

Schools have parent and faculty committees to provide guidance and feedback to principals on important school decisions. Tonghui principal Li Yong told us that when he first took over in 2012, he spent two years in faculty committee meetings debating and discussing reforms. He said that the consensus-building process kept faculty engaged and informed. While parent and faculty committees are formal mechanisms of information gathering and sharing, schools also have many informal ad hoc ones, such as open days for parents, weekly letters to parents, and faculty observation classes. We sat in on an academic meeting at Tonghui in which teachers, parents, and students observed a math demonstration class together, and then discussed and debated the math curriculum and pedagogy.

Complaints hotline

Parents, teachers, and students can make complaints to the district. If there is a complaint, whether in person, over the telephone, or online, district officials must investigate it and provide a report for the district head to read and sign. In this way, the district head is always aware of the concerns of parents, teachers, and students, and of the remedies addressing those concerns.

Third-party evaluation

In 2012, the district started to have third-party assessment for formative feedback. Third-party evaluators conduct surveys on parental and faculty satisfaction, assessing teachers and measuring each school's performance from a variety of perspectives, including academic performance, holistic development of students, creativity, and citizenship. The district also has an online database where principals provide information, and the district is able to track each school's performance and provide real-time diagnosis and feedback.

The district hires service providers that generate the most useful and objective feedback. In 2014, district officials contracted Zhang Yong of Beijing-based Public Education Research Institute because his tests compiled students' performance into school, classroom, and student reports, and pinpointed which concepts and facts students struggled with. Principals and teachers could then use the customized reports to troubleshoot and implement solutions. Although such evaluation tools were controversial when first introduced, principals and teachers now tell us that these assessment reports save time and help them better refine their classroom preparation and pedagogy.

Pull Mechanism #3: Mobility of Ideas

Principals

District officials actively seek and promote effective classroom teachers who have their own vision and ideas. Sometimes, these individuals can be controversial, but district leaders promote them into positions of authority anyway. Tonghui principal Li Yong was a sixth-grade Chinese language teacher in Chengdu Experimental Primary School who openly criticized his school's focus on obedience and discipline when district officials promoted him to run his own school outside the Third Ring Road.[12] The principal of Qingyang's showcase school is not just not a Communist Party member—he's a self-professed and openly practicing Christian.

In their search for school leaders most willing to innovate with curriculum and pedagogy, district officials have experimented with different strategies to hire and train principals. When reform started in 2003, district officials made young talented teachers leaders of their schools without much training or mentoring. Later, officials asked schools to create their own search committees comprising teachers and parents. While that seemed like a good idea, officials discovered that popularity with teachers and parents did not translate into ability, and in 2008, they instituted a talent search process, led by a committee of experts. Today, district officials believe that the best way to train principals is to apprentice them to experienced administrators. When teachers do become principals, there is a two-year trial period, during which they have a lot of support and mentoring.

District officials encourage principals to innovate with curriculum and pedagogy through a variety of means. They provide funding for new programs and give points for new programs in their annual review of each school's performance. Above all, they expect each school to create its own distinctive school culture, and they empower principals with the autonomy to define their own school mission and take risks. For example, district officials let the principal of Shude Experimental School attempt student democracy, despite protests from his teachers.

Education networks

To share ideas, experiences, and expertise, the district mandates heavy cooperation and collaboration among schools. The two best primary schools— Chengdu Experimental Primary and Paotongshu Primary—have started education groups to take over failing schools and to start their own schools outside the Third Ring Road. The district controls personnel and finances, each school principal has management powers, and the group CEO directs school vision, pedagogy, and teacher training.

Besides education groups, district schools work together and share ideas in three other ways: (1) clusters, in which schools share pedagogy and teacher training, but the level of autonomy is much higher than in education groups; (2) partnerships, in which a high-performing school lends its teachers and administrators to help turn around a low-performing school; and (3) friendships or alliances, in which schools share resources and expertise. In addition, principals from six rural schools have started their own network. They felt that QIES teacher training failed to meet their specific needs, which can often be less about teaching twenty-first-century competencies and more about getting students to show up. So they banded together to support each other's capacity building and pool resources to innovate.

Next we provide two examples that illustrate what educational innovation looks like in Qingyang. Tonghui Primary School was an education experiment to teach all students tolerance and citizenship by integrating special-needs children. Located on the rural edge of Qingyang, Wanchun Primary School increased its students' test scores by first increasing their confidence to speak up in class and in front of an audience.

TONGHUI, QINGYANG'S SHOWCASE OF CREATIVITY AND INCLUSION

Built in 2012 outside the Third Ring Road, with a capital investment of 45 million yuan, Tonghui Primary School was an ambitious program to integrate special-needs children into a mainstream setting. The district wanted to teach the 1,200 Tonghui students empathy and tolerance, as well as highlight its commitment to equity. The school today serves 1,500 students and has a special education center that serves 176 students, 100 of whom are autistic. Since its inception, the special education center's students have won twenty-one gold medals, twenty silver, and nineteen bronze in global Special Olympics competitions. Many parents with special education children move to Chengdu to attend Tonghui.

Tonghui is Qingyang's showcase school, and the district often hosts visitors at the school. The beautiful and spacious campus is thirty-three times as large as Paotongshu, one of the two best primary schools in the province. An Astroturf soccer field dominates the front of the school; behind is a four-story teaching building filled with many facilities: music rooms, a Latin dance room, a pottery room, a carpentry room, science labs, computer rooms, and a library. On the roof is a farm where students grow their own vegetables and a park with benches and a sandbox. On the left of the teaching building is an athletic facility with a full-size basketball court and a rollerblade rink around it.

Principal Li Yong, considered Qingyang's most entrepreneurial principal, manages Tonghui. He has introduced many innovations, such as students starting clubs and managing their own activities. Principal Bian Rong, who founded the district's special education program in 2006, manages the special education center. The program's objective is to ensure that special education students finish the nine years of mandatory schooling, learn to live independently, and be prepared for vocational training. The program also enrolls certain autistic students part-time in mainstream classes. There are twenty-one such integrated classrooms in Qingyang.

The program has received favorable publicity, so plans are underway to spread the Tonghui model of inclusion throughout Qingyang. Principal Bian Rong and district vice head Xu Jiangyong will lead the initiative. As Bian Rong told us, there are autistic children in all schools, but parents refuse to come forward. The hope is that, by expanding the program, all teachers will be better equipped to teach autistic children, all students will learn to be tolerant, and parents with autistic children will feel emboldened to acknowledge them. School district officials also believe in focusing resources on the most marginalized and vulnerable because "that's what's fair and right," in the words of Qingyang school district vice head Xu Jiangyong.

WANCHUN PRIMARY SCHOOL, "DELIBERATE PRACTICE" IN PEDAGOGY

Thirty percent of the district's primary students are children of migrant workers, and most are disadvantaged. Migrant children's primary caregivers tend to be their grandparents, most of whom are illiterate. Migrant children also tend to move often as their parents shift from job to job. Their families are too poor to afford extracurricular activities and tutoring. As a cohort, they tend to be low performing and have emotional and behavioral issues.[13] Many urban public school systems in China make it difficult for migrant children to attend their schools, but Chengdu has made a conscious effort to integrate them.

Wanchun Primary School is located at the western rural edge of Qingyang. Next to a provincial highway tollbooth, it is difficult to reach. Three-quarters of its three hundred students are migrant children whose parents work in the nearby factories; the rest are rural children. From the district's test performance data, despite Wanchun Primary School's low socioeconomic level, 71 percent of its students scored "excellent" in fourth-grade math, while only 3 percent failed, making Wanchun one of the district's top-performing schools.

It was a low-performing school six years ago when Principal Chen Shaoguang took over. Under guidance from the district steering committee and experts, Chen was determined to turn its academic performance around by changing the attitude of its disengaged students and teachers by altering their habits. He mentored his twenty-three teachers in preparing lectures, homework, and tests. He suggested they enforce good habits at the school and praise students for their improvements, no matter how incremental. Outside each classroom, we saw a picture of every child, with a note from each teacher, offering praise and advice for improvement, usually telling the child to do homework or be more open and active in class.

As the students' average academic performance improved, Chen also focused on making the school culture more dynamic and creative. He put students on stage to give speeches in which they presented the results of their projects and introduced many different sports activities. His students could not afford extracurricular classes after school, so he worked with experts from the district steering committee to introduce an activity that the students could afford: the art of Chinese paper-cutting. It became part of the school culture and the curriculum. The district built a paper-cutting museum at the school, where students worked as tour guides.

When we visited Wanchun, five students—three fourth graders and two fifth graders—showed us around the museum, which had exhibits highlighting different paper-cutting cultures around the world. They were clearly reciting from a script; when we asked questions—for example, "What does each culture's paper-cutting reveal about the particular characteristics of that culture?"—they balked a bit, but then offered interesting and thoughtful answers. At a roundtable discussion with students, we learned that they had limited activities at home and limited exposure to the outside world, but because of the school culture, they had become more confident, open, and courageous. They also displayed a growth mind-set. When we asked them what success is and how to achieve it, every student answered that achieving success required challenging oneself to be better and overcoming adversity and setback.

CONCLUSION: LIMITATIONS, CHALLENGES, AND OPPORTUNITIES

Because of the surge in demand for more space for students due to China's new two-child policy, rapid urbanization, and migration to the district, the Qingyang school district is under pressure to grow. In Qingyang's rural periphery, it has already built nine kindergartens, nine primary schools, and five high schools. Thirty-two kindergartens, fourteen primary schools, and eleven high schools are under construction.

Critics are pessimistic about the future of the Qingyang school system. Because the district has to grow quickly, they believe that there is not enough talent or time to develop it. They worry about China's booming private school industry targeting Qingyang's most talented teachers and administrators, which could cause a brain drain to private schools and segregation of students into different type of schools by ability to pay.

Xu Jiangyong told us there are two serious constraints to Qingyang's growth. First, teachers' salaries are not competitive with the marketplace, so young and bright teachers opt for private schools. Second, public schools lack enough autonomy to truly experiment and innovate. Overall, he believes that the growth of the private school market will benefit Qingyang District as a whole:

> Qingyang District has succeeded not because of certain individuals, but because of its organizational culture of openness, collaboration, and self-improvement. As Chengdu parents become wealthier and better educated, they want a more holistic and progressive education for their children. Chengdu's economy increasingly depends on creative professionals. As educators, we need to continue to experiment and innovate, especially in the area of assessment, where we need to shift from a focus on cognitive skills to a focus on whole-child education. In my opinion, private schools are a positive development because they create more innovation and diversity within our education ecosystem. It's good that many public school principals are leaving to run private schools because they'll forge close bonds between the public and private sectors. In the future, I will strongly encourage our public school teachers to visit private schools, and study their innovations. As educators, the greatest contribution we can make is to inspire our students with our willingness to learn and innovate.

APPENDIX (CHAPTER 3)

Interviewees and Their Affiliations

Category	Interview participants	Purpose and outcome
District officials (five total)	District vice head Xu Jiangyong and three deputies in charge of teacher management, special education, and migrant children education policy Former district vice head Yao Ming Li Bo, head of the district steering committee	1. Xu Jiangyong has been at his post for eleven years and has overseen much of Qingyang's school system transformation. 2. Yao Ming was one of the first teachers sent to build capacity in rural schools at the onset of reform; as district vice head, she oversaw the introduction of third-party evaluation into the education apparatus. Together, they provided a historical and policy overview of the district's capacity-building. 3. Li Bo studies district policies and strategies, and ensures that they're aligned at a national, provincial, and city levels.
District experts (one)	Liu Dachun, head of the Qingyang Institute of Education Sciences (QIES)	The QIES is responsible for the school system's teacher capacity building and school evaluation. Liu debriefed us on the district's teacher training policies.
School principals (eight)	Principals of the following schools: – Chengdu Experimental Primary School – Caotang Primary School – Caotang Primary West Campus – Wanchun Primary School – Kanghe Primary School – Shude Experimental High School – Tonghui Primary School – Qingyang Special Education School	We visited a range of schools and interviewed the principals to understand their views about Qingyang's capacity-building policies and strategies. They explained how capacity building and school transformation occurred at the school level.
Outside Observers (three)	School principal in neighboring district Head of Chengdu Institute of Education Sciences Zhang Yong, head of Beijing-based Public Education Research Center (one of Qingyang's third-party evaluators)	We interviewed outside observers to understand how Qingyang District's capacity-building policies and strategies compared in citywide and national contexts. They confirmed that Qingyang District was one of the best models of school system transformation in China.

An Inclusive, Whole-School, and Sustainable Approach to Building Teachers' Capacity to Promote Twenty-First-Century Skills

Lessons Learned from the Public-Private Partnership of Escuela Activa Urbana in Manizales, Colombia

Silvia Diazgranados Ferráns
Harvard Graduate School of Education

Luis Felipe Martínez-Gómez
Colegio los Nogales

María Figueroa Cahnspeyer
Universidad Externado de Colombia

Escuela Activa Urbana (EAU)[1] is an innovative education program that radically transformed the quality of public education in the urban schools of Manizales, Colombia. The program has gained increasing national and international recognition for the positive academic and life outcomes it has promoted among marginalized children in the city. Its innovative model, which had its early roots in Escuela Nueva, was developed in an effort to address the high dropout rates and low scores on national tests of students from urban public schools in Manizales, which different research studies had linked to students' disengagement with traditional schooling practices. The EAU model uses a whole-school approach to help students develop twenty-first-century competencies by promoting the core learning principles of active-social learning, participation, and autonomy, and by using a wide variety of multimodal pedagogical strategies and mediations, which include the use of student-learning guides, trapezoidal desks, group projects, self-evaluation charts, and both school and classroom government.

To build the teaching capacity for effectively promoting twenty-first-century skills, EAU has a professional development strategy in the form of a support team, which provides teachers, principals, and schools with ongoing conceptual, methodological, and relational supports and professional development opportunities in order to adopt the three core principles of the program in effective, creative, and context-appropriate ways. A public-private-academic partnership between the secretary of education of Manizales and the Luker Foundation sustains the model; Manizales University–CINDE, a university partner that operates the pedagogical component of the program, provides academic and technical support for program development and implementation.

The success of the program is due to the benefits that EAU obtains from: (1) systematically implementing profoundly democratic and participatory structures and processes of interaction among all community members at all levels of the EAU network, which creates a sense of ownership and a culture of engagement and leadership, (2) adopting a whole-school approach to teaching twenty-first-century skills, where every teacher, in every K–11 classroom, uses a pedagogy, a curriculum, and an evaluation strategy designed to purposefully promote students' active-social learning, participation, and autonomy, (3) creating a highly sustainable model of ongoing professional development and support, which guarantees continuous processes of learning and growth for teachers and schools at all levels of experience, as well as an effective mechanism for feedback and innovation, (4) relying on a public-private partnership model, which allows public and private stakeholders interested in addressing the education challenges of the twenty-first century to together overcome the obstacles they otherwise face when they act within the boundaries of their own sectors, and (5) having a favorable education policy environment that values, encourages, and requires promotion of citizenship competencies in Colombia.

We describe our methods and the sociopolitical and education policy context for twenty-first-century learning in which the EAU model operates and discuss the strategies EAU uses to develop teaching capacity. We conclude by identifying the limitations and challenges of the program and by drawing lessons for practitioners, researchers, and policy makers.

METHODS OF STUDY

In choosing a successful Colombian case for our comparative study, we first talked to different key Colombian educators and policy makers. With their help, we identified the outstanding programs for the development of twenty-first-century skills that some organizations were implementing at large scale with a long enough trajectory (more than ten years) working in the country. In addition to EAU, we considered other programs such as Aulas en Paz, Niños y Niñas Constructores de Paz, Fe & Alegría, and Escuela Nueva. After interviewing the directors of these programs and reviewing different key documents that summarized their work, we decided to conduct an extended case study of EAU for many reasons. Unlike interventions that operate by introducing one class in the curriculum, EAU uses a comprehensive, whole-school approach for the development of twenty-first-century skills. And unlike interventions that aim to transform school practices through a given number of intensive teacher trainings, EAU employs a model of ongoing professional development and support for schools and teachers at all levels of experience. Our interest was further reinforced by the fact that EAU has won several awards and has been widely recognized nationally and internationally.[2] Evidence from multiple quasi-experimental evaluations indicates that the program is having a positive impact on students' development.[3] Finally, we were encouraged by the fact that EAU plans to conduct an experimental evaluation, led by third-party university researchers, to rigorously identify the effect of the intervention on the academic, socio-emotional, and citizenship competencies of program participants.

After choosing EAU as our case study, we traveled to Manizales, Colombia, to visit schools and conduct interviews with different adult stakeholders who volunteered to participate. We used semistructured interview protocols developed with our Global Education Innovation Initiative research colleagues to collect information from twenty-five stakeholders, for approximately sixty to ninety minutes. Given that EAU is a public-private partnership operated by a university ally, we interviewed different groups of stakeholders: (1) key staff from the three institutions that have joined efforts to implement the program (secretary of education, Luker Foundation, Manizales University–CINDE), (2) program participants from four schools (principals, teachers, and members of the support team), (3) program supporters from two schools (parents and alumni), (4) a critic, and (5) external evaluators. Table 4.1 lists the participants in the study, according to the role they play.

We reviewed official documents that EAU has published, which contain important information about the program: "Conceptual and Pedagogical Foundations of the EAU Model," "A Successful Experience: Systematization of EAU," and "Evaluation for Active Human Beings: A Perspective from EAU."[4]

We analyzed the interviews using the software for qualitative analysis NVivo, through a process of thematic analysis where we employed both etic and emic coding. Specifically, we used preexisting categories of analysis that were shared by the larger group of international researchers, but we also allowed other categories of analysis to emerge from the data, to best capture the particular features of the Colombian case study.

CONTEXT IN WHICH EAU OPERATES AND PROBLEMS EAU IS ADDRESSING

EAU operates within the education policy context of Colombia, where, in the 2003, the Ministry of Education, in an unprecedented step, recognized that promoting the development of citizenship competencies among children and young people is as important as teaching math and language. At the time, the government, facing a very difficult socioeconomic and political situation, began to think about the ways in which education could help change the culture of violence and civic disengagement that had emerged and provide children with an education that would help them become constructive citizens, able to work actively and collaboratively with others to address social issues in positive and creative ways. Despite having a long-standing tradition of democratic governance in Latin America, Colombia had been enduring a difficult and prolonged armed conflict, where complex fights between multiple actors (including the army, guerrillas, paramilitary, and drug trafficking groups) had taken the lives of hundreds of thousands and displaced millions of people over the course of six decades. Additionally, Colombia had high rates of violence not related to the armed conflict, and other severe social problems such as poverty, inequality, discrimination, corruption, and low political participation.

The Ministry of Education promoted discussions among a group of experts, including researchers, academics, school teachers, nongovernmental

TABLE 4.1   Study participants, by role, organization, and number interviewed

Role	Organization	Number interviewed
Private partners	Luker Foundation	2 (founder, program director)
Public partners	Secretary of Education	2 (secretary of education of Manizales and 1 staff)
University ally	CINDE	1 (coordinator of the support team)
EAU participants	– Institución Educativa Villa del Pilar – Institución Educativa Divina Providencia – Institución Educativa Asunción – Escuela Normal Superior	3 members of the support team 10 teachers 3 principals
Supporters	– Institución Educativa Villa del Pilar – Institución Educativa Asunción	3 alumni and 5 parents 4 alumni and 2 parents
External program evaluators	– CRECE	2 evaluators
Critic	– Teacher Union	1 teacher

organization leaders, and policy makers, to identify the minimum citizenship competencies that every Colombian student must learn in school. The group formulated national standards, using a notion of competency that implied a shift from knowing facts to knowing *how to do* and *how to be*, with an approach to citizenship education that represents "a shift away from an almost exclusive focus on content to a focus that gives equal emphasis to *skills* and *attitudes* and to addressing the *contexts* in which relationships occur in the school."[5] The group defined citizenship competencies as "the articulated combination of the basic knowledge and the cognitive, communicative, emotional and integrative attitudes and skills that citizens need in order to live and act constructively in a democratic society."[6] As a result, the ministry published the Colombian National Standards of Citizenship Education, which organized citizenship competencies according to different areas of performance: (1) living together and peace: competencies that people need to coexist peacefully (e.g., to identify multiple options to solve conflicts and anticipate the possible consequences of each option); (2) participation and democratic responsibility: competencies needed to understand and participate actively in democratic environments (e.g., to cooperate actively to achieve common goals while understanding the value of agreed-on norms for the same purpose); and (3) plurality, identity, and respect for differences: competencies needed to value diversity and take a stand against discrimination and prejudice (e.g., to identify different forms of discrimination and exclusion in the school, by gender, race, ethnicity, religion, socioeconomic status, and individuals' abilities or limitations). Respect and defense of human rights were seen as a transversal category across all dimensions. Each area was further specified by level of development and type of competency: emotional (e.g., to recognize actions that are related to different emotions and to manage emotions in ways that do not hurt others), cognitive (e.g., to reflect on the consequences of discrimination on people and the community), communicative (e.g., to communicate ideas, feelings, and interests and to listen respectfully to the ideas, feelings, and interests of others), integrative (e.g., to participate actively in cooperation with others in projects for the well-being of the community), and knowledge-based (e.g., to know the difference between conflict and aggression and to understand that aggression is what can hurt others).

According to Colombian national policies, citizenship education functions as a cross-curricular subject that is regarded as part of all content subjects and school activities. The National Standards of Citizenship Education are quality guidelines that establish the topics and skills that schools must teach students, but schools have the right to make decisions about their own teaching programs, curriculum, assessments, pedagogical methods, governance, culture, and so on. However, schools must develop their own institutional education projects and specify how they plan to meet the national standards in the way that fits them best, and they also need to give students opportunities to participate in the school government and student council, and take part in creating and reviewing the schools' code of conduct. Additionally, every year, all third-, fifth-, and ninth-grade students from all public and private schools take the *Prueba Saber*, a standardized national assessment that the government developed to determine whether students are gaining the minimum knowledge, attitudes, and skills they need for competency in the domains of literacy, mathematics, science, and civics and citizenship. The results, which schools, municipalities, and departments receive in aggregate form, are intended for their use in developing plans for improvement.

The national education policy context in Colombia we have described favored the development of a vast variety of education programs that go beyond teaching the basics of math and language to help teachers acquire pedagogical skills for promoting the citizenship competencies students need in the twenty-first century. The Ministry of Education created a portfolio that compiles the best national and international programs and practices for schools to implement, which include (among others) some programs we initially considered for the present case study. The ministry has also organized a series of national forums and conferences to promote capacity building among teachers, to help them adjust their teaching practices to meet the National Standards of Citizenship competencies.

In summary, EAU has grown and gained public and private support and recognition thanks to a favorable national education policy context that encourages, requires, and supports schools to adopt educational approaches for the development of twenty-first-century competencies.

PROGRAM DESCRIPTION

EAU was created in 2002 by a public-private partnership of the secretary of education of Manizales and the Luker Foundation, which together provide the resources for funding the implementation of the innovative education model in public schools of Manizales. The founding partners also rely on the strong support of the Manizales University–CINDE, which operates the program and provides technical support. The program uses a whole-school approach to help students in K–11 develop the twenty-first-century skills they need to become lifelong learners, able to successfully integrate themselves into the labor market, and make meaningful contributions to society.[7] Specifically, EAU works by systematically promoting the key learning principles of active-social learning, participation, and autonomy in all school dimensions (pedagogy, curriculum, school activities, evaluation, and professional development) to develop critical life and labor competencies: (1) intellectual competencies such as decision making, problem solving, and creativity; (2) relational competencies such as leadership skills, teamwork, communication, conflict resolution, and environmental responsibility; (3) organizational competencies, such as management and administration, information management, service, and technological management; and (4) personal and socio-emotional skills, such as empathy, appreciation for diversity, and inclusion.

Core Audience

EAU works in Manizales, a small city of approximately 400,000 people in the coffee-growing region of Colombia. The city's Education Master Plan 2032 indicates that in the year 2012, there were 114,263 people between the ages of zero and nineteen living in Manizales, among whom 56,184 were enrolled in school. It also reports that the secretary of education had 2,277 teachers and schools administrators and 76 schools, among which 70 percent are public. Of all students enrolled in school, 70 percent are attending public schools and 30 percent private schools.[8]

As of 2016, EAU was working in 19 public urban schools of Manizales, serving approximately 800 educators and more than 17,600 students. Both founding partners work together to choose participant schools EAU network by identifying those public schools that serve disadvantaged children and are struggling to provide them with a high-quality education. Santiago Isaza, director of education of the Luker Foundation, described the principles and the process for identifying participant schools:

> We don't see equity as equality so we don't think all students should receive equal opportunities. Instead, we try to give more and do more for students who have experienced more disadvantages. So we use different criteria to select schools. When we started the program, we first chose public schools because our aim is to close the gaps in the quality of education that exists between public and private schools in Manizales, whereas public schools have always shown lower performance than private schools. Among public schools, we selected the schools that have the lowest levels of performance and the schools that serve vulnerable students from highly marginalized backgrounds. We then offer low-performing public schools attending vulnerable populations with the option of adopting the program.

The partners fund the program only in schools where more than 80 percent of teachers agree with the principles and foundations of EAU. The selection process is important for the success of EAU because the program requires a whole-school transformation, where every member of the school community actively takes part in implementing the model. Once a school decides to join the EAU network, all teachers must learn the model and adopt it in their classrooms.

History and Context Pivots

EAU has its early roots in Escuela Nueva,

> a pedagogical model that transforms conventional schooling and learning practices, by changing teacher roles and promoting active, student-centered learning strategies that respect different learning rhythms while encouraging creative collaboration and democratic values, through teacher trainings and student-learning guides that help students learn how to learn, feel happier, become more capable and confident, and gain the cognitive and social competencies that are necessary for a more peaceful and democratic society.[9]

The flexible and active pedagogical model, which EAU adapted to the urban context of Manizales, had been successfully implemented for many years in the region with support from the Federation of Coffee Growers and the government of Caldas, in an effort to help teachers from rural schools respond to the challenges of educating children in those settings. Given the low density of the population, rural schools in Colombia often rely on a single teacher to help students (from different grades and levels of development but grouped within the same classroom) achieve their learning goals with the help of learning guides that they develop autonomously but through collaborative practices. Escuela Nueva is known for effectively counteracting the high dropout rates of students from rural schools who miss classes during cropping seasons and are unable to catch up because it provided teachers with flexible student-learning guides that facilitated the process of reengaging the students academically after repeated absences.

The Luker Foundation, a nonprofit organization established and supported by a group of business leaders, with a long story of investments in education, identified Escuela Nueva as a potential program to prevent children from dropping out of school in the city of Manizales, because the model provided a highly flexible, engaging, and participatory methodology, with an emphasis on life and occupational skills. At the time, leaders of the Luker Foundation were highly concerned by reports showing that between 1995 and 2000, the education system in Manizales had "pushed out" 30 percent of students who had dropped out of school before graduating from basic education, and had failed to enroll 50 percent of school-aged children. In trying to understand the roots of the problem, they learned from a study by University of Caldas researchers, that the high dropout rates and low scores on national tests among students from public schools were driven by students' disengagement and discouragement about schools with authoritarian education practices.[10] The students felt that the schools taught irrelevant content through boring pedagogical methodologies, where they were unable to acquire the skills for succeeding in life and finding a job. Pablo Jaramillo, founding member of EAU and director of the Luker Foundation, commented:

> If the school is an authoritarian and boring place where students don't learn much, and if whatever little they learn is good for nothing, then a great deal of students feel inclined to drop out of school. At the time, dropping out of school in Manizales was a simple decision without much transcendence. Parents from poor children didn't get upset if their children did not go back to school because they were not learning much and after dropping out, they usually started working and bringing money to the home.

Given the low quality of education, public schools in Manizales were only screening students who already had good home supports and a good academic record, so they could access jobs and get promoted to the best positions. For this reason, teachers often sent students from marginalized backgrounds home and discouraged them from completing their studies. Whereas children from privileged families in private schools had access to a high-quality education, children from poor families in public schools only had access to a low-quality education that was not helping them develop the skills they needed to get a job, so they often ended up in the street and vulnerable to recruiting by powerful illegal armed groups operating in the region.

In order to address the high dropout rates in Manizales, the leaders of the Luker Foundation decided to identify a successful education program to prevent children from leaving school. They searched for an integral, highly engaging model that would offer vulnerable, high-risk children the opportunity to receive a relevant education for acquiring job skills, participate actively in their society, and succeed in life. After exploring different options, they decided to finance the adaptation and implementation of Escuela Nueva in the urban context of Manizales, because the program had a flexible and participatory methodology emphasizing the development of life and labor market skills. The Luker Foundation decided to carry out this project by developing strong alliances with the public sector and with actors from civil society.

In 2002, the Luker Foundation and the secretary of education of Manizales created a public-private partnership to cofund and pilot the methodology of Escuela Nueva in four public urban schools, with the support of the Federation of Coffee Growers, which had extensive experience with Escuela Nueva in the rural area of Caldas, in what became known as EAU. Many were skeptical about the idea of implementing a model of education originally developed for highly marginalized children from rural areas in an urban context, as they considered rural education to be of lower quality than urban education. However, when national tests of academic performance were later released, many stakeholders were surprised to learn that highly marginalized children served by EAU had achieved similar levels of performance as those from more privileged backgrounds in urban schools. Interestingly, the tests did not even capture the life skills targeted by EAU, which had a strong academic component. The unexpected outcomes led the partners to make further investments in the program. In the next years, sixteen additional institutions joined the EAU network.

Throughout its development, the EAU model has transformed itself by changing emphasis and diversifying strategies. For the first ten years, EAU used the learning guides developed by Escuela Nueva for rural areas, with some adaptations to the urban schools of Manizales. The guides explicitly articulate activities around the development of leadership, communication, and participation skills, as these competencies prepare students to find jobs. With time, it added other components related to the promotion of labor skills, such as teamwork, networking, problem solving, information management, and so on. In 2013, the program invested a half-million dollars to develop new high-quality student-learning guides to meet the needs of children in urban areas more adequately.

While the early EAU model greatly relied on the use of student-learning guides in the classroom, as Escuela Nueva does, the current model emphasizes the importance of intense, ongoing strategies of professional development to help educators acquire skills to choose, adjust, and/or develop tools to best respond to their particular students and their context, in ways that purposefully promote the development of autonomy, participation, and active-social learning in the classroom. One significant addition to EAU has been the creation and implementation of a professional development strategy in the form of the support team, in which interschool peer experts become the leaders of the model, providing introductory trainings, coaching, and ongoing support to teachers within their schools, at the same time that they plan activities and test new ideas that can eventually become systematic practices within the network. (In the next section, we discuss the components of the EAU model in detail.)

In 2014, the schools in the EAU network began being beneficiaries of Universidad en tu colegio (University at your school program). After eleven years of implementing the program, EAU realized that in addition to helping students develop twenty-first-century skills, the program needed to give them access to higher education opportunities. The program had noted that in 2013, only 33 percent of the EAU graduates were enrolled in higher education programs. The EAU alliance developed an agreement with several universities in the city of Manizales, which made it possible for faculty from different universities in the city to teach technical subjects at the EAU schools, using the pedagogical model of EAU. Students who complete the program obtain a technical degree from a university and their tuition is waived, but those who do not complete the program must pay for the costs of enrollment. The tuition waiver is helpful, as EAU students come from disadvantaged socio-economic backgrounds, so many would be unable to pay for the costs of college. To run this program, the EAU alliance negotiates discounted rates with postsecondary institutions, so the EAU alliance pays only one-quarter of the price for each student that individual students would have to pay for tuition if they applied to a higher education program. As a result of this innovative initiative, by 2016, more than 70 percent of students in the EAU network were able to access higher education programs where they can both gain marketable skills and obtain a degree.

ANALYSIS OF THE PROGRAM

Next we present the theory of change of EAU and describe the core components the program uses to build capacity among teachers so they can effectively promote students' competencies for the twenty-first century.

Theory of Change

EAU works by transforming conventional schooling and learning practices to promote the development of twenty-first-century skills among all members of the school community. The model assumes[11] that—

If institutions provide teachers with the resources and the conceptual, methodological, and relational supports they need to effectively promote active-social learning, participation, and autonomy

Through:

- Shifted expectations about the roles and tasks of both teachers and students, which move away from distant, authoritarian, and teacher-centered practices toward caring, democratic, and student-centered interactions, in which teachers act as consultants and students act as agents of their own learning.
- A strategy for teachers' professional growth and development that includes trainings, workshops, school visits, and ongoing processes of coaching and support for teachers of all levels of experience provided by an inter-institutional network of peer experts who meet weekly to study theories about how people learn, share best practices, and brainstorm solutions to problems together.
- Access to educational resources, tools, and opportunities purposefully designed to promote active contextualized learning, participation, and autonomy in the classroom, including:
  - Student-learning guides for all subject matters that respect different learning rhythms but are developed collaboratively
  - Trapezoidal desks to facilitate group discussions and teamwork
  - Self- and peer-assessment charts
  - School government and classroom government
  - Opportunities to develop group projects based on their interests

Then teachers will:

- Develop the meta-cognition and socio-emotional skills they need to transform their role from lecturers to consultants who intentionally and strategically promote student active-social learning, participation, and autonomy

- Learn to gradually share power, and to support and trust students in the process of coordinating, planning, executing, and evaluating their own learning activities
- Become critical about the learning processes of their students and spend time in class actively asking questions and using a wide variety of strategies to problematize the knowledge that students are co-constructing in ways that are relevant to their lives and to their social context
- Use most of their time planning and adjusting the curriculum in ways that consider the pedagogical purpose of the activities, the specific context and needs of their group of students
- Feel happy, confident, capable, useful, loved, valued, and motivated to conduct high-quality work

Students will:

- Become agents of their own learning, who are academically and civically engaged
- Develop the cognitive, socio-emotional, and civic competencies they need to successfully integrate themselves in the labor market and act as constructive citizens who get along with others, work collaboratively, and think creatively about ways to solve the problems of their community, and respect, appreciate, and learn from diversity
- Feel happy, confident, capable, useful, loved, valued, and empowered

And society will be:

- More peaceful
- More inclusive
- More democratic

Realized Outcomes

EAU has demonstrated that students exhibit good results in local, national, and international tests. Fabio Hernando Arias, former secretary of education of Manizales, pointed out that the EAU alliance provided funding to enable the National Institute for the Evaluation of Education in Colombia (ICFES), which administers all the national and international tests, to oversample schools from EAU in Manizales for PISA. As a result, it was possible to determine that EAU students are exhibiting higher performance in math, language, and natural sciences than other schools in the country.

In our interviews, many stakeholders insisted that tests are not capturing the most important competencies that EAU targets, as these assessments have a strong focus on academic competencies. Juliana Toro, a teacher and a member of the support team at the San Jorge School, explains the main differences in the outcomes promoted by traditional models and those promoted by EAU:

> In a traditional model, an excellent student is one that knows a lot, performs well in standardized knowledge tests and obtains high scores in math evaluations. An excellent student in EAU is one that *also* leads and shows creativity and autonomy to guide his or her own learning, one who supports the learning of others, who learns in community and seeks to gain contextual knowledge. A good student in a traditional model does well in the tests, but a good student in EAU also manages other competencies that are not being evaluated by those tests but that will be evaluated by life. They are children with values, who listen to others and express themselves assertively, who adopt collaborative attitudes to work with others to solve contextual issues, and who appreciate differences and know how to include others.

Principals, teachers, alumni, and parents reported that EAU has helped students become skilled team workers, highly assertive leaders, and clear, compelling communicators who are able to express themselves confidently in private and public settings. They also reported that the program has helped students become more creative and better able to take initiative and carry out projects with greater autonomy and motivation. Their confidence, communication, and leadership skills have helped them to succeed in national and international forums, where they have consistently demonstrated competencies that go beyond those captured by traditional tests. Alcibiades Blanco, teacher, Institución Educativa (I.E.) La Asunción, explained:

> I went with my students to a national event of math and that is when you see clearly that the model works. You see your students in charge of themselves, speaking with confidence to an auditorium full of teachers, explaining to large audiences their methods and findings. For me, the most striking part of EAU is to see the autonomy that children develop, to see that students are able to work by themselves, that they become responsible for their own learning.

The autonomy and leadership skills that students in EAU have developed are also evident in their daily school lives in striking ways. For example, Juan de Dios, coordinator, I.E. Normal Superior, recalled:

> In the Normal Superior de Manizales, where some students are being trained to become teachers, we have "Autonomy Tuesdays" which is an innovative and interesting experiment. On Autonomy Tuesdays, students from eleventh grade and those who are being trained for teaching become in charge of the school. They become the director, the academic coordinator, the discipline coordinator, the teacher, etc. On the previous week, they have coordinated and planned the things that they will do that day. And on that day, the school doesn't have teachers on the classrooms. The teachers are in the school, but they are having a meeting somewhere else. Students are in the hands of the student who acts as principal; the student who acts as coordinator; the students who act as teachers. They manage everything that comes up that day. That type of experience is possible in EAU schools because EAU supports individuals to develop citizenship competencies and autonomy.

In the context of a country severely affected by conflict, war, exclusion, and inequality, teachers highlight that students have developed values and ways of living together that are critical for constructing a sense of community, for negotiating conflicts, and for promoting inclusive attitudes in the midst of diversity. According to Juan de Dios Gallego, coordinator, I.E. Normal Superior, "When students have problems among each other, they do not stay upset, they are able to have discussions, navigate relationships, mediate conflicts, and effectively construct possibilities for resolution and action." Nubia Cardona, member of the support team in the Malabar school, commented: "They have learned to see differences as opportunities to grow because they see diversity from the point of view of collaborative work." Cardona reflected on how the model promotes inclusive practices:

> We have institutions with children who have Down syndrome, physical disabilities like deafness, and they work in an integrated environment with the other children as one of them, because the model is collaborative and different children support each other according to their strengths and weaknesses. There are schools with children from very low SES levels, where there are lots of family and social problems, but you go to the schools and you will see the order and motivation with which children participate in the school government and the classroom governments.

In this regard, the Observatory for the Quality of Education officially recognized the Institución Educativa Villa del Pilar, an EAU participant school with many children with mental and physical disabilities, as an example of how to successfully promote inclusion and integration in the school.

The focus group with alumni also supported the perceptions teachers shared. Alumni consistently emphasized that, more than any other skill, attending EAU helped them become empathetic, inclusive, and appreciative of diversity. One remarked:

> The program is excellent and helps us learn how to respect others, how to integrate people who are different than us, how to include people who have cognitive or physical disabilities. That was very helpful because a lot of people don't like to include others and don't like to interact with others, but in this school is very beautiful because we are taught how to share with others in ways that give a lot of meaning to our own lives.

Another student added: "I learned to share with people who we often stigmatize and would not interact with, and I learned to take away those social masks and know how to interact and work and share with other people who are not like me" (Student, focus group, I.E. Villa del Pilar). A mother of a special-needs girl also shared her own experience:

> My daughter has Down syndrome and has been in this school for seven years. The model has promoted her integration and has given her the opportunity to learn. In no other school in Manizales was she able to get an education because she was seen as someone unable to learn. But the EAU model allowed my daughter to learn and now she is able to read, she is able to add, she is able to socialize and have friends, she is able to participate, and she is able to do things that I was always told she would never learn and that I never imagined she was going to accomplish. The program allows and encourages her to participate and to integrate herself because her peers include her and care for her. In other schools she was bullied, so she was not doing well, but in this school all students are able to grow as human beings. (Focus group parent, Institución Educativa Villa del Pilar)

Finally, all community members consistently said that the model has helped them feel happy, loved, valued, capable, and empowered.

Capacity Building for Individuals and Organizations

EAU has developed its strategies for capacity building around the notion that human development is a process that spans from dependence and heteronomy to independence and autonomy. According to this view, individuals and societies often function at high levels of dependency and heteronomy, but with time, support, and continued opportunities to participate and exercise their agency, they can move toward increasing levels of autonomy. Consistently, EAU has developed strategies for capacity building that do not rely on quick fixes to education, but on the realization that if schools and teachers are going to build the kind of structures, processes, and relationships that will facilitate the development of autonomy, they need to embark on long-term, ongoing processes of support and transformation.

We interviewed members of the support team who were highly aware of the ways in which, in order to build capacity for the development of twenty-first-century competencies, EAU needs to transform not only existing teaching and schooling practices, but also social structures and cultural norms. The coordinator of a school and member of the support team eloquently discussed how EAU works to transform systems of beliefs and behaviors grounded in historical and cultural forces that cannot be changed overnight. Juan de Dios, school coordinator, I.E. Normal Superior de Manizales, noted:

> We have mental structures that are historically and culturally constructed, rooted and ingrained in our past of dependencies and colonization. Historically, teachers are a community that comes from those processes and so we teach students to repeat and to memorize. We have been trained in schools that taught us to restrict ourselves and wait to speak. So we grow up and become old and continue waiting for someone to give us permission to talk. EAU is trying to change our attachments to systems of beliefs that have been taught to us for years and which are hard to change. Our main challenge is to transform teachers, so they can make a qualitative jump to new modes of pedagogical relationships, away from directive and authoritarian models based on the idea that they have the truth, to pedagogical relationships based on what Judith Butler calls "feminine logics of action," where the predominant features are not the patriarchal authority and the military rigor, but the dialogue, the experience of sharing different types of knowledge, the proximity, the presence of love and comprehension in relationships. Schools were born and have been highly permeated by processes of control, but schools must transform themselves and provide students with the opportunity to gain disciplinary

knowledge and to construct new knowledge based on their interactions and relationships with others.

Capacity building then is understood as a long-term process that requires ongoing support for participants at different stages of their development. Ligia Inés García, the coordinator of the support team from Manizales University–CINDE, explained:

> When a school adopts the EAU model, teachers do not immediately give students all the autonomy and decision-making power they need to plan, execute, and evaluate their activities. Teachers need to learn how to gradually transfer power to their students. Otherwise, schools would run the risk of going from authoritarian to anarchic, chaotic environments. The support team works hard to promote participation and autonomy, but with a clear understanding that capacity building is a process that occurs gradually, little by little, because change does not occur in one day, but requires time.

This notion of human development has influenced the conceptual, methodological, and relational aspects of how the program promotes capacity building in ways that move it away from adopting quick and simple solutions to education and toward implementing profoundly deep transformations of education practices, which require stable structures and ongoing systems of support. EAU does not rely on the implementation of a single weekly class to promote twenty-first-century competencies. Instead, it uses a whole-school approach that permeates every level of the system, changing traditional learning tools, learning spaces, learning dynamics, and roles for teachers and students, in all classes and school activities. Similarly, EAU does not rely only on the use of intensive trainings to build capacity among teachers. Instead, the program has created a sustainable strategy to provide ongoing coaching for teachers and ongoing opportunities for professional development, no matter how experienced the school and the teachers.

Next we describe the ways in which different components of the program promote active-social learning, participation, and autonomy to support capacity building.

Core Components

EAU uses a whole-school approach for the development of twenty-first-century competencies, which—as opposed to programs that are limited to one single-content subject—permeates every aspect of the school. The core components of the program—pedagogy, curriculum, evaluation methods, and strategies for professional development—promote the development of competencies as they are designed and structured around the learning principles of active-social learning, participation, and autonomy. They are facilitated by implementing mediations that include interlearning student guides, school and classroom governments, progress control charts, group activities, and so on.

Pedagogy

To better promote students' active-social learning, participation, and autonomy, EAU uses a pedagogical model that shifts traditional teaching practices from unilateral, authoritarian, and distant, to interactive, democratic, and proximal.

Active pedagogies and learning by restructuration. EAU is structured around the idea that in order to build capacity and promote learning, people must actively engage in activities so they can gain, through praxis, knowledge that is relevant to their own experience. The program distances itself from traditional top-down pedagogical models of education where individuals are seen as passive learners who are given information through teacher instruction, and who are expected to memorize information with the help of conditioning and reinforcement methods. Instead, EAU aligns itself with bottom-up pedagogical models that recognize that students are active agents who, in their interaction with people, resources, and environments, gain the needed knowledge, attitudes, and skills to solve the existing problems of their own context and to take a leading role in their society.

While there are different types of active pedagogies, EAU believes that the key to learning is connecting new knowledge with intuitive knowledge. To learn, students must participate in activities that help them understand how a given concept is related to what happens in their own lives and to their own context, such that they can see it as relevant and meaningful. Students should engage in activities that have transcendence and that are connected to their own experiences and reality. Classroom activities should help students come up with questions about issues that are part of their world and that will help them make sense of their context, analyze situations with a critical eye, think about solutions to problems, and imagine improved ways of being in the world. In doing so, EAU hopes to create leaders in different disciplinary fields who can make meaningful contributions to the well-being of their communities and of society.

Collaborative learning. EAU also emphasizes interdependency and collaboration. All pedagogical and teaching strategies have been designed so that students will learn from each other while working in groups, in ways that will lead them to gain life skills that only emerge through collaborative work. Consistently, classroom environments are organized to facilitate collaborative learning, with the help of trapezoidal desks that place children in groups where they face each other and work in teams. Within each team, all members have a role that facilitates their collective efforts to learn and engage in learning dynamics where they must interact constantly to achieve their learning goals, and talk with peers who have different assigned responsibilities if they want to succeed as a team. In this way, the program encourages dialogue and interdependency and moves away from teaching and learning practices where silence and isolation are a predominant feature. Santiago Isaza explained how, in order to support these learning dynamics, the program has to transform the structure of the environment:

> Traditional schools in Manizales usually have unipersonal seats, which we exchanged for trapezoidal desks where students seat in groups of at least three people and sometimes in groups of six people. Those desks are meant to unite students as they enable them to face each other instead of having to look at the back of their peers. By structuring the environment in this way and by using pedagogical approaches where students need to count on others to reach a solution, students learn to cooperate and become team workers.

New teacher and student roles. EAU positions teachers and students in ways that significantly differ from traditional approaches. Teachers do not act as lecturers who impart knowledge, but as facilitators who are experts at didactics and who purposefully use a wide range of multimodal teaching strategies to give students experiential activities to become participatory and autonomous learners. To be effective facilitators, EAU supports teachers in establishing horizontal and caring relationships with their students, with open channels for communication that build trust and respect. In this sense, teachers do not act as superiors but as partners who both teach and learn, and as caring figures who support students in their academic and personal development.

Consistently, the EAU model changes the role of teachers, requiring that they prepare the activities that students will work on during class, instead of preparing the information that they would otherwise deliver in a lecture. During class, teachers observe how students work together, intervene and give feedback, and challenge the construction of the social knowledge that students are creating by asking questions and posing problems so they reflect on why they are doing one thing and not another, why they are positioning themselves in one way and not another, and so on. To facilitate productive interactions, teachers need to know about things happening in the local, regional, national, and international contexts, be critical and aware of identity and power issues, develop the ability to have different perspectives, and know how to skillfully facilitate discussions around controversial topics.

Similarly, students are not passive recipients of knowledge who need to be told what to do, but active agents capable of taking charge of their own learning process. In this regard, Santiago Isaza made an interesting observation:

> In traditional education models, a teacher has prepared class and spends fifty minutes lecturing while students copy information. At the end of the week, teachers conduct a test to assess how many students were able to memorize what they were told. Such method promotes very passive ways of learning, where students spend 95 percent of the time in the classroom being quiet and looking at the back of their peers.

Curriculum

EAU gives students interlearning guides for all basic areas—math, Spanish, social sciences, and natural sciences—from first grade to ninth grade. In tenth and eleventh grades, the program provides interlearning guides for chemistry, physics, trigonometry, philosophy, and so on. All interlearning guides correspond to the Ministry of Education's National Standards, which specify what students should be learning at each grade for each subject matter, but in ways that specifically place students as agents of their own learning. While all the guides for all grades use a methodology that promotes twenty-first-century competencies, the guides for grades 10 and 11 have specific activities to promote the development of key career and life skills, such as decision making, creativity, teamwork, leadership, and so on. In this way, the curriculum promotes twenty-first-century skills through two different mechanisms: first, a methodological approach that consistently promotes a dynamic fostering autonomy, communication, and collaboration; second, content-specific activities specifically designed to promote competencies.

The flexible interlearning guides allow students with very different skills and levels of development to learn at their own pace, but with support from others through collaborative learning. Each learning guide is designed to help children acquire disciplinary knowledge in ways that are connected with the development of twenty-first-century skills. All guides—as well as all adaptations teachers have made—are structured around five stages that purposefully connect teaching with learning: (1) initiation—students and teachers identify and explore previous knowledge and experiences about a given theme or issue, which helps them make connections with the new concepts introduced in a lesson; (2) foundations—students are introduced to new concepts related to the intuitive knowledge and experiences they have already discussed; (3) practice—students practice the new concepts through exercises that help them secure the new knowledge; (4) application—students try to figure out practical applications for their new knowledge in their daily lives at home, school, the community, and the world; (5) complementation—students find further information about an issue and share and discuss what they have learned with their family or community members. Each guide covers one theme in about ten to fifteen pages. The academic year has four units, and each unit has approximately five guides.

The teacher adjusts the interlearning guides to the level of the students. Students with very different levels of development can help each other. In a focus group, two different parents shared their experiences. One parent from Institución Educativa Villa del Pilar stated:

> My daughter was losing her patience in the classroom because she is able to learn everything really quickly and other children take a lot more time than her and cannot learn at the speed that she learns. In her classroom, there are even some children with cognitive disabilities. So she was getting bored because she would complete activities and had nothing else to do. So as the teacher got to know all her students and identified the situation, she told us that my daughter has a very high IQ level. She discussed with us the strategy they were going to use: the teacher would adjust the guides for her to make them more challenging. She explained to us that EAU tries to include people with learning disabil-

ities but also people with all sorts of special needs. In the case of my daughter, the teacher has challenged her to learn fast and perform at the level of the teacher. So they spend a lot of time together and get along very well.

Another parent from the same school discussed the benefits of the flexible methodology: "The teacher adjusts things for every student. The teacher has sixteen students and adjusts things for each of them and according to their skills she creates different ways to challenge them. This makes students highly committed to the work they are doing. You would not believe how responsible my daughter has become, I'm totally impressed."

In addition to the content subject matter that students learn with help from the interlearning guides, the curriculum requires students to participate in transversal group projects according to their interests (e.g., the environment, sexual and reproductive health, peace, and reconciliation, etc.). For these projects, students form committees in charge of planning, executing, and evaluating daily learning activities. Transversal activities take place at the beginning of each school day and help students develop leadership and teamwork skills and give them opportunities to practice expressing themselves in front of large audiences.

Finally, thanks to the Universidad en tu colegio program, students in the EAU network can obtain technical skills and a technical degree from local universities. EAU developed an agreement with universities in the city so that students in tenth and eleventh grades of the EAU networks can gain technical skills by attending afterschool classes taught by faculty members from local universities using the pedagogical model of EAU.

School and classroom governments

Children vote and can be elected to school and classroom governments, where they are active in democratic decision-making processes relevant to their lives in school. Within the classroom, all children have a role and are part of committees responsible for improving specific aspects of the environment and the classroom learning dynamics. Both the school and the classroom governments allow children to actively participate in activities that promote the development of their autonomy, as they take on different community roles that enable them to exercise their agency. One teacher described the importance of their roles in the classroom and school governments:

EAU uses an underlying concept of human development that is rooted in the belief that language and symbols are two core components of the human condition. So EAU takes advantage of students' ability to represent the world through symbols, and makes the school a symbolically rich territory where young people are expected to adopt concrete roles: they are not students who wait for some knowledge to be delivered by an authority figure, but "the monitor," "the classroom president," "the group director," "the team member," etc. By making available concrete roles, students are empowered to position themselves in the world as leaders, team members and agents, and in doing so they become those roles and act accordingly. (Juan de Dios Gallego, Institución Educativa Normal Superior de Manizales)

The principles and dynamics of the EAU model have allowed the school and classroom governments to become genuine structures that promote students' participation, cooperation, and agency. As Carlos Arturo López, a teacher at Institución Educativa Normal Superior de Manizales, noted, "The school government is not decorative or make-believe; it's a real space where students have a genuine opportunity to influence decisions, take action and participate." The school and classroom committees make it possible for each student to have a role (e.g., classroom president, classroom vice president, secretary, leader of the journalism committee, leader of the health committee, secretary of the health committee, etc.). These roles allow students to take on responsibilities as in real life and also help them understand the importance of fulfilling their duties and holding others accountable, for the good functioning of the community.

Evaluation

EAU uses a system of evaluation that responds to policies of the National Ministry of Education, according to which institutions should do three types of evaluation: (1) hetero-evaluation, the assessment that the teacher makes about the performance of the student, (2) auto-evaluation, the assessment that students make of their own performance, based on a set of criteria, and (3) co-evaluation, the assessment that peers make of the students. While schools in Colombia give equal weight to these three systems of evaluation, EAU gives more importance to processes of self-evaluation, as the program purposefully tries to recognize students as agents of their own learning. Hetero- and co-evaluations are then used to triangulate the assessment that students make about themselves in ways that can further enrich and support them in becoming aware of what they have accomplished and what they can to do to make further progress.

To guide processes of self-evaluation, EAU uses a progress control chart, which enables students to monitor their own progress, accomplishments, and behaviors. The chart helps students identify their own capabilities and strengths so they can stay motivated to reach a level of high performance. The chart guides students in identifying what they have accomplished, as opposed to what they have not accomplished, and gives explicit indicators of accomplishment, so they can be aware of their possibilities for growth within each discipline or field of work. At the beginning, students use this chart with teacher support. As they gain practice, students evaluate themselves, moving from heteronomy to autonomy.

To guide processes of hetero-evaluation, EAU helps teachers adopt a student-centered approach to evaluation, where they are encouraged to get to know their students and take into account their strengths and difficulties case by case. Teacher Carlos Arturo López, from Institución Educativa Normal Superior de Manizales, described his experience learning about this student-centered approach to hetero-evaluation:

> One thing that had the biggest impact on me as a teacher is the concept of evaluating with love and seeing students as human beings, and not as objects within the classroom whose performance I need to raise. I learned to see each one of my students as a different person, with different strengths and weaknesses, with different possibilities and paths for improvement. I had previously graded exams, without even looking at the name in the paper. I only cared to determine whether a student passed or failed. But when I learned to evaluate with love, I felt filled with that concept and I started to care about the person behind each piece of work. If they did not do a good job, I would find out why and I would ask: "What happened? What strengths does this student have?" And I would come to the table to observe the work of this student and try to discover why the student did not do well in the evaluation or the activity. And after I identified the problem I would come up with strategies and with a plan to strengthen that student. So I became less interested in the grade, and more interested in making sure that the student would develop the ability to improve, to learn, to move forward.

Professional development

The EAU support team, which is critical to the program, is an inter-institutional group of teachers who have become experts in the principles of EAU, introduce their peers to the pedagogical model and curriculum of the program, and provide teachers with regular learning opportunities and ongoing coaching for as long as they are part of the EAU network. Within each school, one outstanding teacher whom peers have recognized as a leader in the institution, and who has a deep understanding of the model, becomes a member of the support team, together with similar teachers from the other EAU schools. Principals of the school choose the members for their good relationships and credibility among their peers and their love and embodiment of the principles of the EAU model; they are known to have implemented it effectively within their own classrooms. By joining the support team, the teachers become the leading experts of the model and develop the ability to educate other teachers and to provide ongoing support in the school.

Members of the support team attend meetings once a week for three-and-a-half hours to study and plan activities together. During meetings, they spend their time in different ways: (1) engaged in activities that strengthen the foundations of the program, such as reading and discussing conceptual and methodological educational and pedagogical frameworks, and thinking of ways to apply them to their classrooms; (2) socializing problems, experiences, and best practices, and thinking together about solutions to those problems, and finding ways to test and adopt best practices across participating schools; and (3) planning activities to develop in the schools. Members are responsible for designing trainings, facilitating school visits, planning micro-centers, and providing coaching to teachers, as we describe below.

Training. The year before a school starts implementing the model, every teacher in the school attends six training sessions, each of which lasts seven hours. Teachers learn about the theoretical and methodological implications of the three key principles of EAU—active-social learning, participation, and autonomy. They also become familiar with the pedagogical model of collaborative work and learning by restructuring, as they learn about the mediations that the program makes available to promote learning: student-learning guides, group activities, school and classroom governments, charts to self-monitor progress, and so on. The support team gives teachers a wide range of strategies that the model uses to promote learning, and it also collects the strategies that teachers already use, which are consistent with the three key, non-negotiable principles of the model. The goal is to help teachers develop a commitment to implement educational strategies that promote active-social learning, participation, and autonomy, even if the strategies they choose are not exactly the mediations that the program makes available to them. EAU recognizes that many strategies promote active learning such problem-based learning. For this reason, the training encourages teachers to identify and collect strategies; this helps them recognize the importance of the pedagogic intentionality of each activity. The training aims to help teachers become thoughtful and reflexive about the reasons why they should choose one strategy over another with a specific group of children, according to their needs. Training is conducted using the same type of experiential method that teachers will later implement with children in the classroom.

School visits. During the first year after a school decides to join EAU, its teachers visit schools that are already implementing the program. In this phase, they are not implementing the model but observing how teachers in experienced schools do it, so they can think about aspects of the model that would work well or need to adjust to the context and students in their own school. The year a school starts implementing the program, peers visit and observe the teachers, providing feedback so they can improve their practice.

Coaching. After teachers have received their training and attended the inter-institutional visits, they are coached by the support team and spend one week per year thereafter reflecting on their experience and adjusting the program to best meet their needs. When a new teacher comes to a school already implementing the program, a school representative of the support team introduces the new teacher to the model; the representative gives individualized guidance and coaching. Members of the support team work daily within their schools to coach teachers and to ensure that every component of the program is implemented effectively in a way that responds to the school's particular needs and characteristics. Coaches are in charge of introducing and reintroducing information to teachers and of giving everyone updated information and strategies to test and implement. Álvaro Maya, director of the education nucleus at the secretary of education in Manizales, reflected on the support team:

Members of the support team act not only as teachers' godparents, but they also serve as the intermediaries between the school, the Luker Foundation, the secretary of education. When there are problems or needs, when something doesn't work, they are the valid interlocutors who can make requests to the EAU alliance. As such, the support team is considered to be the most important component of the EAU model, as it provides the most efficient mechanism for innovation and feedback.

Micro-centers. In addition to the training and coaching, EAU has micro-centers, or spaces in which teachers meet every two months to discuss specific themes that are important and controversial, such as how to best evaluate students' skills and performance.

RESOURCES FOR SUSTAINABILITY AND FEASIBILITY

Both the Luker Foundation and the secretary of education of Manizales provide resources and plan activities together, but the funding is administered by the private partner (Luker Foundation) with supervision from the public partner (municipality of Manizales). (See figure 4.1.) Manizales University–CINDE, the academic ally, operates the pedagogical implementation of the program and provides all participant schools with the technical support, intellectual rigor, and state-of-the-art conceptual and theoretical frameworks to improve the education strategies of the model. CINDE also coordinates the support team that trains and provides ongoing coaching to teachers, and gives principals and teachers the technical support to adjust their institutional plans of education (PEI) so that the vision, mission and activities of the institution are fully articulated to the EAU model so that it can become both visible and sustainable.

As a result of the public-private partnership, EAU has developed an education model with several advantages over other available alternatives. First, public schools in the EAU network obtain more resources than other regular public schools because they are supported by funding from the public-private partnership, and because the funding is managed in highly efficient ways that are not affected by the devastating effects of corruption practices, such as embezzlement, which so negatively affect the management of public funds in Colombia.

FIGURE 4.1   The public, private, and academic partners of the EAU alliance

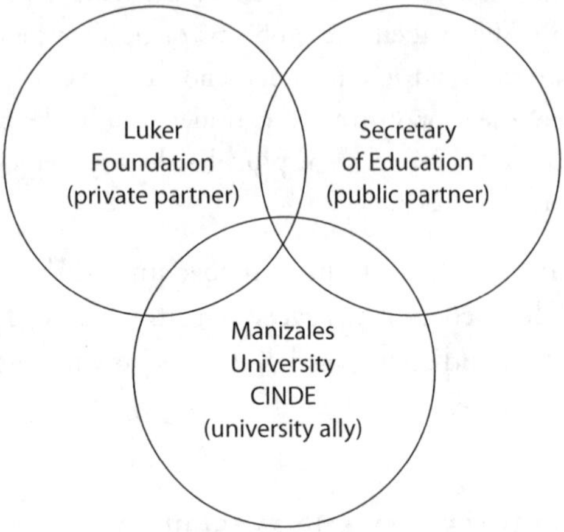

Second, schools in the EAU network have benefited from a greater willingness to pilot new creative initiatives and to take risks because the resources available within the network are not tied to short election cycles. In other words, the public-private partnership of the EAU model has enabled schools in the network to overcome a common obstacle in the public sector, whereby public schools are unable to test innovative but risky projects with money from public funds because politicians are afraid of being held liable for wasting public resources. With access to private resources, schools in the EAU network have been able to grow and learn because they are constantly testing innovative education strategies and initiatives without the restrictions imposed by regulations governing the use of public funding.

Third, schools in the EAU network have also benefited from a greater willingness to conduct evaluations of impact, because there is an interest in learning beyond the short cycles that dominate the public sector. In fact, the private component of EAU has guaranteed the continuity and sustainability of the program and has enabled schools to accumulate wisdom over time in ways that are impossible in the public sector, given the short life span of governments.

The benefits of the public-private partnership between the Luker Foundation and the secretary of education have exceeded the expectations of all stakeholders, and they have allowed an education program implemented in the public sector to accumulate wisdom, despite five changes in the public administration over the course of twelve years. Notably, the EAU alliance has guaranteed the future sustainability of the program by becoming embedded in the planned development of the city. The public-private partnership of EAU has also inspired others to express support for alliances where both the public and the private sector provide funding.

With regard to the costs of the program, the first year of implementation of EAU costs US$66 per child; and the second year is US$5 per child. These figures do not include teacher salaries, because public school teachers are paid by the state. The values include the costs of a bonus income for public school teachers who become members of the support team, as well as the costs of the teacher training and coaching, and the special furniture and materials, such as student-learning guides. The costs also do not include the expenses of Universidad en tu colegio, which is a separate benefit of tenth- and eleventh-grade students in the EAU network. With regard to this program, the EAU alliance pays $533 for every student who joins. The Luker Foundation provides 60 percent, and the secretary of education covers 40 percent of all costs associated with EAU.

PLANS FOR SCALING

The Luker Foundation and the secretary of education of Manizales have solidly committed to continue expanding the model in Manizales. The new master plan of education for the city, which projects what will happen in Manizales by 2032, has included a specific goal for EAU, proposing that by 2020, 80 percent of schools in the city will have adopted the model.

Fabio Hernando Arias, the secretary of education of Manizales (2012–2015), indicated that the city has strongly embraced EAU because the program responds well to three different goals that are a priority at the national, regional, and local levels: (1) improving the quality of education as evidenced by performance in the national Saber tests, (2) promoting the development of citizenship competencies among children and young people, and (3) supporting teachers with professional development opportunities to learn classroom management techniques and pedagogical skills, emphasizing inclusion and integration of children with special needs. With regard to the first two points, he shared his reflection:

We have encountered many family problems, nourishment problems, and learning problems among the children in public schools. But the EAU model allows for children to develop their citizenship competencies, to work in teams and become more participatory, more collaborative, and to act with great solidarity. When someone has a problem, others help. This has made children happier. And you can be absolutely sure that is the reason why we support this model. Also, whether you like it or not, the only way in which we currently measure education is through tests. I go to schools weekly and ask questions to principals, teachers, students, and parents. And I am now convinced that the EAU can help us improve the quality of our education. And I am not making that up, because the tests are showing that.

LIMITATIONS OF EAU

In our discussions with EAU staff, teachers, members from the support team, and a critic of the program, we were identified some limitations, challenges, and risks. Given that all teachers in a school must work according to the principles of EAU, and that principals should be knowledgeable and supportive of the model, one challenge is that when teachers or principals leave or rotate, difficulties and disruptions can result. And when new teachers or principals join a school that has already implemented the EAU model, they do not receive the same intensive training as their peers, and are not equally motivated to implement the program. This situation is especially challenging because the teachers in EAU schools are public servants, and schools cannot choose which teachers to hire, because the secretary of education assigns teachers to schools.

Another challenge is that teachers in other public schools are currently trying to provide active pedagogies to students in their classrooms, so the alternative to EAU against which to compare the program for its impact (the counterfactual) is not the traditional schools prevalent when the program emerged. Gladys Ramos, a non-EAU teacher, member of the teacher union in Manizales, and critic of the EAU program, notes that while EAU has many strengths, most non-EAU teachers and non-EAU schools do not use traditional teaching models, but rely on the type of participatory and democratic pedagogies that EAU promotes and implements, so the contrasts are not stark. However, Ramos acknowledges that EAU provides a systematic set of materials, training, and supports that teachers in other schools do not receive. Instead, the majority of public schools rely on the efforts and skills of their principals and teachers, who try to implement their own cooperative and collaborative work and projects, without the systematic support that schools and teachers who are part of the EAU network receive.

A risk Ramos mentioned is that the secretary of education's desire to bring the program to all schools in the city in the future would limit the choices of students, decrease diversity in education, and limit their ability to identify and understand how the model performs against other pedagogical options. Ramos said, "The idea of homogenizing all schools in Manizales with the EAU model is not desirable, because the city should have as many methods and pedagogical proposals as schools. The idea of making uniform all schools with the EAU model is risky and anti-democratic. Besides, if you make all schools the same, how are you even going to compare their performance against other models?"

LESSONS LEARNED AND RECOMMENDATIONS

EAU's implementation success has led to a long-term, sustainable, effective, and widely accepted program. Based on the case study of this successful model, we identify lessons learned and recommendations for practitioners and policy makers. We conclude that the promotion of twenty-first-century skills requires:

- The systematic implementation of profoundly democratic and participatory structures and processes of interaction among all stakeholders to guarantee a culture of engagement, leadership, and ownership. In EAU, we found that the public partners (the secretary of education), the private partners (the Luker Foundation), the academic partners (Manizales University–CINDE), teachers, parents, and students felt they were playing a leading role in authoring the program, and felt useful and appreciated.
  - Recommendation: Design and implement education models that carefully consider how all structures and processes of communication and interaction at all levels of the system provide avenues for genuine engagement and participation of all relevant stakeholders such that they can actively contribute to the program and feel a sense of belonging and ownership.
- The recognition that the promotion of twenty-first-century skills in schools cannot be limited to one subject taught in one class, but that it occurs in

all interactions. EAU adopted a whole-school approach to teaching skills for the future, ensuring that teaching and learning materials, pedagogy, curriculum, and evaluation strategies that teachers use throughout the day promote students' active-social learning, participation, and autonomy.

> – Recommendation: Assess all components of the school experience, ensuring that they are consistent with strategies that promote twenty-first-century skills and adjust any aspect that is not purposefully and systematically contributing to this goal.

• Teachers can only promote twenty-first-century skills among students if they are highly competent and have acquired the knowledge and developed the skills, attitudes, and behaviors to act as competent twenty-first-century citizens. They also need the pedagogical skills to be effective teachers in the classroom. In order to build this capacity, EAU provides teachers with face-to-face training and ongoing professional development, communication, and innovation carried out by the support team, which guarantees that they are constantly learning, feel supported by their peers, and have access to spaces for meta-cognition and feedback, where they can revise their practices, test and share new strategies, and continuously improve themselves and the program.

> – Recommendation: Create and implement sustainable models of continuous professional development and support that guarantee ongoing processes of learning, transformation, and growth for teachers and schools at all levels of experience.

• Different stakeholders recognize that education is a complex matter that schools cannot manage alone, and create partnerships to overcome the obstacles to education they would otherwise face if not acting collaboratively. EAU functions due to a public-private partnership that enabled it to sustainably fund an innovative program beyond the election cycles. The program also created an academic partnership with Manizales University–CINDE that has ensured the technical components of the model are always improving.

> – Recommendation: Assess needs to understand the obstacles to effective promotion of twenty-first-century skills in your context and create partnerships with organizations that share your values and can help you find solutions to existing barriers.

CHAPTER FIVE

Developing Life Skills in Children

A Study of India's Dream-a-Dream Program

Aditya Natraj and Monal Jayaram
Piramal Foundation, India

Dream-a-Dream, a nonprofit program, is an example of innovation and pioneering work supporting low-income students in India in order to gain twenty-first-century competencies. The organization focuses on developing the life skills of children from disadvantaged backgrounds who have few opportunities to access emotional, physical, cognitive, and mental development when compared to children from advantaged backgrounds in India. In 2015–2016, the Dream-a-Dream program had an impact on approximately ten thousand children directly and around eighty thousand children indirectly. Its partners include seventy-five low-cost private schools, eleven government schools, thirteen colleges, and four nongovernmental organizations (NGOs).[1]

We chose to study Dream-a-Dream because it provides an education that is relevant for the twenty-first century for children aged eight to eighteen. We will discuss how it supports teachers in developing the required abilities in their students. We also describe its organizational model, which has been thoughtfully developed in response to the context of India's education system. We argue that Dream-a-Dream has been effective in building capacities of students and teachers because it has a clear articulation of the twenty-first-century competencies it wants its children to learn, the competencies and classroom practices a teacher needs to learn to be able to support her or his students, and the kinds of ecosystems of support needed so that twenty-first-century learning flourishes. A dynamic organizational culture with a capacity for ongoing individual and organizational learning is necessary for effective teaching and learning in the future.

At a time when the entire country of India is pursuing academic achievement and high grades and when the school system is investing in developing the cognitive abilities of its students and teachers, Dream-a-Dream's model is a unique "action, reflection, redesign, action" approach to the professional development of teachers and staff. While the education system supports quick, short-term, technical skill development of teachers, Dream-a-Dream's approach to professional development is an on-the-job, continuous, long-term process that shifts teachers' mind-sets and practice in their classrooms.

Education for the twenty-first century in India remains a relatively unexplored area that hovers on the sidelines of the national education dialogue. Authors Aditya Natraj et al. argued that the eventual success in implementation of twenty-first-century education in India will require learning from the experiences of small-scale initiatives and public-private partnerships such as Dream-a-Dream. While India's education policies speak of education for social transformation, leaders in the Indian public system have yet to effectively manage the systemic change required for future education.[2]

Natraj et al. also mentioned the country's policy environment, which showcases its readiness in developing students holistically for social and economic transformation. The goal of the policies is to develop learners' individual competencies so they are empowered to make choices to positively transform their lives and society. Twenty-first-century competencies as described in India's National Curriculum Framework of 2005 promote developing students' entrepreneurial attitude, the ability to problem-solve for oneself and one's community by using all the senses—head, heart, and mind—being aware and able to respect differences, displaying an ongoing behavior of equity, being flexible, and using creativity in daily work and life.

While the policy environment broadly articulates twenty-first-century learning, the main stream discourse about education quality in India has been limited for years to a discussion of access for all and improving test scores for basic education. Additionally, investing in twenty-first-century education for children from disadvantaged backgrounds has not yet gained widespread acceptance, reflected in the allocation of financial resources mostly to achieve tangible learning outcomes. The dominant model of standards-based reform in education has earned a critique as a reductionist approach, with little discussion about what might improve upon or replace it.

The Indian education system lacks the capacity to provide effective, contextually relevant, continuous support and professional development to teachers so they can develop the ability to implement twenty-first-century education in their classrooms. Most teacher professional development is not even geared toward preparing teachers to help students meet basic requirements in education, such as literacy. Teachers have no avenue for understanding and developing their technical skills and narrowing the practice gap for achieving basic quality in education.

Keeping the above-mentioned apprehensions in mind, we set out to study several nonprofit organizations and their models of change for teaching and learning in the future. Using a shared research protocol developed with our colleagues at the Global Education Innovation Initiative at the Harvard Graduate School of Education, our study focused on the following questions: (1) At what scale are the organizations working? Is it for a few children in a small area in a city or across several geographies and for children from a range of demographics? (2) Who are the audiences for the organizations? Do they work with students? Do they work with both students and teachers? (3) How do they measure impact? Do they collect anecdotes or have they invested in structured scientific approaches for assessment? (4) What is the organization's history in changing its own structures? Do they encompass a culture of learning and reinventing?

When Dream-a-Dream began in 1999, twenty-first-century learning was not yet a part of the vocabulary of Indian educators. Over a seventeen-year period, the program has continuously learned from its own practice and evolved its organizational structure, climate, and assessment tools for delivering life-skills education to children, especially those from adverse conditions. It has developed a visionary approach to delivering its best practices at scale. Moreover, the program has combined its own expertise in working at the grassroots level with that of two English clinical psychologists—Dr. Fiona Kennedy and Dr. David Pearson—to develop an easy-to-administer Dream Life Skills Assessment Scale (DLSAS). A peer-reviewed scale published in a scientific journal, the tool is the first of its kind to gauge life skills in children from disadvantaged backgrounds. In addition, Dream-a-Dream itself transformed after recognizing it had developed rigid systems that could hamper its ability to scale. Dream-a-Dream changed its system-based and single-founder-driven culture to an idea-based and people-driven culture.

A study of Dream-a-Dream provides insights into what helps students cultivate competencies for the twenty-first century. In Dream-a-Dream's direct program in and around Bangalore, in the state of Karnataka, Dream-a-Dream staff and volunteers work with students. Additionally, Dream-a-Dream provides development to professionals from other organizations and teachers to develop them as educators.

Next, we describe our method for research and then discuss the sociopolitical and education policy context of teaching and learning in India. We then describe the program's broader vision, objectives, and the programmatic and organizational model. We discuss the strategies that Dream-a-Dream uses for supporting students and teachers in developing capacities for twenty-first-century teaching and learning. Finally, we consolidate the limitations and challenges of the program, highlighting lessons about teaching and learning that are relevant for practitioners, researchers, policy makers, and funders.

METHOD OF RESEARCH

We conducted qualitative research for the study, following the research protocols developed with our GEII colleagues. Our methods included the analysis of field interviews, the organization's documents, and field observations.

The research team conducted twenty-six interviews that were then translated, transcribed, coded, and analyzed for the study. The interviewees include three people from the top management of Dream-a-Dream; four from Dream-a-Dream staff; three Dream-a-Dream graduates who are currently part of its staff; two principals of its partner schools; and three teachers from partner schools whose students were the beneficiaries of the Dream-a-Dream programs; eight public school teachers who have participated in Dream-a-Dream's teacher development; one NGO worker who has participated in the teacher development workshops that they offer to their partner NGOs; a principal of a former partner school (this principal has been considered to be one of the critic of the program as the management team of this school adopted the program and then abandoned it; it was important to understand the reasons why a private school chose to discontinue the program); and another critic of the program.

We also interviewed the top management many times to clarify data collected and to discuss deeper questions about certain decisions made by the organization and the program. Dream-a-Dream is a learning organization; as we collected data over the six to ten months of our engagement, we realized that it was continuously refining programs and strategies. We have therefore cautiously chosen the information we share in this chapter. We ask readers to bear in mind that some information may be outdated by the time this book is published.

We analyzed eleven documents from Dream-a-Dream, ranging from impact reports, annual reports, the impact assessment tool, and internal strategy documents. We carried out three field observations: (1) an after-school life-skills session on art; (2) an after-school life-skills session on sports; and (3) a teacher development workshop. We analyzed the interviews and documents using NVivo software for qualitative analysis. We used the process of thematic analysis and preexisting codes that were collaboratively defined by GEII members. In the process, we realized that country-specific data required processing through country-specific codes, so we created our own codes.

As researchers, we also engaged informally with numerous teachers and teacher educators across India for inquiries other than this study. We draw heavily upon the insights developed during those interactions as a lens for analyzing the data collected for the current study.

CONTEXT FOR EDUCATION AND TEACHER DEVELOPMENT

India's Public Education System

The Ministry of Human Resource Development's (MHRD) Annual Report of 2007–2008 suggests that after its independence in 1947, India made considerable progress in the quality of public education in the areas of literacy, infrastructure, universal access, and enrollment. The report shows enrollment figures as high as 82 percent of children aged five to fourteen, of whom 50 percent will drop out before completing grade 8. The report mentions that while the government was able to overcome challenges like access and enrollment, new challenges of social, economic, and gender disparities emerged.[3]

A Dasra research report supports that data: 90 percent of the labor force in India was in the informal sector and was suffering from a lack of focused skills required to succeed in the job market. The report cites the system's inability to give graduates the required quality of skills at a required pace and analyzes this significant threat to the demands posed by changes in market economy and technology.[4]

Worldwide data prove that children pay heavily for growing up in disadvantaged backgrounds. Psychologically and sociologically, the quality of family relationships and parental interactions is better for children from high-income families and thus aids development and their ability to participate and succeed in formal schooling. For children from disadvantaged backgrounds, the challenges are compounded if their schooling continues to provide them with knowledge relevant for previous times or for a different background. Vishal Talreja, CEO of Dream-a-Dream, observed during our interview that "adversity affects children from vulnerable backgrounds and their ability to engage with the world, make healthy life choices, and be successful. The result is poor performance in school, high levels of dropout, and young people ending up either sitting at home or entering unorganized labor markets or taking to crime and violence."

The challenges that social disadvantage creates for the education of low-income students require very high-quality teaching to help them learn, and possibly strategies that are different from those used for other students. Unfortunately, the teachers that serve such students are insufficiently prepared to offer the education necessary to break the poverty cycle, in part because they are inadequately supported.

Teacher Professional Development and Teacher Roles

In India, teacher professional development relies on pre- and in-service teacher preparation. National law and policies require teachers to be professionally qualified with a degree from a recognized institution that is licensed by the state.[5] Once appointed, teachers, especially in government-run elementary schools, are expected to participate in in-service training programs organized and delivered through a centralized system and structured process. National policies recognize that the quality of K–12 education depends on the quality of teacher education; at the same time, the quality of teacher education depends on the quality of entrants to the teacher education programs as they create the social context in which preparation takes place.[6]

Despite many efforts to improve its quality, teacher education in India remains dismal. First, few institutions and universities offer high-quality teacher education compared to the need.[7] The low-quality institutions depend on outdated curriculum and pedagogies that are far from the realities of the schools where teachers will practice and of the children they will teach. As a result, they build little perspective or competence to teach effectively. The MHRD study of teacher education reports:

> Teaching instruction needs to be problem-oriented and not discipline or theory-oriented; approaches such as case studies, simulations, role-play and action research would be more appropriate for the professional development of teachers; emphasis of instruction should not be memorization of content but accomplishment of tasks, insights and competence; open-ended activities and questions could help bring out the vast experiences of the prospective teachers, as also their "personal theories" about knowledge, learning and learners for scrutiny and analysis.[8]

The deficiencies created by initial teacher preparation are further aggravated as the in-service trainings do not meet the needs for a teacher to succeed. Teacher interactions indicate that they would benefit if the in-service program broadened their skills to improve their classroom practice, perspectives about education, and self-learning on relevant topics. However, teachers rarely see the benefit in the in-service training programs provided and find the programs designed with content that is irrelevant.[9]

Additionally, the resource materials cover topics and content that offer inadequate aid for improving teacher practice. Most of the high-quality research on education in the world is available in English, with some translated in Hindi. While Hindi is accepted as the official language of the country, the requirement for resource material in other local languages is high and the availability is bleak.

A fourth reason for the poor quality of teacher professional development is the low skill level of teacher educators. The government requires teacher educators to possess a master's degree in education. However, the number of universities providing these degrees is low compared to the existing need; as a result, many teacher educators lack such preparation.

Natraj et al. have mentioned that the purpose of education as expected in the national education policies is to prepare students with mind-sets that address and rise above inequities and demonstrate an ability to adapt and learn.[10] The MHRD report of 2012 encourages teachers to exhibit practice and mind-set that enable them to achieve the expected objectives of education.

However, as observed, the mainstream Indian education discourse favors traditional methods like rote learning and corporal punishment, which don't help student development.[11] Interviews with teachers from low-cost private schools indicate that teachers, principals, and school management often consider the teacher's role in the classroom to be that of a discipline manager.

Educator Sharon Feiman-Nemser discusses a central task of teacher education: helping teacher candidates examine critically their beliefs and values as they relate to teaching, learning, and their subject matter and as they formulate a vision of good teaching to inspire their learning and their work.[12] Our interviews with teachers revealed that during the teacher preparation programs, teachers were not helped in actively reflecting on their beliefs and therefore chose classroom strategies accordingly.

Mainstream education discourse in India also places unqualified emphasis on academic scores, thus adding to misconceptions about a teacher's role in the classroom. Teacher interviews showcased examples of those who found it difficult and unnecessary to look at their roles as facilitators and organizers of students learning. Instead they believed that their role is to teach the course material to ensure students' high scores in exams. In his interview, Sanjiv Patel, a teacher from a public school in the Dream-a-Dream program, pointed out that teachers prefer to "teach in the class" and "focus on 100 percent marks." Thus, the idea of being a catalyst who inspires independent learning is abstract and challenging for a teacher who is a product of a traditional system and who may not be an independent learner.

Natraj et al. concluded that in India "teachers and school principals reflect a hierarchical and authoritarian mind-set that is antithetical to twenty-first-century learning"; thus the current system struggles to hold a vision and direction to align both teachers and system to the provisions of the existing policy. Working in such a context requires efforts to build a robust system both for curriculum reform and for instituting staff-selection processes to prepare teachers and school leaders with different mind-sets.

PROGRAM DESCRIPTION: HOW DOES DREAM-A-DREAM RESPOND TO THIS EDUCATIONAL CONTEXT?

In responding to the challenges, Dream-a-Dream recognized the need to focus on building capacity for life-skills education. During the post-liberalization period while the public and private sectors were investing in ensuring access and basic quality education for all children, Dream-a-Dream channeled its efforts to holistic development, including life skills like empathy and self-awareness. [13]

In his interview, Talreja explained that children from such backgrounds face multiple adversities including abuse, extreme poverty, poor nutrition, neglect, abandonment, and violence, resulting in slower development compared to their counterparts and often failure to thrive. He added that "[i]ts not just about preparing for life or for the future, but also about preparing a generation of young people who respond with empathy . . . if there is no investment in life skills for [these] children, they are going to grow up in a climate that is unpredictable and challenging and only respond in the way that we have responded which is by not caring at all."

Dream-a-Dream thus designed its program to provide life skills both to children in schools and to those without access to schools. Its hypothesis was that while children from disadvantaged backgrounds needed basic education, life-skills education like thinking creatively, managing conflict, responding with empathy, working in teams, taking initiative, and being adaptable could build resilient individuals who could take charge of their social and economic conditions and adapt to a fast-changing world and succeed, compared to a student with only academic skills. To verify and build evidence for this hypothesis of change, Dream-a-Dream also invested heavily in tools and data systems that provide adequate and continuous information on the effects of the program that it could use to improve.

It also found the need to develop teachers' life skills to this end. Dream-a-Dream discovered that all adults who have an impact on children from disadvantaged backgrounds are themselves products of the traditional system, thus requiring an appropriate developmental approach to engage with them. Talreja elucidates the critical role of teachers' life skills, observing that "the schooling system is going to change not only in this country; it is going to change in the world. Teachers are still catching up to the old system. [Instead] they could actually leap forward to adapt to the new world."

Dream-a-Dream recognized the need early on and registered as a charitable trust to serve both children and adults. It runs direct intervention programs including (1) an after-school life-skills program through sports; (2) an after-school life-skills program through arts; and (c) the Career Connect program. The after-school programs through sports and arts cover 191 different cohorts of students in eighteen locations in Bangalore. There are two Career Connect centers located in the city. While the after-school life-skills program is yearlong, the Career Connect program provides short-term courses. Both programs have personal mentors and intensive learning experiences, encouraging learners to reflect on their concepts of their abilities, choices, and the process they use for making decisions.

Dream-a-Dream reflected on its outreach. In the last seventeen years, it has restructured its programs and strategies for reaching more children, resulting in the design of indirect programs. In the indirect programs, it partners with public and private schools and NGOs offering life-skills training to their teachers and volunteers, respectively. It has trained about 1,200 teachers and more than 2,500 volunteers from different geographies of the country.

The Teacher Development Program (TDP), an eight-month in-service program offering four life-skills workshops of two days each, resulted from these innovations. Dream-a-Dream offers it to all teachers in a school; the teachers and often the school managing boards decide whether to allow all teachers to attend the workshops. This residential learning process is designed around the principles of adult learning, to provide an intensive learning experience to teachers with the facilitators of the workshop and their peers from other schools. Each of the two days provides opportunity to rediscover themselves as teachers, their engagement with their students, and the possibilities of emerging as role models for their students. After two days, the teachers go back to their teaching with an aim to reflect on and change their practice in the classroom.

Organizational Model: The Concentric Circle Approach

The Dream-a-Dream staff has thoughtfully built the organization to operate on the values of accountability, trust, and dignity so that it becomes the role model and hub of empowered individuals for the system to learn from. The Dream-a-Dream concentric circle model is inspired by Urie Bronfenbrenner's model, wherein the American psychologist explains how a child's development and inherent qualities are influenced by the micro-, meso-, and macro-environments, including family, teachers, community, friends, and people in the society.

For Dream-a-Dream, the concentric circle represented its model to scale impact of its work and impact the ecosystem with respect to life skills for children. The immediate sphere is teachers and the school system, the third sphere encompasses the ecosystem including stakeholders such as the volunteers, parents, government, school leaders, and businesses, among others. The outermost sphere consists of the larger society that defines or reframes norms in society, thus influencing the child's education at a macro level.

The after-school life-skills programs and the Career Connect program form the organization's innovation lab, which has a direct impact on students. Insights about pedagogy, learning approaches, and challenges in the application of the life-skills approach to learning arise from the innovation lab and feed into the design of the large-scale TDP. The TDP has an indirect impact on students by training teachers to facilitate the life-skills development of their students. It also runs a volunteer program to bring volunteers from corporations, colleges, and the larger ecosystem to affect young people and become champions of the life-skills education.

In its bid to bring life skills to the forefront of India's mainstream education policy discourse, Dream-a-Dream undertakes activities such as organizing and participating in conferences about twenty-first-century education and contributing to research on the subject. Suchetha Bhat, chief operating officer of Dream-a-Dream, asserted, "If we want to influence policy change, if we want life skills to become part of mainstream interrogations, if we want to re-imagine education, we need to change the frame of society. We need to develop new visions and new frameworks for learning. This is what we are calling framework of change. So, today our programs are aligned in these four concentric circles."

The objective of the TDP is also to help individual teachers develop their own life skills while creating human resources for schools and the education system. In his interview, Talreja clearly explained that if a teacher leaves a school to join another after undergoing the professional development program with Dream-a-Dream, then he or she carries her new mind-set and practice to the new school; therefore the new school benefits from the previous school's investment. While Dream-a-Dream faces a huge challenge in encouraging school management boards to invest in its teachers' professional development, its vision for systemic impact is evident.

How Does Dream-a-Dream Address Constraints?

Teacher professional development in India, as we've mentioned, depends on programs that are either low quality or focused on building technical skills. Rarely do we observe programs where professional development is systematically supported to look inward, reflect critically on the current state of mind and behavior, and identify gaps in practice in the classroom. Emphasis is not on developing teachers with an expertise to be more self-aware and how that action supports student growth.

Dream-a-Dream has responded by organizing its TDP to help teachers learn how to make judgments about the conditions in which their students can develop twenty-first-century learning. The program activates intrinsic motivation and inculcates habits of lifelong learning. It develops a range of capacities including a facilitative approach to teaching, managing teachers' own motivations to find solutions to challenges in the classroom, finding new ways to teach, personalizing instructions, and making instructions relevant to each learner. It also helps teachers break their traditional forms of responding to challenges and bring in new mind-sets for taking action, taking risks, and learning from mistakes.

The program is adapted from creative community model developed by Partners for Youth Empowerment (PYE) Global. The model promotes using the arts to motivate learners to develop creativity, personal power, cross-cultural competency, and skills for leading purposeful lives, through methods like asking questions, reflecting on actions, and visioning. The core principle of the model is to acknowledge that the minds and actions of human beings are influenced by their environments and therefore are open to change.

If the environment is changed, the human mind experiences it and thus learns new action. Thus, if people consciously decide to develop a different mind-set and are empowered with an environment of togetherness and community, then their minds and actions have an opportunity to shift. All programs and the organizational culture in Dream-a-Dream are designed around this principle of change.

As researchers, we have observed Dream-a-Dream using experiential learning as a principle for adult learning. It carefully designs and executes the activities in its workshops to provide those experiences for its learners. The facilitators therefore thoughtfully build the workshop's environment as non-threatening, reflective, and supportive. Music, dance steps, and simple exercises that encourage friendly interaction with a known or unknown fellow participant, and collective visioning of educational goals or schools are some activities used to create the environment.

Teachers' interviews revealed that these experiences were key to their learning from the workshops. They also pointed out that while traditional training sessions would have engaged them only partially, this format helped them learn experientially at their own pace and collectively. Capacities that the teachers appear to learn from experiential learning include facilitating learning, creating a safe culture of learning, reflecting on their own, asking questions, taking initiative to work on a project, working collectively, and collaborating.

While Dream-a-Dream does not create learning communities between teachers in a particular school, it rather creates learning communities and peer networks through its workshops. Teachers make new professional friends, break their inhibitions of interacting with strangers, and learn to respect others' perspectives. Over the eight months through the four sets of workshops, a culture of trust, honesty, camaraderie, and collegiality with new colleagues sets in, and thus a learning community is created. However, active tracking of the continuation of learning communities is not yet in place, and there is sparse anecdotal evidence from the interviews about engagement, with a select few over phones and WhatsApp.

Dream-a-Dream uses the "arc of transformation" as a method for causing change in its learners during the workshops. The concept is used in leadership development, wherein a learner is helped by the arc to move from one point of view to a new one (see figure 5.1). Theoretically, the learner experiences a curved movement when his or her thoughts move from one point of view to the other. During this movement, the learner's mind is busy creating the new learning by bridging the gap.

Suchetha Bhat suggested in her interview that she uses the arc of transformation's process to facilitate any workshop on any topic. Her learners undergo a well-planned structured process of (1) a powerful beginning; (2) reflecting relationship with self, others, and with the world, and thus experiencing transformation; (3) creating meaning of the transformative experience for self; and (4) celebrating the newfound meaning by committing to it. She suggests that shifts happen during the workshop when individuals reach a tipping point and open to reimagining their notions about themselves. Next, we delineate the objectives of the four workshops.

Workshop 1: Discovering your creative potential with key outcomes of—

- Increased self-awareness, confidence in your own creativity, and awareness about life skills
- Understanding the definition of life skills; experiencing the development of your own life skills
- Ability to conduct easy-to-lead experiential activities to develop life skills in young people
- Building experiential tools to facilitate learning

Workshop 2: Engaging with empathy with key outcomes of—

- Increased understanding of early childhood development, adversity, and its impact on learning and development in young people
- Increased awareness on importance of an adult as mentor in a young person's life
- Ability to effectively engage young people through the practice of deep listening and validation skills

Workshop 3: Learning to facilitate young people's learning with key outcomes of—

- Understanding the role of facilitation to develop life skills in young people
- Increased confidence to facilitate learning through experiential learning techniques and tools
- Learning to develop supportive communities within your network
- Understanding and practicing strength-based facilitation

Workshop 4: Celebrating one's role in a young person's life with key outcomes of—

- Celebrating one's role as a teacher, community worker, and facilitator
- Increased confidence to integrate life skills within current teaching, programs, and approaches
- Understanding and developing the ability to design life-skills sessions or programs for young people

FIGURE 5.1   Arc of transformation*

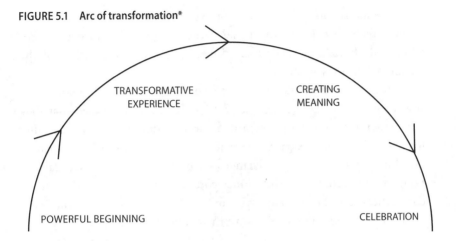

*Adapted from the creative community model developed by Partners for Youth Empowerment (PYE Global).

While Dream-a-Dream facilitators are still collecting and analyzing quantitative evidence, they share many anecdotes of teachers in this journey on the arc of transformation and the learning facilitated. Some shifts in which the arc appears to have an impact on the teachers are:

- From authoritative behavior in classroom to collaborative behavior. Eight teachers mentioned that their behavior changed in the classroom. They realized that they had been operating in authoritarian ways before participating in the Dream-a-Dream workshop.
- From "what" to "why." Four teachers referred to the change in the questions they ask. Before attending the workshop, their curiosity to learn new things was limited; this seemed to change after the Dream-a-Dream workshop where they developed the habit of asking a "why" question.
- From "I will tell you" to "we all learn." Some teachers and facilitators confirmed their didactic attitude in classroom, where a teacher assumes the role of passing on all the knowledge to students. However, the Dream-a-Dream workshop engaged the teachers as learners and helped them become learners.
- From "give me answers" to "let's ask more questions and find answers together." Teacher interviews and beneficiary interviews both revealed that the workshops encourage learners to ask more questions and find answers.

- From the status quo to "I am the pivot to change my own situation." Interviews with both teachers and beneficiaries captured the learners' acceptance and efforts to change their situation as a continual effect of the Dream-a-Dream workshops.
- From implementer of others' ideas to building one's own implementing strategies while collaborating with others. Teachers mentioned that they overcame their fear of implementing their own ideas and problem solving for themselves. One teacher experienced a feeling of liberation. Her relationship with others has now changed from dependence to collaboration.
- From disconnected with their inner core to connected with their inner core, others, and the external environment. A few teachers shared an experience of renewed relationships with their environment.

While conventional teacher training in India aims to improve teachers' skills, Dream-a-Dream's teacher professional development aims to improve their potential for their current jobs and their effectiveness for the future and increase ownership of their learning and change.

What Is Dream-a-Dream's Theory of Change?

Dream-a-Dream's theory of change isn't as yet been published anywhere. As researchers, we have derived this theory of change based on our analysis of the programs and the interviews. Dream-a-Dream aims to transform the conventional education system to promote a life-skills approach for all in the system. Talreja's belief that "[w]e do not want to be a reflection of the society the way it is today. Instead we want to be a reflection of the way we wish to see society," signals change among all members of the society and the education system. He proposes completely tearing down previous structures and reinventing individuals and the systems they follow.

Theory of change for teachers and teacher development

If an education system wants holistic development for children and wants children to grow as whole individuals, then, first, teachers will have to be systematically helped to shift from practicing conventional teaching strategies to facilitators of teaching and learning. Bhat says that "we want the teachers to stop teaching. In today's world teaching is no more required; rather, facilitating of learning experiences is required." Teacher interviews and Bhat's interview confirm that teachers believe their role in children's lives is to fill an empty vessel. Teachers are also pressured to deliver the syllabus, so thus choose to disseminate information through textbook-based, didactic lectures. The delivery instead needs to build from students' understanding of the concepts and experiences in the classroom that inspire students to create their own learning path.

Second, teachers will have to be systematically helped to be self-motivated and self-learners. The professional development of teachers needs to encourage learning and motivation to act in difficult situations. Current training has to stop providing technical inputs and, rather, engage teachers in dialogue and with the contexts of the classroom to find contextual solutions.

Third, teachers have to be intentionally helped to become creative and to plan for the future. Student needs are dramatically changing. For example, over the last fifty years, more people from different parts of India have moved and settled into other parts. Teachers do not necessarily teach students from their own communities or cultural background and face multiple challenges. Preparation to address such complexities in the classroom requires creativity and preparation.

Theory of change for students

If society wants students from adverse backgrounds to experience equity in opportunity and success in life, then, first, learning for students from adverse backgrounds has to intentionally focus on life skills as a foundation for learning along with academic scores. Bhat asks, "[W]hat good are academic scores or if children are in schools, if education is not giving them skills and tools to deal with complex life challenges?" To this, Talreja comments:

> We care more if children excel in academic scores but are rendered ineffective when they are seeking job opportunities. We don't believe that such schooling is of any importance and in fact believe that such schooling needs to be urgently stopped. Recently I read a newspaper article that mentions that people with engineering background are forced to eventually take up a Uber taxi driver's job. The alumni from Dream-a-Dream are possibly better placed than these people who took up engineering studies. So in short, we need to build them as people who can find ways to overcome their poverty and take a leap beyond their current economic conditions.

Theory of change for education system

If India's educational system wants to align its practice with its curricular goals, then it must align the culture of the current system with the expected curricular goals. Paradigm shifts in the schooling community's practices depends on specific features of the organization in which they exist. Research on organizational development has shown the connection between an organization's culture and the behavior of individuals. The organization encourages building of relationships of trust, dignity, and respect to individuals' behavior. Talreja refers to this learning from experts:

> If you are expecting your staff and teachers to be more accountable and constructive then you need to create this consciously as a culture of the organization. We want to role model a space where dignity and respect are earned by deeds and action and not by hierarchical position or role and responsibility. We firmly believe it is possible for creating a culture of accountability without someone having to push it through, without an authority to monitor people's engagement. The current system of accountability is a top down approach; in Dream-a-Dream it is exactly the opposite, where each individual is believed to own her role.

To practice its theory of change, Dream-a-Dream recruits individuals who are willing to engage in self-awareness and reflection. Both Talreja and Bhat shared the understanding that behavioral shifts in adults are directly linked to the meaning they place on their actions. An organization needs to look for people who show some basic abilities to reflect, be empathetic, and be open to feedback. While it does not have clear recruitment processes, its engagement with volunteers and the students who graduate from its programs emerge as potential resources for recruiting. In fact, 50 percent of Dream-a-Dream staff and facilitators are program graduates and beneficiaries of the direct-impact program, who have themselves surmounted adversity and therefore have an opportunity to lead their trainees by example.

What Are Dream-a-Dream's Realized Outcomes?

Dream-a-Dream has tracked and demonstrated during the last three years that students benefiting from its direct programs exhibit gains on the DLSAS. Its arts, sports, and Career Connect program have all contributed to students' improved performance in life-skills assessments. Personal stories show how each child seems to be changing. In an informal engagement with some children who were part of Dream-a-Dream programs, we observed a marked difference in the levels of confidence, engagement, and initiative compared to children from similar backgrounds elsewhere in the country.

The DLSAS, developed by Dream-a-Dream along with clinical psychologists Kennedy and Pearson is a standardized, observation-based scale to measure life-skills development in disadvantaged children.[14] It is based on five of the ten skills identified in the World Health Organization's life-skills framework. The five life skills (interacting with others, overcoming difficulties and problem solving, taking initiative, managing conflicts, and understanding and following instructions) are observable across programs, age groups, gender groups, and contexts. The designers used a five-point Likert scale to measure each item for easy administering. Initially, the staff used the scale to observe students from the program. After collecting the data, professional market researchers used the scale to observe the same children. Both data sets were then collected and analyzed to check on inter-rater reliability and test-retest reliability.

Facilitators and teachers use the scale to conduct baseline and end-line assessments each year to track the life skill development of students in the programs. The designers also devised a fourteen-item self-evaluation tool called the Prepared for Life scale for the beneficiaries of its Career Connect program. For teachers from the development program, Dream-a-Dream collects self-reported stories of change in a structured format. At the time of data collection for this research, the organization was experimenting with developing a self-evaluation tool for teachers to establish a causal relationship between the life skills of teachers and students.

Students' realized outcomes

Some examples of change, a range of immediate and long-term impact, can be observed in the students associated with different programs of Dream-a-Dream. Table 5.1 shows the percentage of the gain between the baseline and end line from 2011 through 2014, when the program intake of students increased by two thousand students, and 100 percent of the previous years' students were retained in the program, as against the loss of 11 percent in the previous years. The gains in the five life skills remarkably improved over the three years, clearly proving that Dream-a-Dream's programs make an impact and its theory of change works. Year-on-year, a minimum of seven out of ten young people have shown an improvement in life skills measured using the DLSAS.

While Dream-a-Dream initiated organized tracking of the life skills learning outcomes since 2011, sporadic observations of students and collection of change stories indicate that learning of life skills may have occurred during the previous years, too. A good indicator is that twenty of the beneficiary alumni are now part of the Dream-a-Dream staff. About 50 percent have leadership roles one step below the chief operating officer. Bhat points out that this only proves that the program "worked well and caused impact" in its previous years and also indicates that life-skills approach has the potential to make a "long-term impact" on the beneficiaries. Our analysis of individual stories of change showcased the relevance of the life-skills approach for students within the social and educational context of the country.

Students' immediate life-skills learning and academic learning outcomes

Students developed resilience for pursuing academic learning outcomes. For example, his principal and teachers saw Vinay, a student from the Stella Maris School, as an underperformer. His teachers had observed that he was experiencing the pressure of his performance in ninth grade. He took a long time to read single lines from his textbook. He was unable to concentrate on academic work. After attending the Dream-a-Dream program, he displayed different behavior; he seemed more courageous and confident. After speaking with him, his teachers realized that Vinay had developed confidence in himself. He was able to refocus on his academic work, too.

Students also overcame difficulties in problem solving. Talreja summarizes that as the students are growing up, they discover that their challenges in life do not decrease. The risks of dropping out from the school because of adverse challenges at home and of violence and crime continue in their lives. However, after Dream-a-Dream engagement, their responses to these challenges change.

For example, Prasanna, who came from a violent family background and used violence to deal with all conflict in his life, participated in the life-skills program for seven years. While violence in his family continued, he was able to graduate and joined Dream-a-Dream to support other young people like

TABLE 5.1   Improvement of life-skills learning outcomes 2011–2014

	2011–2012	2012–2013	2013–2014
General indicators			
Total students enrolled	3066	3050	5357
Attendance	NA	83%	89%
Retention	NA	89%	97%
Life skills—Gains between baseline and endline in percentage			
Interacting with others	44%	42%	60.40%
Overcoming difficulties and solving problems	36%	49.38%	59.50%
Taking initiative	50%	42.62%	61%
Managing conflict	43%	40.26%	57.50%
Understanding and following instructions	42%	40.69%	56%

him. The students grew up in Dream-a-Dream's environment of positive role modeling, empathy, and building their own abilities to make a choice and manage conflict. Today, twenty-five-year-old Prasanna is a program facilitator managing eleven other facilitators and a program for five thousand young people.

The students have also learned to take initiative. At Dream-a-Dream, children from challenging backgrounds are systematically taught to celebrate and understand what they are capable of within their constraints. The pedagogy used is a simulated project on problem solving at an outdoor camp site. This practice then becomes a lifelong learning experience to return to, each time they meet a challenge.

For example, the example of a female student shows how she developed resilience in the program. The student faced a tough financial challenge. Her father was a drunkard, and she was the single breadwinner for her family. She took the initiative to find her own solutions to her problems and chose to leave school, find work, and continue education by correspondence. Her cited reason for not giving up related to what she had learned at the Dream-a-Dream life-skills program—a "never give up" attitude to life and taking initiative to find one's own solutions.

Students transforming their own lives for lifelong change and impact

The students learned to be responsible. For example, Pavi, a female student, is currently a manager of the Career Connect program and also a member of the mentor team at Dream-a-Dream. As a young person, she had been through Dream-a-Dream sessions as a mentee herself. Her experience of her mentor and the mentor's role in shaping her life choices encouraged and inspired her to do more. Her mentor's influence had encouraged her to feel equally responsible for the next generation of mentees. Pavi said, "I eagerly look forward to making that new special friend and build a relationship with my mentee similar to what I have with Manisha. I want to be change maker in this society and I am going to assist my mentee also to be change maker in this society."

The students have learned to aim high. For example, Vishwa, the son of a security guard, embarked on a life-changing journey after joining a Dream-a-Dream program. It provided life skills and mentoring, which encouraged Vishwa to go on to pursue a one-year course at a community college in the United States on a full scholarship. Vishwa commented, "I now have the certificate of having studied in US, have best friends in more than fifteen countries, have visited many places in US which I had just dreams of going to, have gotten the experience of studying with American students, and have learned about different cultures of different countries. I also interned and volunteered in many places. With my qualifications I got a job as an editor in an editing company called MetaCog Solutions and am continuing my education."

Realized outcomes for teachers, staff, and volunteers

While it is easy to capture quantitative data, analyze it, and represent the realized outcomes with students, it is difficult to do the same when considering realized outcomes for adults. While Dream-a-Dream collects data on the students using a scientific tool, it is in the process of designing a tool for assessing the learning outcomes of teachers, staff, and other adult participants of its programs. We collected anecdotal evidence during our interviews and review of the stories of change Dream-a-Dream collected.

Our analysis of the limited data shows that teachers, volunteers, and staff possibly demonstrate shifts in mind-set, although it is difficult to determine whether these shifts are long term or short term. What is clear is that there is an urgent requirement for a scientific system to collect evidence of the learning outcomes of the adults, particularly because Dream-a-Dream is spending most of its energy and resources on the TDP. Its teacher workshop and its staff training involve helping adults examine their roles, potential, and creativity within the existing constraints. For example, a crucial element in educating for transforming lives is to be able to build deep connections with each other and with young people. Participants are encouraged to rethink their actions as teachers and reflect on what adults need to change in themselves to empathetically help young people learn. The engagements with adults resulted not only in learning ways of becoming different teachers but in taking charge of their own life transformation. Some clearly articulated realized outcomes that we share here with supporting interview notes.

The adults stopped corporal punishment in their classroom practice. Corporal punishment is a rampant behavioral trait of teachers in Indian schools. The belief and practice possibly come from an Indian social belief—*Bhay bina preet nahi*—that there is no scope of demonstrating love without demonstrating fear. In the school system, however, the existence of *bhay* (fear) has caused students to lose interest in schools and damaged their psychosocial well-being and possibly their capacity to learn, with lasting implications for their lives.[15]

At Dream-a-Dream, transforming a teacher's action toward corporal punishment is the best first step toward change. While adequate data are not collected to track the number of teachers ending the use of corporal punishment, nine of eleven teacher interviews indicated that they have become more aware of corporal punishment and their role as discipline manager in the classroom and attempted to stop the practice. For example, when Daval Nilgund, a seasoned teacher with almost sixteen years of experience first attended Dream-a-Dream's workshop, he honestly shared that "I used to beat my students up earlier. After the training, I stopped doing so. After the training I stopped carrying a stick to the class; I would rather encourage my students by giving a morale boost. I stopped punishing them and now I am happy to share that 100 percent of times I do not use punishment."

Many adults experienced personal change. For example, Manisha, a former volunteer with the mentoring program, believed that she was imperfect and always wondered how she could contribute to making someone else's world a better place. While undergoing training to become a mentor to students,

Manisha experienced a change in her perspective about herself. In the on-the-job training, she was conducting mentoring sessions for her mentee Pavi. Interactions with the mentee helped Manisha reengage with her self-concept.

Pavi, who was mentored by Manisha and is now a mentor herself, mentioned that her experience with her facilitator and experience of being a facilitator has helped her become a better human being in her personal life, too. She finds herself being a facilitator at home, building strong relationships, communicating in depth with the family members, and leading the problem-solving process there.

Adults now practice reflection. For example, Puja, associated with Dream-a-Dream for the last eight years, learned to practice reflection and accountability for each of her actions. She said, "I think I am continuously developing my life skills because when I go and tell someone else that a particular thing is important, then it is actually important [accountability] for me to do it myself. For me I find it hard to say I am reflective only at work. Reflection is something I do at work and I do in my life—it is really helpful."

How Does Dream-a-Dream Leverage Networks, Funding, and Scale?

Leveraging networks

Dream-a-Dream leverages its networks with institutions to strengthen its own program activities and advocate for life-skills education. Networks for the exchange of ideas at the international, national, organizational, and teachers' levels have informed its program design. The TDP and after-school life-skills program curricula have resulted from a partnership with two international organizations working on art and sports—Partners for Youth Empowerment (PYE) Global and South Africa–based Grassroot Soccer.

At the country level, Dream-a-Dream has received mentorship support from senior leadership at Ashoka India and the Lego Foundation to scale its model. Currently, Dream-a-Dream has begun to explore collaborations with other organizations to build teacher assessment tools. At the organizational level, facilitators brainstorm and find solutions for the program-related challenges facing them at monthly meetings. At the teachers' level, TDP workshops lay the foundations for peer-learning networks of teachers to cross-share insights from their creative experiments on the field.

Dream-a-Dream actively organizes and participates in learning communities to identify and experiment with large-scale approaches to impart twenty-first-century education. Dream-a-Dream holds an annual "Change the Script" conference that is a platform to delve deeper into problems and innovative approaches to prepare young people for the future. Dream-a-Dream actively participates in other initiatives for twenty-first-century learning, for example, the Lego Idea Conference where top academicians, researchers, educationists, nonprofit leaders, and corporate leaders deliberate about ways to provide life skill education at scale.

Funding and scaling effort

Dream-a-Dream has revamped its fund-raising and scaling strategies to maximize the spread of life-skills education. Grants, corporate social responsibility funding, corporate foundation funds, fund-raising events, and individual donations form a majority of Dream-a-Dream's resources. The organization faces challenges in communicating the value of life-skills education to potential donors, who are more likely to fund programs for academic achievement. Therefore, it has tailored its fund-raising pitch to the needs of corporate donors.

Talreja explained:

> We are pitching for HNIs—"high-net-worth individuals." We see the CEO of a company who is struggling to hire good talent. He is struggling because that talent does not have life skills. So we go to that CEO and say we need to start at grade six and even more, at grade four. Do not try to solve the problem at the age of nineteen or twenty. Because by then the person would have learnt or stopped learning what is needed to be learnt. So let's start as early as possible.

Scale for Dream-a-Dream is not about increasing its impact. Impact would mean training more adults in the life-skills approach. Dream-a-Dream recognizes that the challenge of strategically moving from providing direct-impact programs to hosting indirect programs training teachers and staff from private schools and other partner NGOs across the country. Ramanan, a senior leader in Dream-a-Dream, considers the TDP as "a force multiplier" strategy. He adds that "if teachers in schools demonstrate the skills, the chances are that they increase the number of children to be impacted." The scale advantage of this strategy has infact helped Dream-a-Dream reduce the per-child cost from $43 to $1.15.

What Are Dream-a-Dream's Limitations and Challenges?

We based the limitations we identify in this section on our analysis of the interviews and perspectives of two interviews with critics. The critics asked questions about the existing nature of the program. As researchers, we recognize the limitation of conclusions from only two critics. We therefore present the limitations observed in other interview data as well.

Workshops need to equip teachers to implement their learning in actual classroom environments

The teacher interviews reveal the shortcomings in the TDP design. While teachers believe that the TDP helps them grow into believers in life-skills education, and also learn to become facilitators of secure environments, they feel ill-equipped to use those life skills in their own classrooms. Ravi, an interviewed teacher, explained, "Without beating students up, how it is possible to bring discipline in the children? This is challenge for every teacher, and while Dream-a-Dream provides the understanding why corporal punishment should not be practiced, we find it difficult while actually practicing it."

Development of teacher life skills and mind-sets requires sustained, multiple interventions

Providing post-workshop on-site support and consolidation of practices can help teachers feel more confident about improving their practices. Interviews show that teachers have a need for more support interventions in the form of on-site follow-up after the workshops to reinforce their learning. A critic also mentioned that sustainable change in the larger community is possible with varied efforts other than just providing the training to teachers and then leaving them to deal with their practice alone.

Dream-a-Dream fund-raising showcases the need to challenge deeply ingrained mind-sets in India

Life-skills education is unfortunately neither understood nor resonating well with prospective donors. It also does not help when governments do not support the idea of life-skills education. It is a chicken-and-egg situation; with governments not on board, donors may not be on board, and vice versa. While Dream-a-Dream's rebranding based on the concentric circles is a big step toward changing the perceptions, the challenges continue.

To improve teacher and government investments in life skills, Dream-a-Dream
needs to reexamine its assessments

Interviews revealed that the teachers from government schools find administering of the Life Skill Assessment Scale an additional burden to the existing
CCE tool that the government requires, despite its simple format and limited
number of items. CCE-based testing and interventions are slowly becoming
mandatory in government schools. Expecting interventions and assessments
of tools that are different from the government recommendations only makes
Dream-a-Dream's case weaker with the government, especially when Dream-
a-Dream chooses to not necessarily sign up memorandum of understanding
with the authorities but to rather accept teachers self-initiate themselves into
TDP. At the time of data collection and analysis the organization continued
to grapple with external challenges to introduce life-skills education as part of
the national dialogue on education.

Institutionalization of teaching life skills depends on the life-skills approach
permeating all facets of the education system

Mr. Gurumurthi, principal of a former partner school and one of the critics
of the program, expressed his reservations about life skills being a separate,
after-school, one-off activity without the participation of his teachers. He
shared that the after-school program's lack of integration with the rest of the
curriculum was one reason his management discontinued the program. However, in his interview, Talreja also expressed his concerns with adoption of life-
skills approach in the current structure of a school day: "Today a teacher is
expected to complete a massive syllabus in a limited time. They do not look
at the needs of the child or the local context. We do not want life skills to
become like that."

Assessment of realized outcomes of capacity development will direct improvements
to the TDP

Tracking what and how adults are learning from the program and analyzing whether changes in mind-sets are long term or short term will become
an essential strategic step in order for Dream-a-Dream to move ahead. While
anecdotal evidence provides motivation to continue doing the good work,
the sustainable impact of the program depends on what the data about the
adults show.

Dynamics between academic scores and life-skills scores of children must establish sustainable impact and correlation of life skills

Failing this, life skills and academic scores will each continue to suffer.

KEY FINDINGS AND CONCLUSION

Our study shows that the following factors are essential in facilitating systemic change at scale:

- *A mind-set shift and action change is key for the professional development of teachers.* Teacher development for the twenty-first-century in India is not about improving the skills in teaching better differently; it is rather about shifts in individual mind-sets and ac**tion**. It requires teachers to analyze (1) their role with their students; (2) the impact of their roles on student lives; (3) defining their own self-concept; (4) their willingness and ability to adapt to new ideas and innovations; and (5) being able to translate what they learn to change action in their classrooms.

  The professional development process needs to support the individual's personal experience during the change process. It requires understanding what needs to change, how to make the transition from the current status quo, and what messages teachers need to feel motivated to make the transition. It also requires all teachers to be mentored and coached in the new behaviors to make this new behavior consistent in their current professional work.

- *The changes required for twenty-first-century teaching and learning depend not only on individual efforts but also on a culture change in the organization.* At a large scale, management of person-by-person change is impossible and resource intensive. It requires that principals, management boards, and the education system accept, embrace, and adopt the teachers' professional development process at large scale. This requires a culture of group effort, mutuality, trust, and support between different stakeholders. Driving individual transitions through large-group processes need to be the focus of school system's culture.

- *Systemic change for twenty-first-century teaching and learning depends on the system's ability to adapt to the ever-changing world and to recognize the interrelationship between the system and the community of stakeholders.* The professional development of teachers for the twenty-first century would, therefore, mean changes in the roles, structures, processes, projects, and leadership competencies of those in the system. It depends on the role that several actors from the system play to support the acceptance of the new methods. And the lack of involvement of various members in the system can weaken the acceptance of the life-skills approach.

- *People in leadership roles above the teachers have key roles in managing the teacher professional development.* Development of teachers requires such activities as (1) aligning principals and other leaders with the educational goals; (2) consciously neutralizing the disagreements with the educational goals; (3) envisioning and communicating the advantage of the educational goals; (4) converting the educational goals into actionable steps; (5) being aware of one's own accountability to reach the goals; (6) diligently determining how to reach the goals and how to help others do the same; and (7) constantly tracking and measuring the deliverables with metrics. The leader must create conditions for teachers to succeed in the new paradigm.

CHAPTER SIX

Developing Twenty-First-Century Competencies in Mexico

How UNETE and School Communities Broaden the Goals of Education by Using Educational Technology

Sergio Cárdenas, Roberto Arriaga, and Francisco Cabrera
Centro de Investigación y Docencia Económicas/CREFAL

Revising a national curriculum is a difficult task for politicians, policy makers, and school communities. It requires knowledge of trends in national and international job markets, awareness of perceptions about social challenges and, drawing from those analyses, clarity about which competencies are necessary in an increasingly globalized society. It also requires an ability to reconcile the different, often conflicting demands of several interest groups frequently voicing opposing views about educational goals. Furthermore, it needs the management of consultations aimed at building a shared vision among the different educational stakeholders and interest groups.

Reaching such an agreement is a complex but essential step in the process of enacting a curriculum designed to develop new competencies relevant to a changing world, as recent efforts to update the national curriculum in Mexico illustrate. After a series of legal amendments were enacted in 2013 to increase accountability in the national education system, the Ministry of Education initiated a national consultation to capture the perspectives of different actors, including leaders of nongovernmental organizations (NGOs), parents, scholars, teachers, and students enrolled in public schools. Among the stakeholders included in this consultation were NGOs implementing interventions aimed at developing a range of competencies among students deemed relevant to contemporary demands, such as citizenship skills, entrepreneurship, and tolerance.

In Mexico, the lack of "alignment across grades, subjects, and domains" in the current official curriculum for basic education regarding twenty-first-century competencies increases the relevance of fostering the participation of stakeholders, such as educational NGOs, in designing and implementing new instructional models promoting the development of these competencies.[1]

The open and thorough participation of NGOs in implementing different interventions in public schools in Mexico is a relatively recent activity. Such NGOs typically partner with local governments, targeting low-income communities across the country. These public-private partnerships usually aim at improving educational quality through the following interventions: (1) the distribution of educational materials (e.g., books or computers); (2) the organization of professional development activities for teachers; (3) the modification of instructional practices and nutrition and health programs; and (4) the organization of additional instructional activities for students (e.g., teaching foreign languages).

One NGO using these four approaches while implementing educational interventions in Mexican schools is the Union of Entrepreneurs for Technology in Education (known as UNETE by its acronym in Spanish). Created in 1999, it has the specific goal of increasing student access to educational technology in public primary schools, a pertinent goal to achieve in Mexico if we consider that in 2005, only 23 percent of primary schools and 62 percent of secondary schools reported using computers for educational purposes. Computers are even less accessible in public schools located in rural or indigenous areas.[2]

Considering its goal of reducing the gap in access to technology, UNETE is an effective organization. It provides technology access to nearly 2.3 million students per school year, equivalent to nearly 11 percent of the total national student enrollment in basic education.[3] Encouraged by their achievements in reducing these gaps during the last few years, its leaders decided to expand and diversify their goals from the acquisition of basic technological literacy to supporting the development of noncognitive competencies such as teamwork, collaboration, critical thinking, and creativity. To achieve these goals, they modified their implementation model to include professional development activities, educational content design, and new instructional practices.

Such attention to organizational learning and change in schools is rare among Mexican institutions involved in this type of public-private partnership. For this reason, even though this is an ongoing effort in the early stages of implementation, it is a promising intervention for study, particularly because it is an opportunity to learn how to manage the process through which organizations interested in including the development of twenty-first-century competencies in their institutional goals manage their transition. Additionally, learning about this shift is important in the context of Mexico, not only because of the ambitious curriculum reform currently underway but also because of the limited studies about the role NGOs play in promoting the adoption of relevant competencies in public schools.

In this chapter, we describe the main characteristics of UNETE as an organization currently working to learn about how to best support the development of twenty-first-century competencies in Mexican public schools. We also explicate how it managed its transition after including new educational goals, a relevant aspect considering that other organizations have reason to add twenty-first-century competencies to their educational goals, as they are part of the new national curriculum. We describe how UNETE: (1) realized the necessity of including twenty-first-century competencies; (2) aligned its organizational structure to respond to the new challenges resulting from this shift; (3) dealt with the main barriers during the transition; and (4) drew lessons from this experience.

METHODS FOR STUDYING THE CASE

To analyze how UNETE expanded its goals for school improvement to include twenty-first-century competencies, we conducted a descriptive case study. As noted by Robert Yin, this approach allowed us to understand a current "real-world" phenomenon when the limits between the context and the studied occurrence might not be "clearly evident." In addition, this approach is useful when there is no control of "behavioral events," as in this organization.[4]

We selected the case to analyze after considering different programs implemented across Mexico. We initially reviewed programs aimed at promoting twenty-first-century competencies implemented within the country. Once we identified these programs, we specifically looked for programs that were a collaboration between public agencies and NGOs or other private organizations.

Next we conducted a more detailed review of specific activities, evaluations if available, and information about the programs' target populations and implementation processes.

We selected the case of UNETE, considering the publicly available information regarding its intervention model, such as previous studies and external evaluations, descriptions of competencies to develop, the collaboration with government and other international organizations, and the duration and operation of the program. Furthermore, this case creates an opportunity to study a management and transition process that might interest other organizations evaluating the inclusion of twenty-first-century competencies in their institutional goals.

Next, we decided to collect and analyze data from interviews with school principals, teachers, main staff, the CEO, and external evaluators (twenty-one interviews). We also reviewed documentation such as external evaluations, internal technical reports, and other studies. We performed a content analysis of UNETE's websites, repositories, and electronic forums. We also directly observed coaching activities conducted during field visits to primary schools where UNETE programs are implemented. We followed a semistructured interview protocol co-created and shared with our GEII partners. (The appendix at the end of this chapter includes a complete list of the data sources we used.)

CONTEXT OF THE MEXICAN EDUCATION SYSTEM AND UNETE

Education System

On average, the Mexican students complete 8.6 years of schooling, although in poorer states, it is only 6.6 years.[5] Such regional inequalities, stemming from the unequal quality of schools and variations in socioeconomic conditions and local capacities, constitute one of the greatest challenges for the system. Furthermore, of every one hundred students starting the first grade in primary education, approximately sixty students graduate from lower secondary school and then enroll in a high school, although 13 percent of these students will drop out during their first semester in that educational level.[6] In addition, in 2012, 57 percent of fifteen-year-old Mexican students performed at level 1 or below in PISA scores in mathematics, while only 4.3 percent performed at advanced levels in the same subject (level 4 or above).[7]

Unfortunately, there are limited examples of governments and other organizations making effective long-term and deep interventions to promote the development of twenty-first-century education among Mexican children and youth in basic education.[8] This dearth of existing interventions results in limited opportunities to better understand how to develop this type of competency (e.g., noncognitive competencies), consequently increasing the importance of analyzing how school actors and organizations work together in implementing initiatives aimed at developing twenty-first-century competencies in public schools.

UNETE

The success of the educational reform approved in 2013 depends on the adequate design of new educational materials and the implementation of effective in-service professional development programs. The new curriculum to be piloted in the coming years includes several twenty-first-century competencies as educational goals for the public education system (e.g., socio-emotional development, creativity, critical thinking, teamwork, appreciation for diversity). Including these competencies may result in additional public interest and further initiatives from governments and NGOs like UNETE.

As described in one of its recent annual reports, UNETE was founded by Mexican entrepreneur and philanthropist Max Schein. After observing children interacting with computers during a visit to Israel, Schein personally decided to provide computers to public school communities in Mexico, which he began to organize on his own in 1995 and through UNETE four years later.[9]

In its early years, UNETE had a very simple purpose: to organize businesspeople to donate computers to the poorest public school communities in the country, in collaboration with the Ministry of Education. UNETE successfully collected donations to provide access to technology for school communities. In the last sixteen years, UNETE has built a significant network of supporters to achieve its goals, including international companies such as Dell, PepsiCo, Ford, Nissan, Hewlett-Packard, Microsoft, Sempra Energy, and Deutsche Bank, as well as foundations such as the Larry D. Large Foundation, the W.K. Kellogg Foundation, the American Express Foundation, the Televisa Foundation, and the Natural Gas Foundation. UNETE has also built partnerships with local governments, signing agreements with thirteen of thirty-two state governments in Mexico to support the implementation of the program across the country. In this regard, local governments facilitate access to schools in deprived areas and to financial resources to equip a computer room, while the school community constructs or assigns a classroom. UNETE also provides professional development and teaching capacities to introduce the use of information and communication technology (ICT) in schools.

As UNETE reached more students and schools, the orientation of its intervention model gradually evolved, mainly because of learning from constant interaction with teachers and schools, feedback from school principals and facilitators, and a better understanding of school management. From its original role as a donor of hardware and software and a provider of basic training to help teachers use technology, UNETE shifted to create what they call a "learning ecosystem" in each school it supported by organizing professional development activities, designing and disseminating curated pedagogical content, organizing and managing teachers' virtual networks, coaching in schools, and providing technology and connectivity to public schools. As its current mission statement describes, UNETE now aims to "introduce technology into [the] teaching-learning processes, . . . creating and supporting an environment designed to improve the digital proficiency of students and teachers alike, to later develop certain cognitive and non-cognitive skills."[10]

The most significant modification of this model occurred when UNETE's executive board looked to expand its type and number of institutional goals. It responded to an ongoing concern about the possibility that providing technology might not be enough to improve the education quality in the schools it supported.[11] As the current CEO of UNETE explained, at that moment, he "had to initiate a debate around different pedagogical theories and international frameworks" to identify and select competencies "close to our reality" and linked to UNETE's mission. To improve its model, UNETE reviewed models from international organizations such as the OECD. As it is described in their own report, when its staff was looking to increase and modify its goals, it "turned to the most recent educational theories outlined in OECD's 21st Century and Innovative Learning Environments, that recommended placing students at the center of the learning process and evaluating under real conditions, different models of equipment and digital content to benefit the teaching-learning process with the use of ICT."[12]

UNETE's selection of the new competencies to develop was validated based on feedback from teachers working at the schools participating in the intervention. UNETE decided to promote the development of several cognitive and noncognitive skills, thus, in practice, selecting and emphasizing an additional set of twenty-first-century skills, using technology as both an incentive and a tool to promote the use of new content and the adoption of new instructional practices in schools.[13] Although this shift is still in the beginning stages of adoption at UNETE and, therefore, is not fully implemented in every school that it supports, there is an organizational shift in switching from the support of basic technological literacy—such as using word processors or software for presentations—to including educational activities aimed at developing additional cognitive competencies such as problem solving or critical thinking, as well as intra- and interpersonal competencies such as communication, conflict resolution, and self-direction.

PROGRAM DESCRIPTION

The educational model that UNETE designed is based on the organization of parallel professional development activities along with the provision of technology infrastructure and internet access (see figure 6.1). Specifically, the intervention provides training for teachers and grants access to relevant content, such as tutorials and teaching plans, gathered in an ad hoc educational portal where teachers can collaborate with other colleagues. Moreover, monitoring allows UNETE to provide technical and pedagogic support to principals and teachers, both on-site and remotely. Finally, the intervention considers the constant evaluation of its impact on technology literacy and noncognitive skills.

Generally, UNETE selects schools every year, corresponding to the available financial and institutional resources, from two different groups of schools: (1) a pool of poor schools with low levels of academic achievement, provided these schools have a classroom available to transform into a computer lab; and (2) a group of schools explicitly chosen according to the donors' or funders' interest, for example, the Ford Civic Committee, which supported schools located near Ford dealerships only, maintained by the Ford Motor Company. Specifically, UNETE selects all participant schools based on a cost-effectiveness evaluation, assessing not just socioeconomic aspects

FIGURE 6.1   UNETE's model

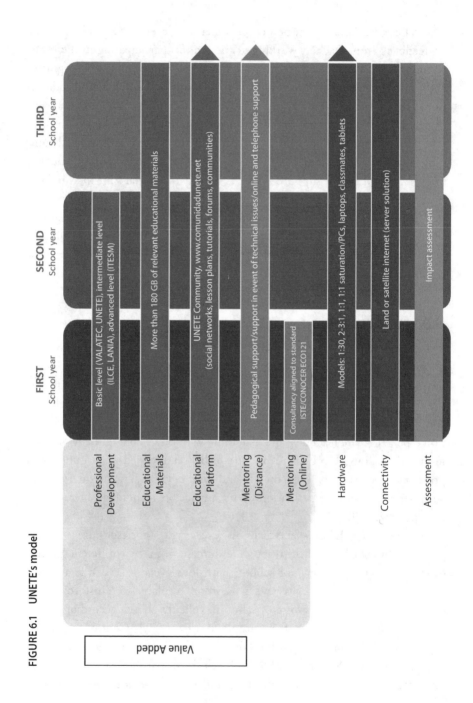

Value Added

	FIRST School year	SECOND School year	THIRD School year
Professional Development	Basic level (VALATEC, UNETE); intermediate level (ILCE, LANIA); advanced level (ITESM)		
Educational Materials	More than 180 GB of relevant educational materials		
Educational Platform	UNETE Community, www.comunidadunete.net (social networks, lesson plans, tutorials, forums, communities)		
Mentoring (Distance)	Pedagogical support/support in event of technical issues/online and telephone support		
Mentoring (Online)	Consultancy aligned to standard ISTE/CONOCER ECO121		
Hardware	Models: 1:30, 2-3:1, 1:1, 1:1 saturation/PCs, laptops, classmates, tablets		
Connectivity	Land or satellite internet (server solution)		
Assessment	Impact assessment		

of school communities but also other issues such as the school community's interest, the motivation of teachers and school principals, and school management practices. A key aspect to consider in this process is the characteristics of school principals, given their expected role as pedagogical leaders in the intervention.

After UNETE defines participant schools, it donates and delivers free technological devices, including PCs, laptops, mini laptops, or tablets, to each school, along with prepaid access to the internet for three years and a server containing preloaded pedagogical content for teachers and facilitators to use as a local resource.[14] Once the equipment is available, UNETE hires and pays a facilitator to train teachers in using the resources during instructional activities, following a school-based model: as the manager of training and educational services noted, UNETE maintains a consistent core of practices and provisions across schools via facilitators, but it "adapts [its model] to teachers' instructional practices" to intervene in the school in an undisruptive way.[15] Finally, a team of regional supervisors, also hired and trained by UNETE, monitors and accompanies each facilitator while working at schools. In addition, facilitators create informal virtual networks for exchanging experiences and available resources among teachers in the school.

The role of the facilitators is crucial for the implementation of UNETE's model, since they organize weekly in situ activities over a school year. Usually, they are graduates from teachers' colleges or from bachelor programs with a major in pedagogy or psychology. After organizing a selection process, including interviews, a training seminar, and observations to identify how they relate with colleagues and students and other social skills, facilitators are hired based on assessment by central supervisors, who provide ongoing assessment and virtual coaching once they are allocated to schools. Each facilitator can support up to three schools at the same time.

The facilitators look to achieve four main goals. Regarding the use of technology, they work as instructors for teachers, especially when teachers have no experience with the computers and educational applications or platforms. In assisting teachers with instructional practices, facilitators work mostly as advisers, as they respond to needs to connect learning goals included in the curriculum with specific programs or activities to be conducted in computer labs. In their work with students, although it is not their main responsibility or intended activity, facilitators usually adopt roles as teacher assistants in activities such as reading comprehension workshops or any other activity aimed at developing competencies on subjects not necessarily included in the curriculum, such as appreciation of the arts. Finally, they serve as a permanent liaison between UNETE and schools.

Facilitators are the main resource for teachers. Teachers frequently interact with them regarding the use of computers or about how to better utilize the instructional resources and educational materials that UNETE has curated. Therefore, facilitators show teachers how to effectively use computers during instruction, help them appropriately use all the educational content provided, and show them how to adapt their teaching practices to foster the development of relevant competencies. Although the design assumes full cooperation from teachers, facilitators face additional challenges when working in schools. For instance, one facilitator described how, initially, "some teachers hid from him, or even refused to work by arguing they were in the middle of other school activities." From this facilitator's perspective, this attitude was a consequence of their lack of experience with educational technology, while other facilitators noted that UNETE's structure to support school communities is still under development.[16] In addition, facilitators agreed that gaining access to schools is complicated, given that teachers report being overwhelmed by their workload, especially due to the enactment of a new national teacher assessment process and the fact that they are unfamiliar with the use of educational technology, although this attitude changes when they perceive the benefits.

Consistent with this goal, when facilitators arrive at any school supported by UNETE, they conduct a diagnostic evaluation of school conditions and interview teachers before designing a local plan and organizing activities for the academic year. Based on these annual plans, which facilitators design and school principals and teachers approve, the facilitators visit each school once or twice a week during the school year to coach teachers and to staff the computer lab. The objectives for each visit are determined according to their workload and the specific needs of each school regarding subjects or instructional activities needing improvement.

During the school year, facilitators support teachers in adopting and using technological applications as well as pedagogical content that UNETE developed or curated. A first step in this process is to introduce teachers to the use of software and computers. Once the teachers master the basics, the second step is to teach them how to organize educational activities using technology, such as reviewing a class plan in Prezi software or using multimedia resources to improve their instructional practices. While practicing, teachers and facilitators also discuss how to use some of the available software to better use educational content. Finally, teachers suggest new activities to implement in a real setting; for example, one biology teacher uses Jeopardy software to administer an exam simulation.

These activities are not necessarily sequential. Teachers may ask to spend more time reviewing or working with a specific software program or move forward to learn how to use a specific educational tool in class, given that some are already familiar with basic technology. The program's built-in flexibility and adaptability are the main reasons UNETE's staff affirms that its model is school-centered and responsive to the needs teachers identify.

Facilitators also help teachers improve their teaching skills by showing them how to address specific issues regarding the use of technology in classrooms. Through the facilitators' interventions, teachers have access to different sources of information suggested by the facilitators, new tools to use during instructional activities, and the ability to systematically exchange ideas with their peers. In addition, facilitators help not only to implement new practices within classrooms and schools but also to inform UNETE about the progress of teachers and schools toward the goals included in annual plans.

Teachers have access to additional sources of support and distance education, such as the website Comunidad UNETE (UNETE community), with free membership to a web portal with different instructional resources organized by grade and subject, such as (1) videotaped lessons, tutorials, or online workshops; (2) guides on creating lesson plans, including different lesson formats; (3) a platform to exchange ready-made lesson plans; and (4) supplementary educational materials such as videos, presentations, and recommended websites. For instance, resources such as Eduteka and Educare—from Argentina's Ministry of Education—are suggested to develop information literacy and critical thinking skills while evaluating the content of a website or a TV program. Similarly, the Anti-Defamation League in the United States proposed an activity to host a debate about the presence of sexism in various video games; the activity aims to develop students' active listening skills, tolerance, and civic engagement, if the teacher is an effective moderator.

Through this web portal, teachers also receive remote support from technical staff trained and supervised by UNETE about how to use any available electronic resources listed on the Comunidad UNETE's website. In collaboration with the Latin American Institute of Educational Communication (ILCE) and other educational organizations, UNETE also organizes short-term online courses, known as *diplomados*, to develop skills such as professional leadership and competency-based teaching, among others.

The final component of UNETE's model is evaluation. It designs evaluation activities to demonstrate how teachers use available technological resources to modify instructional practices. For instance, facilitators require teachers to identify a real-life problem in their community—for example, water scarcity, in which students conduct a research project to thoroughly understand the problem and identify feasible solutions. This kind of evaluation helps children use the specific skills that UNETE wants them to develop, such as critical thinking, collaboration, and problem solving. The final product includes a brief report and a videotaped presentation using the technology UNETE provides. With this activity, UNETE monitors and assesses students' progress.

ANALYSIS OF THE PROGRAM

Theory of Change

According to UNETE, providing facilitators, technology, professional development, access to new educational content, examples of different instructional practices, and continuous technical support helps teachers better plan, manage, and guide their lessons. This also modifies how teachers motivate students to learn different academic subjects and participate in instructional opportunities. All these activities are oriented toward the development of new competencies, including those categorized as most relevant to thriving in the twenty-first century. UNETE assumes that effectively supporting teachers during the full school year will have a greater potential to modify instructional practices, as findings from TALIS suggest.[17]

In UNETE's description of its theory of change, the main goal of its model is to motivate students to learn and develop new skills that explicitly include twenty-first-century competencies.[18] As one supervisor explained, although "the list of twenty-first-century skills is long, we take the first step to develop these skills by using technology, encouraging communication and collaboration, and stimulating critical thinking [skills]. We believe that if we start with a first step, both the teacher and the student will intuitively and independently move forward and will continue to do so even after we are no longer present in the school."[19]

This goal responds to a specific vision regarding the role, capacities, and resources available to public schools in Mexico that positions UNETE as a local facilitator of organizational change within school communities without substituting the role of the local government, teachers, and school principals. Furthermore, as its CEO explained, it sees its role as an external, temporary, and nonintrusive support intervention for school communities with the aim of creating opportunities to modify instructional practices and build capacity, all while caring about the schools' and teachers' autonomy and self-direction.

School principals also described a flexible and adaptable implementation model that corresponds to UNETE's view of its role as a temporary intervention in public schools. However, implementing its model in a short time (up to three years) while promoting self-direction is also one of the main challenges UNETE faces, given the short time in which facilitators must earn the trust of school community members, convince teachers to participate and adopt its model, and create capacities and foster adequate engagement to guarantee sustained implementation, all while respecting school autonomy and decisions.

Although UNETE's own definition is a broad description of its orientation and goals, based on information collected through interviews and observations, we identified additional steps and intermediate procedures and goals that may better represent how its model will result in schools aimed at "strengthening 21st century skills and competencies." Figure 6.2 depicts the theory of change we built, based on perceptions from staff members at headquarters and facilitators working at the schools.

UNETE makes three main interventions in schools: technology provision, represented by the first column in the figure; professional development activities (column two); and the distribution of new pedagogical content aligned with new instructional practices (column three). In this model, each intervention has different expected intermediate outcomes. Providing educa-

FIGURE 6.2   Theory of change based on the three sets of inputs defined by UNETE

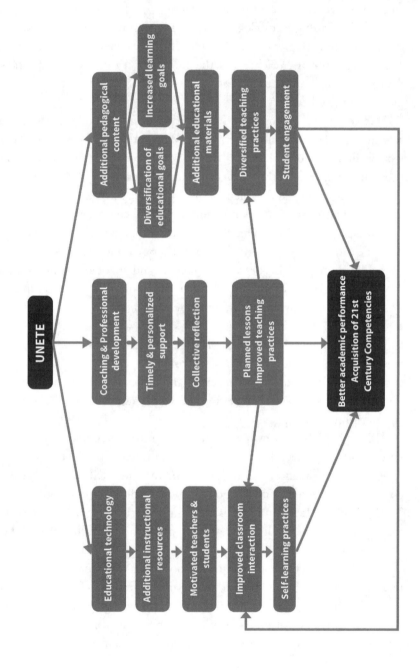

tional technology is supposed to become an incentive to develop openness and recognize the teachers' need to learn new ideas and methods. According to UNETE's theory of change, these conditions will then result in increased student engagement, better interaction between teachers and students, and autonomous or independent study, along with a favorable disposition toward the implementation of UNETE's model within school communities. The second channel (the more likely to modify instructional practices) aims at ensuring adequate and effective teacher support—one year in situ and three years of distant activities—through contributions from facilitators and external advisers or peers. The third and final component, educational content curation and delivery, aims to increase and diversify learning goals by distributing lesson plans, presentations, and other electronic resources and encouraging the adaptation of instructional materials to individual teaching needs. These interventions have the goal of creating conditions within schools and classrooms to develop new competencies among students attending UNETE schools.

Therefore, according to their conceptual design, if all three different components are in each school, the school will reach intermediate goals, resulting in improved instructional practices and, therefore, the development of new competencies. The UNETE model explicitly promotes twenty-first-century competencies as expected learning goals in each school, frequently in addition to those educational goals included in the national curriculum. This may be innovative in a context where fostering competencies beyond those included in the official curriculum is an exceptional practice.

Audience

UNETE's target populations are low-income school communities (identified based on national government statistics regarding poverty thresholds and information about school infrastructure from the Ministry of Education's national surveys) throughout the country that lack computer labs, computers, or Internet access. Within this type of school, UNETE frequently selects schools based on specific requests from national and international donors. Based on these criteria, UNETE works in many schools in the poorest states in Mexico, such as Chiapas, Oaxaca, Puebla, and Veracruz. However, variation occurs among states with similar levels of poverty, a condition usually explained by local government and donor support for this initiative. An important aspect to note is that school principals, teachers, and the community must agree and communicate their consent to be in the program, while local governments cannot force schools to participate.

UNETE staff considers its model as increasing educational effectiveness through an external, temporary, and flexible intervention, where school communities make decisions and will never be replaced by external actors. As its CEO described, "One of the great lessons from our pilot studies is that if you arrive to schools with an inflexible model, where teachers must follow exactly what you say to get some results, the implementation will fail . . . instead of being helpful, you become a burden; it won't work."[20]

The director of education explained, "Selecting schools is a big challenge. We have improved this process, but by experience, we provide the equipment only if the school community agrees to participate in the program.[21] That is the only way we can ensure they will open the doors and commit to participating."[22] As expected, this condition determines characteristics of school communities, resulting in a self-selection process, where UNETE will not invite or select schools lacking the proper organization, parental involvement, or a committed principal to participate in the program.

Expected Outcomes

UNETE promotes the development of seven skills among students in participating schools. Its model assumes three categories to develop by implementing this intervention (see figure 6.3). The rationale behind this expectation is that technology will work both as an incentive and as a pedagogical tool to develop skills if explicit educational goals are defined and included in the educational content UNETE curates or are included as a part of subjects to be taught during professional development activities. For instance, educational materials aimed at developing information literacy can be found on the Comunidad UNETE website, thus creating opportunities for teachers and school principals to expand traditional educational goals. The competencies promoted by UNETE (except, perhaps, for technological literacy) were not widely included in the national curriculum before 2013, thus increasing the value of this type of intervention for public schools. [23]

FIGURE 6.3   Expected effects on learning

Type of skills	Skill	Description
Digital skills	Technological Literacy	Ability to analyze and critically evaluate data and information, using devices to process, organize, maintain, and interpret in a more effective way
	Designing projects using technology in teaching & learning processes	Ability to analyze and critically evaluate data and information, using devices to process, organize, maintain, and interpret in a more effective way
Cognitive skills	Problem solving	**Critical thinking** Ability to use knowledge and skills to devise solutions to unfamiliar problems
	Critical thinking	**Learn to learn** Achieve effective learning in innovative ways
Non-cognitive skills	Communication	Ability to articulate in oral and written communication for a large audience
	Collaboration	Ability to be an effective team member. Help your teammates to complete their tasks and achieve a common goal; take shared responsibility in collaborative work.
	Interpersonal	Ability to work with similar team members in an environment of respect. Negotiate and solve problems.

CORE UNETE COMPONENTS

Based on observations and revised documents, we can identify different components that are fundamental to the successful implementation of UNETE's model. We consider the following five aspects as key inputs for implementation of the model.

1. Effective Staff: Characteristics, Orientation, and Capacities

UNETE's relatively small staff is distributed across the country. It includes a pedagogical technical group located in Mexico City that works from headquarters, producing educational materials for use in schools, organizing training activities for personnel in the field, and providing technical support for any technical or pedagogical problem in schools. Although it is possible to identify other interventions from NGOs based on the design of educational materials (in addition to those provided by federal and local governments), we consider UNETE a remarkable intervention due to its efforts based on expert advice. In addition, UNETE hires staff in each state where its model is implemented.

Local staff people provide support and collaborate with facilitators working directly in school communities. They are responsible for selecting, hiring, and promoting facilitators. For this reason, UNETE decided to hire young professionals, usually recent graduates from normal schools, or college graduates with majors in psychology or pedagogy. A focus on service orientation, the willingness to become a teacher, social awareness, appreciation for public education, and knowledge about the communities where they will work are considered important characteristics determining who will become a local UNETE associate.

2. Technology as Incentive and Strategy

While providing technology to public schools was the initial goal, the staff at UNETE learned that technology was a tool for influencing how schools operate and teach students and for developing competencies not currently addressed in the national curriculum. Under the UNETE model, technology becomes an incentive and catalyst for organizational change within schools, especially because the high expectations of parents and students for the use of technology in classrooms and the provision of free hardware and software facilitates access to school communities and opens opportunities to expand

educational goals, modify instructional practices, and encourage a new pedagogical orientation in some courses. As a facilitator from a rural school noted,
computers and training represent an external shock for schools, thus resulting
in additional motivation for teachers to adapt instructional practices.

Technology became an effective way for UNETE to guarantee access to
school communities in the neediest regions of Mexico, to promote different teaching practices, and to support students and teachers in developing
basic technological literacy while exploring different ways to expand learning goals in the enacted curriculum. Once technology was accepted, used,
and included by school communities in instructional practices, the teachers, encouraged by facilitators, began to include new classroom practices.
According to the facilitators we interviewed, technology helps teachers promote "children's creativity, [and even influence] the way they work as a team."
Using new technology also helps to promote lessons about problem solving and critical thinking, debates and collaboration with peers, the development of basic metacognition skills, and self-directed learning. For instance,
while we conducted an observation in an elementary school, we saw students
making a multimedia presentation about marketing and misleading adver-
tising. After each presentation, their teacher guided a discussion about the
sources' reliability and the consistency of the students' argument and their
use of audio and images. The class also provided feedback for future presentations. Their teacher highlighted the role of the facilitator in adding this type
of activity in the classroom.

3. Facilitators

Some facilitators are graduates from pedagogy, psychology, or engineering
bachelor's programs. Candidates take part in a four-day, thirty-hour training
program. Facilitators are taught to emphasize the importance of continuous
learning and fostering professional growth. In addition, they receive external distance support from specialists working at UNETE's headquarters to
address some of the challenges they will face in their daily activities at each
school.

Facilitators are responsible for training and supporting teachers as well as
encouraging them to innovate, broaden the learning goals for their students,
and change instructional practices. A facilitator explained how his initial goal
was that students develop basic technological skills as a preliminary step in

performing activities in the computer classroom according to the national curriculum. Then he promoted the use of different free software tools, such as Hot Potatoes, Audacity, and Movie Maker, to develop teaching and learning activities linked to daily class content. In addition, he identified and encouraged the implementation of extracurricular activities to strengthen reading comprehension and the use of different software programs to help students improve their English language skills and to interact with parents. In their work with teachers during the school cycle, the facilitators continuously implement training activities, adjusting the content and goals while responding to how teachers dominate different activities, or how new interests arise within their groups. In scheduled working sessions, facilitators and teachers have the flexibility to deepen the exploration of a subject or to change its content, depending on the reactions from the students.

Toward the end of the cycle, when the students work independently with computers, facilitators and teachers request the participation of students in a final capstone research project. In teams, students investigate and diagnose the causes of a community problem to suggest how to solve it. With this problem-based educational activity, facilitators and teachers develop three sets of skills while working together in organizing this activity under UNETE guidelines. First are technological skills, followed by skills for encouraging collaboration and communication among students, including the development of socio-emotional skills and teamwork. Finally, the process of identifying a real problem, the consequences of the problem they experience, and possible solutions helps them to develop cognitive skills such as critical thinking and problem solving. Collaborative projects also function as a motivation to develop twenty-first-century skills. In the diagnosis of the problem, they aim to develop critical thinking skills; finding solutions is essential to developing the ability to solve complex problems and decide on the best solution to present. Metacognition, communication, and teamwork skills are developed during the discussion with members of the project on alternative solutions and ways to present information. Finally, students develop technological literacy at each stage of the project, as they must search for information, analysis, and presentation with different software programs.[24] Although teacher involvement and participation is crucial in implementing these activities, school communities still depend on the effective intervention of facilitators, who are responsible not just for pedagogical and technical guidance but also for the involvement of all school actors (including school principals).[25]

An additional component of UNETE's model is the implementation of a monitoring process. Based on their observation of teachers' activities, facilitators gain access and influence teaching practices. However, it is unclear whether this type of labor-intensive collaboration will be financially and technically sustainable and whether teachers will modify instructional practices in lessons that do not require the use of educational technology.[26]

4. External Networks (donors and public officials)

A key characteristic of UNETE since the beginning has been the ability to attract additional financial resources for the public education system. For instance, UNETE received support from Dell, IBM, Intel, and other technology companies. In addition, the focus of the organization has recently shifted from delivering computers to training teachers to effectively use technology to improve instructional practices.[27] Consequently, since 2007, UNETE has reached new academic and public institutions to develop teacher training programs. In a first stage, it participated with the Instituto Tecnologico de Estudios Superiores de Monterrey and the Latin American Institute of Educational Communication (ILCE). Currently, it includes in its network educational institutions from the Aliat universities system, formed by local educational institutions in several cities across Mexico. According to its records, it has trained more than twenty-five thousand teachers in person or remotely. Furthermore, it gains access to schools in every case with authorization (and sometimes funding) from local governments. This example shows how building external networks and establishing a solid reputation have been key components that explain the effectiveness of this intervention.

5. School-based Approach

By design, every school community adapts UNETE's model to its conditions. UNETE organizes and provides facilitators, educational content, hardware, and coaching following the main principle that schools determine how they use these resources, avoiding a "one size fits all" approach.

In this broad approach, activities occur with significant variations among schools. Beyond the differences in infrastructure and human capital across schools, one important variable seems to be the school principal's commitment. Schools with committed school principals who interact with teachers usually have strong participation in training activities, with principals even taking part during the main sessions. This characteristic explains how schools may freely and enthusiastically adopt their model, especially because this implementation strategy contrasts with many practices commonly promoted by local authorities, where school communities are neither consulted nor included in decisions.

IMPACT EVALUATIONS

UNETE has funded four external evaluations to estimate the effects of its programs (see table 6.1). It conducted the first in 2013, comparing the academic results its school achieved against the performance of other schools in the country, using test scores from a national diagnostic examination (ENLACE, a test administered by the federal government). It conducted the second evaluation during the 2013–2014 school year, assessed effects on noncognitive skills, and used surveys to collect data on different practices and perceptions among students. The third available evaluation assessed digital skills and motivation in a sample of high-poverty schools in southern Mexico. Finally, the fourth evaluation identified the possible effects of the program on a set of noncognitive skills. All these studies report positive results on students' motivation and certain cognitive skills. Although the interpretation of the results requires further analysis, it is an opportunity to learn how to measure the development of different competencies and how to support programs diversifying learning goals.

Regardless of the methodological complexities of identifying UNETE's effects, it is important to highlight some key lessons from these evaluations. First is UNETE's interest in diversifying learning goals for evaluation processes by including twenty-first-century competencies. Second, conducting evaluations is a routine process for UNETE, providing evidence and information used for redesign purposes. A key characteristic of the organization is its constant interest in collecting information on the possible effects of educational technology. During its fifteen years of operation, it has conducted pilot tests with different devices at schools, such as PCs, laptops, and tablets

TABLE 6.1   Evaluations of UNETE's model

Author	Methodological design	Findings
Valora Consultoría (2014)	158 Schools (131 treatment/47 control), located in poor areas from Chiapas, Campeche, Quintana Roo, and Yucatán. Self-reported questionnaire (learning motivation, digital skills, critical thinking, problem solving, communication, and teamwork)	Learning motivation, problem solving, critical thinking, teamwork (+), captured through self-reported surveys
Banuelos, A. (2014)	Pilot study, mobile technology model, (CISCO and INTEL). Two schools located in Hidalgo. Knowledge and skills according to PISA	Reading comprehension (+)
SIEME (2014)	168 schools, 7,000 students. Measuring creativity, communication, information literacy, critical thinking, digital citizenship and TICs management	Communication, teamwork (+), with no effect on other competencies. Effects measured by self-reporting
IFIE (2013)	Mathematics and language scores, comparing all UNETE schools against the schools from the rest of the country	Math (+), mostly for experienced schools

using different applications and preloaded content, as well as internet use in schools. The pilot studies, with different devices at different educational levels and subjects, promote organizational learning and support the redesign process of its model. In addition, the organization documented how its intervention affects the development of cognitive skills, teacher motivation, and expertise in using technology for instructional purposes. However, it appears that UNETE has not developed a "healthy cycle of data processing, integration, and analysis," due to the lack of a systematic approach to support, conduct, and use all the available evidence and information.[28]

In the process of the evaluation and redesign of UNETE's interventions, facilitators are the main source of information to use in any adjustment of the model or adaptation of the organizational structure. UNETE's internal monitoring and evaluation activities are mostly focused on its perceptions and how schools perceive the quality of the program. As a member of its staff described to us, "[W]e know if we are successful because of the feedback we get from schools; we must listen to the teachers to verify if children are motivated because of the computer labs and to observe if teachers use technology while they teach students."[29]

LIMITATIONS OF THE PROGRAM

Just as in any intervention, some conditions may reduce the effectiveness of the program or increase implementation costs. Based on the conducted observations, we identified the following components as factors demanding close monitoring to ensure adequate replication of this program.

Technology Support

Even though Comunidad UNETE is an important component for distributing learning resources such as games, videos, apps, and other learning objects, having the flexibility to suggest and include new content from teachers results in an important variation with regard to quality. After reviewing available resources on the website, we found, for instance, that content related to noncognitive skills requires more teacher involvement to guide activities or provide feedback to students. Therefore, to adequately use these resources, teachers require the development of other skills first, such as metacognition or critical thinking, thus demanding further support from facilitators or external advisers.

UNETE's proposed resources are significantly limited in several ways, especially in the development of noncognitive skills. First, because the model requires teacher involvement, the assumption is that teachers will develop a set of competencies. However, this does not always occur, despite the support from facilitators during the school year (mostly feedback and suggestions for using curated educational materials). Second, this structure reduces the ability of students to develop these skills at their own pace or outside the classroom. Third, due to constant changes in the website content, it is difficult to have resources available all the time. However, the compilation of the sources allows students and teachers to obtain information that they could not access on their own or through official channels.

Teacher Skills

According to the UNETE model, teachers have access to different technological tools, internet resources, and learning objects to keep students motivated during lessons. However, in Mexico, teachers' technological skills are often still extremely basic, thus increasing the costs of implementing the model.[30] As the interviewed UNETE staff has reported, the professional development activities UNETE provides is frequently the first experience in using technology for educational purposes.[31] Furthermore, if teachers are to promote the development of twenty-first-century competencies among their students, they must carefully develop lesson plans and activities, identify the best ways in which they can use new educational resources during lessons, and prepare a plan in collaboration with facilitators. All these activities require competencies not fully developed during preservice training. Although this is a relevant barrier, it seems that UNETE's intervention is not yet sufficient to overcome this problem.

In addition, the interviewed facilitators reported the prevailing problem of self-selection: teachers who were the most capable and interested were also the most interested in participating in the courses and training activities that UNETE organized. Based on this observation, UNETE has explored different implementation strategies, including hiring private companies to coordinate these activities or inviting college students to organize training activities. Based on the results from these experiences, since the 2015–2016 school year, UNETE has decided to organize training activities directly, with its own staff and supervision, to respond more accurately to the needs of the teachers. In this implementation model, it obtains relevant information about which goals are achieved, immediately adjusting its model to each school context. Despite these changes, from the perspective of facilitators, several challenges remain:

> Teachers have been limited to adopting a "traditional" role, without further considerations of twenty-first-century competencies; UNETE wants to train them, but sometimes teachers do not have the time; others work double shifts. In addition, teachers are not very open; they say, "We will not spend more of our time on training activities." However, if you work with them with a gradual strategy and they realize how technology transforms students to become more interested in any of the subjects, then they participate with us.[32]

This situation has several policy implications, particularly regarding the role of facilitators as external promoters of organizational change, as well as the need to explore different tracks within the professional development activities, including introductory activities aimed at sensitizing teachers to the impact that effective use of educational technology may have on students.

Continuous Support at the School Level

Creating an effective network for school-based support is perhaps one of the greatest challenges UNETE faces. By design, it assumes that school communities must decide how to adapt and implement the model, and therefore facilitators play an important role within schools in the adoption of the model, but they should never substitute teachers or principals as pedagogical leaders. Consequently, the adoption, adaptation, and promotion of the adequate use of educational materials, along with constant participation in professional development activities, are contingent upon acceptance by principals, teachers, and the continuous engagement of school communities. Therefore, the simple provision of additional resources or the implementation of external interventions alone will not transform instructional practices.

As a consequence, this implementation model, although interesting and innovative, may represent additional costs for facilitators and UNETE staff, given that it results in different levels of commitment and adoption of educational goals. Although UNETE's approach seems to acknowledge the capacity of school communities to identify their own needs and to have a voice in adapting the program to their local context, it may still result in inadequate implementation of the program.[33]

Self-Selection and Equity

One key problem detected during the implementation of school-based management programs in Mexico is that schools with better organizational cultures are usually those ready and willing to effectively participate.[34] Given its implementation model, UNETE may face a similar problem, thus inadvertently contributing to reproducing certain inequities within the school system by promoting the engagement of school communities that are already motivated and organized.[35]

Connectivity problems in rural communities represent further challenges for the implementation of this model. Although UNETE decided to provide servers with preloaded content to schools located in poor communities, it is still redesigning its model to reduce emphasis on the use of technology and to focus its efforts on the development of teaching skills.[36] This process is ongoing, with effects still to be evaluated, but it certainly poses additional costs for the organization.

Continuity and Sustainability

A main concern emerging from our observations in schools is whether UNETE will be able to support the implementation of its model in schools in the long term, particularly when, by design, coaching and training at the school level cannot be a permanent component of the intervention, under the conceptual assumption that school communities must develop their own internal capacities. As we have described, providing technology equipment is the main incentive, followed by the provision of curated educational content and the participation of a facilitator that UNETE hires and funds. However, although changes in the operation of schools and instructional practices are reported, it is still uncertain whether teachers and school principals will permanently adopt these practices. For instance, some facilitators about to be relocated to a different school thought that up to 50 percent of teachers from their current schools required personal support to continue leading a class based on the use of technology. Furthermore, it is still unclear whether parents will value the new competencies their children are developing, and therefore, it is unclear whether they will demand and support school communities looking to expand educational goals beyond the national curriculum. In addition, there have been issues arising during the implementation of other school-based interventions where state education agencies ignore the requirements of programs such as UNETE. For instance, UNETE's orientation toward the development of new competencies not explicitly included in the curriculum may discourage teachers' engagement, given that teachers' evaluations are based on traditional competencies.

Costs

As expected, UNETE demands substantial investments. The transition from simply providing technology to improving teaching practices along with the technology definitively increased its costs (see table 6.2). This increase is mainly due to the key support from facilitators, the operation of virtual communities, and the organization of training activities. Even though UNETE appears to conduct adequate planning activities (for instance, defining the number of schools to support in consideration of available resources every year), the increasing costs of the program may limit its rapid expansion, thus affecting equity and perhaps reducing its impact. This dilemma is also faced

TABLE 6.2   Total costs per school, per components, and program

Partner	Main expenditures	Mexican pesos (MXN)	US dollars (USD)
School	Computer lab (built or modified); part of short-course fees	15,300	700
UNETE and partners	Teacher's training design, short courses, and software	152,200	6,970
Donors	Computers	36,500	1,671
	Internet	24,500	1,122
	Logistics	95,000	4,350
	Teacher's training	131,700	6,030
Total		455,200	20,843

1 USD = 21.84 MXN

Note: This cost structure is only a model, due to enormous variations across school contexts. It is based on a medium-sized school, with ADSL wideband internet and no special school conditions. This cost rises if the number of students increases, if satellite internet is needed, or if students present different pedagogical requirements.

by public education systems, which might prefer low-cost policies to more effective interventions demanding more investment.

LESSONS LEARNED

UNETE's experience in implementing a program based on the provision of technology, educational content, and coaching helps identify possible policy options to support the introduction of educational goals related to twenty-first-century competencies in developing countries and to increase collaboration with school communities and teachers in implementing this type of reform. The following aspects summarize some main lessons we learned from the UNETE experience:

- *Use of incentives to adopt innovations.* Usually considered as an inadequate substitute of effective learning practices, educational technology seems to be an effective incentive to expand educational goals and revise instructional practices within school communities. From the UNETE experience, we can conclude that teachers in the program agree on the need to develop other skills along with the traditional curricula and that the use of technology is a powerful means to trigger the development of such competencies. However, the supplementary coaching provided in every school to adopt technology might not be replicable, due to financial costs, and the dependency on the initial teachers' skills in using technology may contribute to a delay in other school communities' full adoption of the model.

In addition, organizations interested in identifying incentives they might use to foster twenty-first-century competencies in public schools have to consider other aspects. For example, incentives may have different effects across different school systems. There are also disparities in various actors' perceptions about the relevance of twenty-first-century competencies; thus they respond differently to different incentive-based interventions. Finally, it is important to consider the cost of including such competencies as institutional goals given that, for example, some education systems, as in the case of Mexico, evaluate their teachers based on their competencies in traditional subjects and may therefore not see the advantage of fostering twenty-first-century skills among their students.

- *Efficiency and quality concerns.* As the UNETE experience suggests, expanding educational goals to include twenty-first-century skills while adapting former traditional programs may result in significantly higher expenditures, compromising the replication of these programs. Further research is needed to estimate the costs of developing twenty-first-century competencies under different conditions as a necessary step to conducting cost-effectiveness analyses that may result in better decisions. In addition, expanding educational goals to include twenty-first-century competencies represents a change in the definition of educational quality, thus increasing the complexity of the implementation process and creating additional challenges for monitoring and evaluation.

- *Lack of alignment with educational systems.* Interventions such as UNETE underscore a problem frequently faced in the management of innovative school-based programs: other schools and upper administrative levels might focus on different goals and educational activities, isolating UNETE school communities. Even though UNETE has intentionally designed an intervention to work at the school level, with little or no intervention from state education agencies, a lack of alignment with state education authorities' priorities may represent additional risks and costs for UNETE schools. This situation may result in challenges for the continuity and sustainability of interventions promoting the development of twenty-first-century competencies. In contexts such as Mexico, where the central government controls curriculum design and teacher evaluations, it is necessary to carefully explore and identify how to design effective school-based interventions while guaranteeing a homogeneous implementation. Given the multiple definitions and taxonomies related to twenty-first-century skills, we recommend that a widely accepted definition be adopted as guidance for defining new educational goals.[37]

- *Networks and external supporters.* A key lesson in this case is the role that external actors play in supporting the introduction of new educational goals among school communities. As described, external supporters were key to the implementation of this model. Any initiative aimed at supporting the development of twenty-first-century skills in public schools as one of its educational goals may benefit from designing a plan to create a network of external supporters. Furthermore, this network may help in later stages of the plan, particularly when sustainability in schools might become an urgent policy goal.

- *NGOs as promoters of policy changes or experimental approaches.* Based on this case, we underscore the importance of the role of NGOs as promoters of relevant competencies in the national curriculum as well as in school practices. UNETE has successfully attracted attention and promoted the implementation of interventions aimed at fostering the development of twenty-first-century competencies, regardless of the few educational goals promoting these competencies in the official national curriculum. NGOs may have an important job supporting schools when local and national governments are not involved in exploring new competencies to develop in public schools.

UNETE also illustrates the importance of organizational learning, experimentation, rapid prototyping, and evaluation to support such learning on the part of schools and of UNETE, something not commonly observed in the actions of local and national governments. This approach allows facilitators to invent school improvement alternatives in partnership with teachers and to evaluate how they work, even as they monitor progress in the schools' yearly plans and extend the lessons learned throughout the network of schools where they work.

FINAL COMMENTS

Diversifying learning goals in schools to include twenty-first-century competencies requires sustained collaboration among public officials, parents, students, and teachers. It also requires continuous technical support, tutoring by qualified staff, and additional resources, all oriented toward supporting processes aimed at producing significant changes in instructional practices. Given the complexity that this activity represents (particularly when national curricula and policies do not fully include new competencies), public and private partnerships with NGOs create an opportunity to raise awareness about the importance of including twenty-first-century competencies and exploring different policy options and innovations for school communities.

UNETE's experience provides some lessons regarding the implementation of a transition from traditional to twenty-first-century competencies in schools. Incentives, professional development activities, and the provision of external support and educational content seem to be potential means for gaining access to school communities, developing capacities, and promoting changes in instructional practices to foster the development of these competencies among students. However, concerns about the feasibility of implementing this intervention at the system level (mainly because of financial and technical constraints) resemble the challenges any education system faces when implementing educational reforms.

Beyond learning about the provision of additional resources to schools, UNETE's experience suggests three aspects to consider in any design of interventions promoting the development of twenty-first-century competencies in schools. First, it is necessary to support school communities, including teachers, principals, students, and parents, in starting a continuous process of self-assessment, experimentation, and learning. In this process, teachers and principals have the opportunity to revise current educational goals, explore and learn from new competencies to develop, and learn from materials and props useful in adopting new educational goals and modifying instructional practices. Second, it is necessary to overcome the perception that school communities will fully embrace new competencies because of their intrinsic relevance; therefore, additional efforts should be made to create an environment where everyone clearly understands how traditional and new competencies interact and how developing both types of competencies should be a shared goal among public officials, teachers, and parents. Finally, external support will never sustainably replace local capacity, especially when the development of twenty-first-century competencies among students is contingent on the development of the very same competencies among teachers.

APPENDIX (CHAPTER 6)

Interviewees and Their Affiliations

TABLE 1   Interviews conducted for this study (UNETE)

Name	Position	Location
Alejandro Almazan	CEO/UNETE Headquarters	Mexico City
Cesar Loeza	Director/UNETE Headquarters	Mexico City
Alberto Dávila	Director/UNETE Headquarters	Mexico City
Rubén Martínez	Director/UNETE Headquarters	Mexico City
María Altamirano	Director/UNETE Headquarters	Mexico City
Lluvia Martínez	Director/UNETE Headquarters	Mexico City
Israel Vázquez	Facilitator	State of Mexico
Guadalupe Romero	School principal	Mexico City
Miguel Iván Cruz	Facilitator	Mexico City
Uriel Álvarez	Facilitator	Hidalgo
Perla López	Facilitator	Hidalgo
Hugo Mercado	School principal	Aguascalientes
Benjamín Herrera	Facilitator	Aguascalientes
Bernardino López	School principal	Hidalgo
Leticia Castillo	School principal	Puebla
Nélida Alcocer	Facilitator	Puebla
Angélica Moreno	School principal	Tlaxcala
Adriana Cervantes	Facilitator	Tlaxcala
Carmen Martínez	School principal	Jalisco
Mario Aceves	Facilitator	Jalisco

TABLE 2   Interviews conducted for this study (external actors)

Name	Position	Relationship with UNETE
Felix Martínez	General coordinator at SIEME	Evaluator

TABLE 3   Schools visited

Schools	State	Municipality
Julian Villagran	Hidalgo	Tepeji del Rio de Ocampo
Ignacio Manuel Altamirano	Hidalgo	Acaxochitlan
Mariano Jimenez	Aguascalientes	Aguascalientes
Fundación Beatriz Velasco Alemán, IAP	Mexico City	Venustiano Carranza
Heroes de Chapultepec	Tlaxcala	Chiautempan

CHAPTER SEVEN

Creating Cultures of Learning in the Twenty-First Century

A Study of EL Education in the United States

Connie K. Chung
Global Education Innovation Initiative,
Harvard Graduate School of Education

E L Education, a network of approximately 150 schools in the United States, provides contextually relevant, ongoing systematic support, and professional development to teachers as they cultivate relevant twenty-first-century competencies in students. The key argument of the chapter is that as the goals and purposes of schooling broaden, focusing on increasing the individual abilities of teachers is not enough. Capacity building needs to include the school, with attention paid to increasing the organizational capacity of schools to create the kinds of climates and cultures in which teachers and students are teaching and learning the competencies, attitudes, and values needed to thrive in the twenty-first century.

OVERVIEW OF MAJOR FINDINGS

In different contexts, capacity building can mean any of the following and more: schools receive more financial, administrative, or professional development resources; teachers continue teaching the way that they have taught, but get better at doing the same activity; teachers expand their repertoire of how they teach because of professional development sessions, including coaching; teachers take ownership and create something new, whether it is curricular content or pedagogy, and so on. In this chapter, I propose that capacity building for twenty-first-century competencies is a multidimensional endeavor, requiring not only acquiring expert knowledge, but also developing the interpersonal and intrapersonal skills and dispositions of school leaders and staff, including their commitment to persist through difficult challenges to improve their schools over time. Effective capacity building requires not just the effort and improvement of individual teachers, but the effort and improvement of the school as a whole, including deliberately shaping its culture so that students and teachers can do good and better work.

In this sense, capacity building is necessarily a collaborative and consensual process, requiring mutual, relational work among different stakeholders, including teachers, principals, students, and community members. Further, in this context, leadership for capacity building involves paying attention to and cultivating a particular kind of organizational culture in which staff and students relate well to each other as they take on engaging and challenging learning tasks. It involves the understanding that leaders "create the conditions in which good teachers stay and where good learning and teaching happens."[1]

Capacity building for schools also takes into consideration the existing capacity of people and organizations, including local needs and contexts, and by necessity is grounded in practice and in partnership with the stakeholders. Because twenty-first-century competencies are more complex than the traditional literacies, professional development that is done "to" schools and teachers is limited; rather, competencies are developed as staff and students commit to and take on challenging learning tasks. Capacity building, in this sense, also develops over time.

RESEARCH METHODS AND DESCRIPTION OF EL EDUCATION

To determine which program to study in the United States, we canvassed leaders in education in the country and asked who was educating students well at scale. We asked for nominations of organizations that were developing not just students' cognition, but also their interpersonal and intrapersonal competencies; almost all nominated EL Education.

EL Education's model for teaching and learning "challenges students to think critically and take active roles in their classrooms and communities."[2] The staff members believe that learning should "be active, challenging, meaningful, public, and collaborative." To support these notions, they work with about 152 schools in 30 states to design and implement their education model. They serve about 4,000 teachers in these schools, offering professional development workshops and conferences that focus on practice and learning from other teachers and principals in their network, and host an online repository of high-quality student work. Most recently, they worked with EL Education teachers to translate the Common Core standards into curriculum, and half the state of New York implemented this curriculum. The curriculum, provided free online, has been downloaded more than 8 million times as of 2018, used in 44 states, by over 40,000 teachers, and they are building a suite of online offerings, including videos.[3]

EL Education is part of the Deeper Learning Network. Barbara Chow, former education program director of the Hewlett Foundation that leads the network, noted that EL Education stands out among other school networks because it was unique in working with both district (48 percent), charter (46 percent), and independent (5 percent) schools, in urban (60 percent), rural (17 percent), and suburban and town (23 percent) settings, according to data from 2012–2013.[4] As of 2016, it was working with 152 schools in 30 states and Washington, DC, which included 50,000 students and 4,000 teachers.[5] Elementary schools compose 43 percent of its schools; middle schools, 37 percent; and high schools, 20 percent; it serves a diverse population of students, with 44 percent white, 24 percent black, 26 percent Hispanic, 3 percent Asian, and 3 percent other.[6] We wanted to choose a school network that reflected the demographic diversity of the United States and the American public education system, and EL Education appeared to fit this criterion well.

EL Education is one of the bigger networks of schools in the United States, having been in existence for more than twenty years. Other organizations working on education in the twenty-first century are newer and thus smaller and, in the case of EDLeader21, not yet fully realized in their theoretical model and not yet ready for study when we began this research project in 2016.

EL Education's documentation of success strengthened the case for our choice of this network for our study, having been recognized not only by President Barack Obama and Secretary of Education Arne Duncan, but also by external evaluators who found that, on average, EL Education students perform better on state tests than their district peers. In reading, elementary school students score seven points above their peers; middle school students, eleven points; and high school students, twelve points.[7] In math, elementary school students score six points above their peers; middle school students, nine points; and high school students, eight points. These differences are even larger when comparing students in EL Education's "mentor schools," those schools within the EL Education network as having a deep implementation of the EL Education model, strong student engagement, and school leadership.[8]

According to one study, when broken down into scores by student demographic groups, in reading, white students in EL Education mentor schools outscore their white peers in other schools by eight points; black students outscore their black peers by fifteen points, and Hispanic students outscore their Hispanic peers by sixteen points. Students from low-income families outscore their peers in similar economic situations by fourteen points, and special education students outscore their peers by nine points. In math, the results are similar, with white students outscoring white peers in other schools by seven points; black students outscoring black student peers by thirteen points; Hispanic students outscoring Hispanic students in other schools by eight points; low-income students outscoring other low-income students in other schools by ten points, and special education students outscoring their peers by nine points.[9]

To study EL Education and the ways in which it builds the capacity of its teachers and schools, I interviewed twenty-seven people, including nine EL Education staff members, sixteen teachers and principals in EL Education network schools, a funder, and a potential funder who ultimately chose not to fund EL Education, as way to seek the viewpoint of people who might have a critical perspective on EL Education.

I also conducted observations, attending the three-day EL Education Leadership Induction Institute in Amherst, Massachusetts, in July 2015. I also visited four schools in the fall of 2015: one charter high school, one district high school, one charter middle school, and one district middle school. I sought the recommendation of a number of EL Education staff before settling on these four schools, and I deliberately asked to see schools that, in their opinion, would provide clear insights into what EL Education was trying to achieve. During the course of these school visits, I interviewed people and also observed a number of classrooms, and attended schoolwide meetings, staff meetings, and other key components of EL Education schools. I was not seeking to evaluate the schools on their effectiveness in executing the model, but instead was gathering data to understand how EL Education worked and what staff and these schools said they valued about being part of the network. The unit of analysis and focus was not individual EL Education schools, but EL Education, including its network and professional development offerings.

I also received from EL Education staff members a number of documents describing their program; I read pertinent newspaper articles about EL Education schools or EL Education itself and contacted EL Education teachers and staff who had previously conducted their own research studies. In addition to formal interviews, I also spoke formally and informally with people familiar with EL Education's work.

CONTEXT FOR TWENTY-FIRST-CENTURY LEARNING AND TEACHING

Next, I discuss the policy and other relevant contexts that contributed to EL Education's existence and why it functions as it does. For example, the United States has several challenges in education, but those most resonant with what EL Education is trying to address in its practice are the following: (1) the need to expand the definition of "achievement" in schools; (2) the need to understand that teaching is a complex activity requiring in-context, personalized, continual professional development throughout teachers' careers; (3) the lack of attention paid to the development of interpersonal and intrapersonal competencies at the staff and school levels, and the connection between personal and social competencies with the intellectual competencies.

A recent history of a narrow definition of "achievement" as documented in our findings from our first book, *Teaching and Learning for the Twenty-First Century: Educational Goals, Policies, and Curricula from Six Nations*, shows that the United States is just coming out of a period of testing and accountability policy measures that focused mostly on test scores.[10] Ron Berger, the chief academic officer for EL Education, discussed the implications of such policies: "Most of the other [education] organizations [believe that] if your test scores are good, then you're working [well]. If you're closing the achievement gap, you're working. And we absolutely don't believe that. We believe that our mission is creating good human beings who are deep and thoughtful intellectually but also have a core of character and citizenship in them that they are contributing to a better world."[11]

In addition, there is a lack of understanding and practice that teaching is a complex activity and is a profession that requires practitioners to continually study, refine, revise, reflect on their practice, and learn from others. This misunderstanding leads to very few opportunities in schools that provide the time, space, and the means for teachers to document, reflect, revise, and ultimately improve their practice in a systematic, collaborative way. For example, UCLA professor Jim Stigler observed that "teaching is a complex system. There is no one variable, or even an additive group of variables that are going to determine whether teaching is of high quality."[12] EL Education, in this context, emphasizes the idea that "learning is collaborative," and that it is an activity in which "school leaders, teachers, students, and families share rigorous expectations for quality work, achievement, and behavior. Trust, respect, responsibility, and joy in learning permeate the school culture."[13] It cultivates a national network of practitioners and goes to extraordinary lengths to document quality student work, to begin to codify effective teacher and school practice, and to iterate on these documented activities to continually improve.

In addition, another challenge is that in the United States, education is valued primarily as a private, individual good, rather than a public good. Furthermore, the mechanism for how teaching and learning works is assumed to be at the individual level, so the policy and practice foci are greatly imbalanced to weigh on mechanisms that increase individual student achievement, rather than on the multiple and multidimensional factors at the organizational or cultural level that contribute to not just individual but community and organizational flourishing. Indeed, the cultivation of interpersonal and intrapersonal competencies at the organizational and cultural levels is virtually ignored.

However, scholars like Anthony Bryk and Barbara Schneider have shown how critical such factors as "relational trust" are in creating a culture where learning and improving practice are part of working and being at a school.[14] EL Education teacher Mallory Haar commented that in her experience, in many schools, "It's very easy for teachers to feel some shame and protectiveness sometimes, [saying to other teachers,] 'oh, this is my thing I'm doing [in my classroom]. You wouldn't necessarily understand.'" In contrast to this perception, EL Education explicitly pays attention to creating positive cultures in its schools that provide the soil in which students and teachers can grow. When asked how they felt they had grown as teachers in EL Education schools, the majority of teacher respondents spoke about the importance of the context in which their growth took place, which they specified as a particular kind of culture that the model EL Education schools provide.

These are some of the key challenges that EL Education is solving around developing competencies relevant to the twenty-first century. In addition, in a policy climate where education can often solely focus on the product in the form of student test scores, EL Education focuses equally on ways to be and the process of learning and teaching that can produce works of high quality and character. For example, EL Education staff members often refer to "Austin's Butterfly" as a way to communicate what they are trying to do in all of their schools. It is a video that describes the process of how a first-grade student in one of their schools drew a beautiful butterfly, after six drafts, with feedback from peers.[15] They use the video as an example to show that the process of producing high-quality work combines the development of cognitive, social, and emotional competencies. They teach students to persevere through producing multiple drafts; effectively and empathetically give and receive peer feedback; and collaborate to produce works of quality. Remarkably, the video demonstrates that when guided by knowledgeable teachers, even students as young as first graders can think critically and give effective feedback to their peers to produce excellent work.

In other words, in a century when the abilities to take on difficult challenges and to persist in creatively solving them by collaborating with others to produce high-quality work that is valuable to society are more important than ever, the teachers of EL Education explicitly cultivate in students ways to behave, be, and belong with others in the world. Perhaps twenty-first-century competencies ultimately are not discrete skills but are powerful habits of mind and work that serve students well, no matter what the particular task or challenge.

WHAT DOES EL EDUCATION DO?

What does EL Education do to develop capacity in teachers and schools? EL Education sees the competencies pertinent to the twenty-first century as an expanded notion of achievement that encompasses three components: (1) mastery of skill and knowledge, (2) character, defined as both process and relational, and (3) high-quality work and craftsmanship. As such, these components align with the three domains outlined in a 2012 National Research Council report: cognitive, interpersonal, and intrapersonal.[16] In layman's terms, at EL Education, students cultivate the ability and the disposition to take on and persist through challenging tasks, iterating multiple drafts of their work, with reflection and feedback from others until their work is of high quality. They cultivate the ability and disposition to relate well with others, so that they are able to not only work with others, but also seek to understand them. They have the ability to self-regulate and practice engaging in reflection. Students are also able to understand and apply their learning to take positive action to contribute to their communities.

The EL Education handbook, *Expeditionary Learning Core Practices: A Vision for Improving Schools*, has an explicitly "different approach to teaching and learning"; for EL Education, "learning is active, challenging, meaningful, public, and collaborative."[17] It states that the practices outlined in the book "create school environments that promote deep engagement in learning and support students to achieve at high levels, [gaining] skills critical to college readiness and life success—literacy, numeracy, problem-solving, critical thinking, collaboration, creativity, persistence toward excellence, and active citizenship, as well as mastery of knowledge."[18]

To this end, EL Education partners with individual schools and assigns a "school designer" or coach to the school, who then visits and works with the school leaders and key teachers to set the overall strategy, determine a few key priorities on which to focus their work for the year, and also assist in planning professional development priorities and activities that align with the goals outlined. In tandem with the work of the school designer, the school might also involve instructional coaches and send its staff to EL Education regional and national conferences and workshops. EL Education has also identified mentor schools that operate as models and resources to other schools in its network. A regular and systematic assessment that benchmarks the school's progress along thirty-eight core practices in five domains (instruction, curriculum, leadership; culture and character, student-engaged assessment) is also part of the process. Throughout the program, teacher and student voices are valued, included, and prioritized.

Where Does EL Put These Goals into Practice?

EL Education works with entire schools, including all staff and students across the United States, as I summarized earlier. It also offers curriculum and other resources such as videos about instructional practice online. It offers a network of schools to inspire and to serve as models and mentors to other schools and staff. It influences policy as it collaborates with other organizations such as the Deeper Learning Network, and as it is invited into such conversations as those about the Common Core. Though its outreach is intentionally broad and widespread, in its core practice in schools, it is almost a self-enclosed and self-sufficient system, in that EL Education network leaders and members set the overarching vision and mission; provide curricula, professional development, and other resources; and cultivate model schools.

How Does EL Education Work?

EL Education has a deliberately broad vision worth changing to and consistency and clarity in the practice of its core mission, vision, and values. As with any organization that is successful, EL Education is clear about its vision, mission, and values, and its schools take the time to also articulate their own vision, mission, and values. For example, over the doorframe of the cafeteria of Codman Academy in Dorchester, Massachusetts, is a statement directly from one of the ten design principles seen in many EL Education–affiliated organizations: "We are crew, not passengers." In other words, practical engagement and effort to make the community work are both explicitly stated and practiced. For. example, EL Education's chief schools officer and former EL Education school principal Mark Conrad and Janine Gomez, school designer for the Atlantic region and former EL Education school principal, conducted a three-day leadership institute with minimal staff support. Conrad and Gomez both took part in arranging and organizing the chairs and facilitating discussions, and encouraged the participants to do the same, referring explicitly to the value of everyone's contribution to making the leadership institute a success.

EL Education intentionally cultivates cultures and values of respect, responsibility, humility, engagement, and ownership of the community in its schools. Many organizations have vision, mission, and value statements painted on their walls, but successful practitioners of the EL Education model put them to practice in their actions. EL Education also expects that student work will be of high quality and supports its teachers in helping students produce that kind of work. EL Education also believes learning should be active, purposeful, authentic, and meaningful. For example, students engage in "learning expeditions" that consistently result in original reports and presentations to real audiences, such as government officials and community members. These projects make an impact beyond the classroom. EL Education believes that "learning with a purpose helps students develop the academic skills and work ethic that prepare them for college and beyond."[19]

EL Education originated in a collaboration between Outward Bound USA and the Harvard Graduate School of Education (HGSE). It joined Outward Bound's emphasis on experiential education and HGSE's expertise in the theoretical and practical approaches to teaching and learning.[20] EL Education was first built on ten design principles that reflect the values and beliefs of Kurt Hahn, founder of Outward Bound. I have grouped them thematically, emphasizing the key ideas that emerge from them.[21]

The importance of creating particular contexts for learning that places student self-discovery, construction of knowledge, nurturing of both the emotions and the intellect, and the process of learning at the center.

- *The primacy of self-discovery.* Learning happens best with emotion, challenge, and the requisite support. People discover their abilities, values, passions, and responsibilities in situations that offer adventure and the unexpected. In EL Education schools, students undertake tasks that require perseverance, fitness, craftsmanship, imagination, self-discipline, and significant achievement. A teacher's primary task is to help students overcome their fears and discover they can do more than they think they can.
- *Having wonderful ideas.* Teaching in EL Education schools fosters curiosity about the world by creating learning situations that provide something important to think about, time to experiment, and time to make sense of what is observed.

Here, in its first two principles, EL Education recognizes and articulates the necessary blend of emotions and intellect in learning, recognizing that intentionally creating contexts in which "adventure" and "the unexpected" are an important part of the learning process. It reaches beyond the traditional role and expectation of teachers to deliver knowledge and instead states that the teacher's role is as much about providing emotional and social support as it is to nurture the intellectual development of students. Thus, in two short paragraphs, it has placed students at the center, emphasizing that learning is about self-discovery and learning facts about the world, and emphasizing the process of learning—that is about practicing "perseverance, craftsmanship, imagination, self-discipline"—as much as the product of learning or significant achievement. It also stated that the phenomena of developing such capacities require a context of learning, where—as in real-life contexts outside the classroom—"situations that offer adventure and the unexpected . . . and that provide something important to think about, time to experiment, and time to make sense"—are a critical part of constructing a meaningful learning experience.

The importance of emphasizing the social nature and mission of schooling, where students learn just as much from each other as they do from individual activity.

- *The responsibility for learning.* Learning is both a personal process of discovery and a social activity. Everyone learns both individually and as part of a group. Every aspect of an EL Education school encourages both children and adults to become increasingly responsible for directing their own personal and collective learning.
- *Empathy and caring.* Learning is fostered best in communities where students' and teachers' ideas are respected and where there is mutual trust. Learning groups are small in EL Education schools, with a caring adult looking after the progress and acting as an advocate for each child. Older students mentor younger ones, and students feel physically and emotionally safe.
- *Collaboration and competition.* Individual development and group development are integrated so that the value of friendship, trust, and group action is clear. Students are encouraged to compete, not against each other, but with their own personal best and with rigorous standards of excellence.
- *Diversity and inclusion.* Both diversity and inclusion increase the richness of ideas, creative power, problem-solving ability, and respect for others. In EL Education schools, students investigate and value their different histo-

ries and talents as well as those of other communities and cultures. Schools and learning groups are heterogeneous.

Following research literature that shows the importance of small learning communities in creating not just effective cultures of learning but development of trust, EL Education emphasizes the benefits of each child having a "caring adult" and advocate at the school. The physical and emotional safety of students and the value of friendship are as much part of the explicit curriculum as are English, math, and science. EL Education explicitly sees diversity as a source of strength and an aspect to intentionally seek and practice in creating school communities and learning groups.

The importance of developing the whole self—with challenges and failures as an explicit and central core of the curriculum.

- *Success and failure.* All students need to be successful if they are to build the confidence and capacity to take risks and meet increasingly difficult challenges. But it is also important for students to learn from their failures, to persevere when things are hard, and to learn to turn disabilities into opportunities.
- *Solitude and reflection.* Students and teachers need time alone to explore their own thoughts, make their own connections, and create their own ideas. They also need to exchange their reflections with other students and with adults.

Even before the recent emphases on growth mind-sets and grit, EL Education has emphasized the importance of learning from both success and failure. Such explicit attention to a more holistic view of the learning process in its core design principles document forms a clear contrast to recent education policy contexts in which achievement has been narrowly defined as performance on summative evaluations such as high-stakes tests. By virtue of articulating the principle so explicitly in its core document, EL Education creates the capacity or the room for students, teachers, and schools in the EL Education network to structure contexts in which failure is valued and embraced, rather than denigrated and avoided, and where the creation and construction of knowledge—rather than imbibing and reproducing facts—can take place.

The importance of an education that intentionally orients learners toward the world and toward the future.

- *The natural world.* A direct and respectful relationship with the natural world refreshes the human spirit and teaches the important ideas of recurring cycles of cause and effect. Students learn to become stewards of the earth and of future generations.
- *Service and compassion.* We are crew, not passengers. Students and teachers are strengthened by acts of consequential service to others, and one of EL Education school's primary function is to prepare students with the attitudes and skills to learn from and be of service.

True to its roots as an Outward Bound organization, EL Education values outdoor experiences and respect for the environment. Many of its schools take students on camping trips and ropes courses as part of its explicit efforts to build community. Thus, in its design principles statement, it values nature not just as an end to itself, but as a valuable learning resource that captures for students the importance of "recurring cycles and cause and effect," including mindful attention to the impact of choices and actions on "future generations."

In addition, EL Education schools focus on service to others and to the larger community, so that success and achievement is not just about developing the self, but about learning how to build better communities. One example of this emphasis is the project that King Middle School in Portland, Maine, embarked on, in which middle school students learned about the importance of caring for the environment. They marched to city hall and called for their entire community to take action on climate change.[22] "We're the first generation to feel the effects of climate change, and the last one to be able to do anything about it," said Satchel Butterfield, an eighth grader. "Climate change isn't the biggest problem. Changing it is."[23] Demonstrating a kind of thoughtfulness that is one of the aims of EL Education, the middle school students' march was not just a protest to raise awareness, but considered a larger global context and was timed to coincide with the United Nations climate talks in Paris. In this and other ways, King Middle School enabled students and the broader community more aware of the relevance of what they were learning in the classroom to key global issues. The students were able to connect knowledge with action and skills with which to create a better world for themselves and others.

HOW DOES EL EDUCATION BUILD CAPACITY?

Capacity building includes the notion of constructing an environment in which inspiration, camaraderie, trust, collaboration, clear expectations, and agreements are fostered, in pursuit of a "vision worth changing to." EL Education believes that articulating and putting in practice "a vision worth changing to." It also feels that adults and young people in a school need support, encouragement, and skillful coaching to become better teachers. Mark Conrad noted that EL Education believes teachers need to "be engaged, supported, and held accountable" to change their practice. Thus, its "professional development is designed to provide these three things: Deep engagement around the ideas, deep levels of support to actually help and scaffold the process of implementation, and then the right forms of accountability to ensure that teachers are following through."

When asked to explain the phrase "right forms of accountability," Conrad answered that these forms of accountability "hinge on agreements. So, what is it that we all agree to strive to have instruction look like in our classroom?" Thus, EL Education encourages its schools to emphasize explicit and clear expectations for both adults and students. For example, EL Education staff often end professional development sessions with questions about what participants will do next in their classrooms, given what they have learned. Encouraging people to make public their commitments and then follow through to see that they execute on these agreements is their version of accountability. Conrad noted, "One of the things we see most often in ineffective schools is that leaders don't follow through on initiatives in ways that show people that this [change they are adopting] matters, and that this [initiative] isn't something else that will pass." In a national context where reforms come and go rapidly, this explicit emphasis on asking teachers to make clear, public commitments and agreements on next steps and plans and also see them through is a large part of how EL Education builds an organizational culture that both fosters and ensures professional growth and better teaching and learning that makes sense to teachers.

In putting to practice its theory that people benefit from clear expectations and descriptions, EL Education schools focus on modeling, establishing clear expectations, articulating, documenting, and codifying good and best practices. Conversations, open dialogue, agreement as a school and faculty about where they are headed are a regular part of school practice. EL Education's theory of change is that growth occurs in a supportive culture and structure. Casco Bay High School (CBHS), in Portland, Maine, for example, is centered around an open area called "The Great Space," with tables and benches where students and teachers alike sit for informal conferences. CBHS teacher Matt Bernstein noted, "There is a bunch of teachers always around and everyone is willing to lend an ear [to another teacher] whether it's 'Hey, I had a really rough class this morning, can I just talk about that?' Or 'Can you help me look if there's a rubric that I'm rolling out in a couple of days, get me some feedback?'" The school is designed to enable casual interactions and takes these kinds of conversations away from more formal observations. Bernstein continued:

> Just the whole idea of the way the school is set up . . . is rooted in . . . this idea that we're all connected. Kids, teachers, all sitting around, milling about, quick conversations. A couple of TAs sat down over there while I was doing some work during prep and they were like hey, remember when you were a student teacher? That was a thirty-second conversation that would have never happened if I was in my own classroom with my door closed because of my prep and I'm working. So the fact that we are bringing into this space and then opening it up to communication, I think helps teach and develop this idea of we are community so we care about each other. We're invested in each other. And that I think is a really key social-emotional development.

Not all EL Education schools have a "Great Space," but other schools I visited had restructured their schedules to allow for faculty collaborations, and for students to work on complex projects like learning expeditions in longer blocks of time.

Thus, in its emphasis on developing culture, EL Education puts to practice what researchers who study effective school reform have observed. For example, Richard Elmore writes that "the development of systematic knowledge about, and related to, large-scale instructional improvement requires a change in the prevailing culture of administration and teaching in schools. Cultures do not change by mandate; they change by the specific displacement of existing norms, structure, and processes by others; the process of cultural change depends fundamentally on modeling the new values and behavior that you expect to displace the existing ones."[24]

Similarly, Michael Fullan has written: "Capacity building concerns competencies, resources, and motivation. Individuals and groups are high in capacity if they possess and continue to develop knowledge and skills, if they attract and use resources (time, ideals, expertise, money) wisely, and if they are committed to putting in the energy to get important things done collectively and continuously (ever learning). This is a tall order in complex systems, but it is exactly the order required."[25] Thus, the conditions for improving teaching and learning include not just learning more and better skills but also paying attention to the conditions—such as time and resource allocation—that enable a culture of continual learning and improvement.

Capacity building includes creating a culture of learning, rather than focusing merely on tactics and teaching strategies. This priority is rooted in EL Education's theory that, to the extent that these competencies are not inherited, they develop over time. Thus, EL Education's capacity-building practices include the notion of creating conditions in which long-term learning can take place. The theory is also that the work to teach these competencies not only takes more effort, but also that people "have to open [their] hearts, to take risks. Conrad noted, "It's more fulfilling but you can't be a slacker to do it. And if you don't have a leader that inspires their faculty to work hard and if people don't trust the leader to really be a great leader," they "just know" that it is difficult for EL Education to externally impose the learning on the faculty. Conrad was quick to point out that they are looking for faculty who say they are willing to try.

Conrad observed that when adults see growth in students as a result of changes in their own practice, it is "deeply motivating for adults." He believes that the "vast majority of teachers are motivated primarily by wanting to do what they believe works for kids." Thus, EL Education encourages teachers to experiment with new practices even as they learn about developments in research.

Core to its theory of change for adults is the importance of building "relationships, relationships," Conrad said. EL Education staff development practices are based on coaching, and its "theory of change is that teachers need that job-embedded side-by-side coaching support in order to take what they learned in more traditional forms of professional development, and actually implement it."

EL Education believes that the reason many teachers think that most professional development is a waste of time is that, according to Conrad, it "doesn't penetrate the impermeable membrane of the classroom, because there isn't that level of support to break down the barriers, and the habits in the routines that get in the way." Thus, to EL Education, capacity building is about building trust and relationships so that it can tackle the areas where teachers may feel most vulnerable in terms of sharing and changing classroom practice: they believe "the building of human connection between individuals . . . drives change in practice."

Conrad noted that job-embedded coaching "just absolutely" has to be present at a high level. This coaching can happen within a school, ideally over time, but it has to be "consistent enough, and implemented in a way that is strategic, and thoughtful, and really pushes change in practice." EL Education sees coaches as critical friends and thought partners pushing practice, looking at evidence of student learning together, and having tough conversations about identifying students for whom it is not seeing shifts and improved instruction. In all four of the schools I visited, both teachers and students were seemingly unfazed by having visitors come in and out of their classroom. They were used to them, and seemed to understand the value of sharing practice. They trusted that classroom observations were not "gotcha" moments, but part of the learning process for both students and teachers.

In addition, EL Education's theory of change and assumptions about learning for both students and teachers is that people are growing, not performing. Teaching and learning are both activities that are about making mistakes and getting better. Bernstein, the novice teacher at CBHS, noted that "the idea of the growth mind-set is really prevalent here." He further explained:

> I'm not afraid to go to a teacher and [say], "I really didn't do well in that class. Where did I go wrong?" I don't need to hide that I didn't do well and I can focus instead on improv[ing . . . This] has been great for me as an intern and as a young teacher because I feel like unfortunately I've made a lot of mistakes. [But] I'm not willing to say oh, "It's no problem". . . I always want to get better . . . and it's been nice to be in a place where the focus is, "Hey, that wasn't the best way you could have done that. Here's how to do it," instead of, "Now

you're on probation" or "We're watching you." That's been really helpful, I think. It's allowed me to focus on my growth and development as a teacher rather than focus on "they'll hang me."

Sydney Chaffee, a teacher at Codman Academy who was the 2017 National Teacher of the Year, echoed these sentiments, observing that such a culture creates a better experience for both teachers and students:

> I think it's really important that the adults collaborate with one another, both in terms of talking about kids, because then you can better support kids. But also just in terms of is there a culture where it's okay to reach out to your colleagues and say I need help with this. I think that's really important. And that filters down to the kids, because that makes better teachers and less frustrated teachers.

EL Education staff members say that they emphasize creating this kind of culture in schools because they believe deeply in challenging students with complex problems. Complex work, like teaching, requires continual trial and error, reflecting, iterating, and improving practice. Berger noted, "We have always said kids should be taking on high-level work right away, and they should be struggling together with it. We've just said that's our core."

According to Codman Academy teacher Ed Yoo, building trust with students is critical to their work as teachers: "It's the close relationship that you have with your students, [that makes] a lot of things possible. I think even with the best training and best strategies, if the student doesn't trust you, then nothing can happen. So I do think it's just building the trust and the foundation and then all the little conversations that you have over time allows you to then have . . . —when it does happen—the more difficult conversations."

For Bernstein, his school is "just a really supportive environment for both students and teachers. I really appreciate that it feels like a family, like we're all invested in each other's success. And the students are invested in the teachers doing well and the teachers are invested in the students doing well, and the students are invested in each other. And it feels very supportive in that way."

EL Education's belief that culture is critical to its mission is so strong that when it agrees to work with a school, it runs a two-week summer institute to "reimagine who [the staff] are as teachers." It makes public the answers to such questions as how staff members decided to teach in the first place to how they are going to rebuild their professional culture. Berger notes that these institutes are often "very emotional" experiences in schools where the teachers had often "siloed themselves off into their classrooms and they haven't confronted the fact that they don't all trust each other, all respect each other [and/or] treat each other well." They will bring up "issues of race and class and gender and the kinds of prejudice."

When asked why EL Education devotes such time and attention to these matters, Berger says that they "feel like the student culture can't be ahead of the faculty culture. The students are not going to become respectful, outgoing, courageous people if the faculty members are not respectful, outgoing, courageous people. We have to bring the faculty culture forward if we expect the student culture to follow." Because its aim is to create a particular kind of school culture, rather than a classroom culture, EL Education is mindful to include everyone in the school in the staff development sessions, including "the cook, the custodians . . . so that everybody in the school feels honored in a different way and responsible in a different way. Because the crew leaders may be classroom teachers, but they might be a nurse, they might be a counselor, they might be the principal. We feel like everyone in the school should feel like every kid's behavior is their own—it's like changing the dynamic of what the school feels like."

Indeed, EL Education as a whole tries to walk the talk in how it tracks the changing needs of its partner schools and how they learn. It is in close, long-term partnerships with its schools, and its staff members are regularly in schools. It surveys teachers and students in its schools about their experiences in learning and teaching. It has an implementation review process that explicitly outlines a number of criteria, or in EL Education parlance, "Power Practices," for schools to assess five key areas: (1) curriculum (mapping skills and content, case studies, projects and products, learning expeditions); (2) instruction (effective lessons, supporting all students, reflecting and structuring revision, culture of reading, culture of writing, culture of mathematics, integrating the arts); (3) assessment (learning targets, assessment for learning; quality assessments, communicating student achievement, analyzing assessment data); (4) culture and character (community of learning, crew, fostering character, engaging families, beautiful spaces); (5) leadership (school vision, using data, supporting, planning, assessment, and instruction, positive school culture, professional learning).

EL Education has a humble attitude about working and learning from others, including those outside its network. Its employees speak honestly with each other—Scott Hartl (president and CEO), Ron Berger (chief academic officer), and Mark Conrad (chief schools officer) have been working with EL Education and with each other for decades. When they had an interim executive director who they felt was taking the organization in the wrong direction, the staff made the decision to go directly to the board to express their thoughts. As they believe students cannot learn what teachers do not practice, EL Education staff explicitly attempt to practice the qualities they encourage in their schools.

Former deputy minister for education for Ontario, Canada, and professor at the University of Toronto, Ben Levin writes about capacity building: it "requires a thoughtful, sustained approach that will create and support the changes in behavior or practice that we want to see. Because schools are social settings, change is not just a matter of giving people new ideas but of creating the social conditions that foster and support changed practices."[26]

Capacity building means assessing and taking into consideration critical baseline capacity measures and identifying key criteria necessary to set up for success. So central is EL Education's belief in the importance of nurturing a particular kind of culture that it does not take on every school that applies to be part of its network. EL Education turns down 90 percent of the schools that come to it. Its selection process is grounded in its learning from practice. It is based on its experience working with dozens of schools under various conditions, and realizing that simple baselines conditions need to be met in order for EL Education to feel as though it would make a difference in the school.

EL Education looks for the following conditions during a yearlong "courtship," to see if the school can be a good partner:

- Eighty percent faculty buy-in to the process of engaging with EL Education and the kind of broad vision that EL Education espouses
- School leader that faculty believe in
- Autonomy in administration for the school, or at least the permission from the district to make changes in the curriculum and the professional development offering at the school
- Expression of intent to work with EL Education for four to five years, even if the contracts can only be one-year contracts

EL Education believes that in order to engage in whole-school change, it needs staff people who are motivated to work with it, and that in engaging with multiple facets of a school, it needs multiple years in which to build relationships and engage in developing the leadership and the faculty. As Berger notes, "We can't be a 'force fit' program. If every teacher is going to be a crew leader, for example, then every teacher is a teacher of social and emotional learning skills, interpersonal and intrapersonal skills, every day." Teachers need to accept that as part of the job and not be tied solely to their identity as subject-matter teachers. Expectations for teachers and staff are as clear as they are for students entering an EL Education school. Berger emphasizes, "We need a school where people say, I want to be a teacher of students, not a teacher of math, even though I happen to teach math." While EL Education has helped to found brand-new schools where it asks for the ability to co-hire the principal and the teachers with the district, the majority in its whole-school network are existing schools.

Indeed, EL Education's theory of action hinges on having articulated the kind of expanded vision of student achievement that it expresses in its core design principles document, and then working to actualize and further express the kind of adult, student, and organizational behavior and practice that enable achievement of these end goals. Conrad noted:

> We work backwards from [the] student—from goals around student achievement, and we think about what are the shifts in student achievement and student learning that we want to see? But then we build a theory of action that says, well, what are adults going to need to do differently in order to implement, or to achieve this student achievement goal?
>
> And so we build that theory of action through learning targets for staff, and through thinking about leadership supports, and supports from EL Education staff, and what's the evidence that we're going to be collecting? So, we create this work plan each year, and those work plans build on the needs and assets of the school going into that year. We build in cycles of looking at student work, of collecting evidence around student character, of assessing more traditional modes of assessment to make decisions as a leadership team about where are we going to get the most high-leverage impact in a given partnership year?

EL Education also "build[s] primarily on the assets in any given school site." It thinks about how it can take what is working well and build on that success, as opposed to a deficit-focused model where it is hunting for the problems and then trying to solve them.

Its organizational structure reflects the value of helping schools develop holistically and authentically. EL Education national staff are organized in geographical clusters, because its theory of change includes coaching, building relationships, and learning from others as effective capacity-building practice; it feels it should be in close proximity, to facilitate access to school coaches, regional mentor schools, and other resources.

How it recruits staff and hires people also reflects the emphasis on looking for a particular level of baseline capacity and beliefs. The core staff attracts people who believe that education should be about transforming society and creating people who care about others. In addition, because practice is crucial at EL Education, the staff, especially school coaches, comprise former teachers and principals.

Indeed, EL Education has structured itself as an explicitly capacity-building organization, publishing curricula and videos on its website in addition to providing in-person professional and whole-school development. Its list of resources is quite long; it is agnostic in borrowing, but it takes theory and research and emphasizes the implications for practice. Conrad noted:

> Over time our goal is to put ourselves out of work in every school where we're partnering. We want the [schools] to develop the capacity to understand this work deeply, to lead this work, to be creating sustainable structures within the school, where they don't have to rely on us in the same way that they do early on. They may still have, obviously, the affiliation with Expeditionary Learning; they obviously in most cases would still have some form of partnership with us, but it's not that intensive transformation focus, as in the early phases.

SCALING EL EDUCATION'S IMPACT

EL Education knows that scaling such an intensive work plan for changing a school culture and professional practices requires high intensity and resources that it alone cannot provide. But in providing curricular resources, making public its design principles and practices, it provides a clue as to how it wants to make an impact in the field of education.

Berger noted,

We decided scaling should be a different paradigm for us. If we're going to scale our impact, it shouldn't be through adding schools and desperately trying to make them great. It should be taking the greatest features of those schools and seeding them nationally, knowing that we don't have control of how well they're implemented, but hoping that good things will go viral and that will be a useful thing for the country. And that's maybe our best value proposition for scaling is to scale our best thinking and best resources versus scale by making more schools.

What EL Education wants to scale is the vision of why and how it thinks its schools are working, which is "the culture, how [it] build[s] the culture in those schools, how [it] do[es] classroom instruction." Berger says that while the curriculum is important, he and his staff put their focus on something else.

Berger noted that rather than scaling physical schools, EL Education wanted to scale vision and ideas. For example, he noted that core to EL Education is a vision of schools in which "character and scholarship are never separated." In this strategy for scale, they write documents and books and make videos about what it looks like to fuse character and scholarship in teaching and learning and how to do it. Similarly, EL Education shares the video, "Austin's Butterfly," as a vision and strategy for how young people can learn by making multiple drafts and giving and receiving true critique. Berger notes that if this approach "spreads around the country, that will be a big contribution for us . . . It's the ideas and structures we want to have scale, rather than building more schools."

Berger notes one particular metaphor he uses when talking to people about scaling:

One way to scale is the way Starbucks has scaled; —you try to get a Starbucks on every street corner. But we don't want an EL Education school on every corner; that's not what we're trying to do.

Another way of scaling is . . . when I was young, there was no ethnic food anywhere except in tiny enclaves in cities, which meant that in my town there was no sushi, there were no bagels, there were no burritos, not in the whole town. And now you go into any supermarket and there's sushi and there's burritos and there's bagels, because those foods have scaled on their own because they're a good idea, like they've just gone viral. And no one is taking credit and making profit from that scaling because the fact that everyone eats burritos and sushi now is just what it is.

[So] we're hoping that our ideas can be like sushi and be like burritos, just like whether or not people attribute it to us, it doesn't matter. Our mission is to scale those ideas, not to own more schools.

CHALLENGES FOR EL EDUCATION

As part of an organization that values and practices reflection, EL Education staff were humble in naming the various challenges they faced. Conrad reflected that, at the school level, they face "competing priorities, ineffective leadership, insufficient resources, teacher turnover, leadership change at the district level, which brings in other initiatives." Because these structural challenges are not EL Education generated, they are mostly uncontrollable and yet are "predictable . . . factors that interfere with the ability to help schools." Indeed, the flip side of the fact that EL Education is able to operate in a variety of district, charter, urban, rural, and suburban schools is that it does not "control any of the hardware of the school" but is, in fact, "the operating system for the school."[27]

Its second big challenge is how to create consistency of outcomes across a portfolio of over 150 schools. According to Berger, narrow definitions of achievement with narrow targets are easier to achieve than its "expanded definition . . . and [a] sophisticated vision of pedagogy that we believe gets to that higher, more relevant vision for achievement." Berger notes that because the tools, strategies, and structures needed to achieve the vision are varied and because "scale and quality are typically the enemies of each other," its biggest future challenge is to figure out how to effectively and strategically scale its vision for teaching, learning, and design.

THE VALUE PROPOSITION FOR EL EDUCATION

Given all these challenges and the complexity of the EL Education model, why does it persist? Berger described how EL Education is different from other models of school reform. While they share similar outcomes such as high academic achievement, EL Education has a fundamentally different approach:

Our mission is to take [young people from challenging settings] and equip them to make a better society. So [while other school networks are] building kids that will fit in[to existing society], [w]e want to build change agents. And that's different. Like we want rabble rousers. We want kids who stand up for what's right. We want kids who will challenge the universities they go to . . . to be more inquiry based and to be better. We don't want kids that will just get good jobs and make money. We want to build kids that are committed to making a better world, not just fit into the existing world. And it seems like a small difference but it is partly why we're a little more threatening than some of the other organizations and partly why we get a tenth of the funding that most of those groups do, is that what they're doing is replicating society but giving more low-income kids access to it. And we want them to make a more just society. We want them to be the kind of kids who fight for justice everywhere they go. It's a little different value proposition.

LESSONS FOR PRACTITIONERS, RESEARCHERS, POLICY MAKERS, FUNDERS

School Culture Matters

School culture is a capacity to intentionally build when considering teaching and learning for the twenty-first century. Perhaps adding a strong social-emotional or inter/intrapersonal component to schools means that a focus on creating a particular kind of school culture is a foundational aspect of learning. If some of the emerging challenges of the twenty-first century persist—assuming that the current trend of a shrinking planet is true and growing inequality continues to be a challenge, for example—then the competencies to share well, to consider others' welfare along with one's own, to get along with others, to work collaboratively, to hold multiple points of view, to understand and negotiate differences, and, as EL Education says, "to get not just myself to the top, but to bring everyone else along as well," might have to reside at the group, organizational, and systemic levels as well.

For example, EL Education cites Bryk's work on trust, and trust came up repeatedly in interviews with teachers, along with comments about how the school culture encourages them to stay, even as the hard work required to sustain the EL Education model may lead to high staff turnover. The complex, challenging work of teaching in the twenty-first century requires a collaborative team effort by students and staff as a way to both model but also address some of the more engaging, relevant, curricular and pedagogical challenges.

What is happening in the classroom matters, but from these interviews, what is happening among the school, staff, and student body at large also matters as well. All four EL Education schools I visited have learning expeditions that involve travel. The entire student body goes off campus at the beginning of the year to build community. Through whole-school assemblies and "crew" (EL Education's name for advisory groups), the school cultivates a particular kinds of relationships and values. The teachers talk as much about the "Habits of Work and Learning" as the academic content. The social-emotional aspects of learning and teaching that enable, facilitate, and make possible high-quality, challenging, and engaging work are deeply intertwined with academic rigor. The students at CBHS cited not just classroom experiences but their experiences in the school as a whole, including ones formed outside the classroom in enrichment activities with peers.

School Resources Matter

Does adding a strong social-emotional and civic component to schools require additional money or, at least, money spent differently than in traditional schooling that confines itself to the school building? EL Education schools have a strong experiential and community-building component in which they take the whole school to a multiday, off-campus experience. One of the themes is intentionally building a strong, caring, cohesive school culture. The four schools I visited had devoted intentional time and effort into raising money to support such ventures.

If not adding more money, then schools may have to think deliberately about reorganizing existing resources. For example, in setting up advisories for students, where there is a smaller staff-to-student ratio than in classrooms, schools may deploy all available staff, including librarians, to lead a group of students. Certainly, further research about how existing schools manage to redeploy existing resources and find ways to add more would be helpful.

School Structure and Organization Matters

Do twenty-first-century schools need a fundamentally different structure? The EL Education schools I visited designed the weekly schedules to support collaboration and the development of intra/interpersonal competencies. For example, at Codman Academy, the whole school takes an hour each week to assemble and celebrate; everyone at school has daily crew meetings where students talk about their lives, goals, struggles, and receive some kind of mentoring as well as community building. Do *all* schools need to think carefully about how their structure aligns with their goals and values? Currently, at least in the United States, there are either traditional schools or people discarding those altogether to establish highly individualized learning. Is it possible to do both? Can we find a hybrid middle-ground?

Fidelity to Implementation Matters

With twenty-first-century schooling and the multiple associated outcomes, goals, and purposes constituting so many important pieces of a student's experience and of an effective school, fidelity to implementation is challenging. The critic of EL Education I interviewed emphatically said that she was *not* critical of the EL Education model, but of how challenging and uneven the implementation process is or might be. Almost all EL Education interviews stressed the challenge of implementation, and the ways EL Education is trying to help schools implement the model well.

EL Education appears to be aware of this challenge, having recently developed an implementation rubric with data points. Its awareness has led to more explicit articulation of everything, starting with curriculum and pedagogy, for example. The critic interviewed felt that EL Education needed to work significantly on this aspect and thought that EL Education had taken on too much with its whole-school model. Yet the alternative—a focus just on academics—is unduly narrow for the twenty-first century, as we argued in the first book. Twenty-first-century learning organizations will have to find a way to quickly address this concern.

The Important Role of Policy

Federal policy helped to give birth to EL Education when it encouraged comprehensive school reform, but almost ended its existence when policy came to focus solely on test scores as a measure of a school's success. But a shift in policy also gave EL Education new life.

While EL Education first has its roots as Kurt Hahn's Outward Bound program that emphasized the wilderness and the cultivation of character, it arose as a specifically school-based program when it wrote a grant in response to a request for proposals (RFP) issued from New American Schools, a federally started program under President George H. W. Bush in 1991. It was a policy decision to encourage the development of designs for the "break-the-mold" schools to increase student achievement.[28] Eight hundred organizations around the country responded to that RFP. It offered a million dollars immediately to schools to flesh out the model if they liked what they saw in response to the first RFP, and then another $3 million for the next three years if they approved after the first year. EL Education was one of eight organizations that received the grant.

As a result, EL Education grew from ten schools in year two to forty schools by year six. Then it grew quickly around 1999 as a result of another policy when Congress passed comprehensive school reform legislation, the Obey-Porter Act. The act gave schools that were failing a lot of money to align themselves for three years with an existing model approved by the federal government to transform low performance to a high performance.[29] EL Education took on many turnarounds, about fifty of the worst-performing schools. "Big mistake for us," Berger noted. There was only one metric for its success that was dictated by policy, which was whether the students' test scores were going up in math and English language arts (ELA). While EL Education schools might have become much more humane places where students were happier, the test scores did not turn around quickly.

"At that point," Berger said, EL Education realized that because of policy changes "[t]he whole world is turning to test scores. That's all that matters. We've been not focusing on it at all." EL Education then consciously decided it needed to focus on basic literacy and numeracy skills in addition to its social-emotional and character work and its inquiry and high-quality project work. By the early 2000s, as a response to policy incentives, it started running workshops specifically about increasing skills in numeracy and literacy. In the mid-2000s, most of the other grantees from the original RFPs started disappearing because they were not raising test scores quickly enough. EL Education leadership wondered if their test scores were "even good enough to keep [them] afloat." Fortunately, EL Education's data were good. It actually gained credibility in the mid-2000s because its test scores looked "really good. Otherwise, I think we would have gone out of business, to be honest," Berger noted.

The policy push to look at test score data made EL Education realize that there was a strong correlation between how long a school had been with the network and how well it was doing in terms of academic results; the schools that were implementing its program most deeply had the highest test scores. Berger noted that outside observers who came in to give advice to EL Education remarked, "The schools that take you seriously do really well." EL Education found that there was a direct correlation between how well a school cultivated the interpersonal and intrapersonal competencies and how well the students did on cognitive measures.

EL Education's reputation for most of its twenty-two years, its staff members explained, was that it was "really good at building character, really good at building good citizens, good human beings" but "[it was] never seen as leaders in the cognitive area." But when the Common Core came out, rather than oppose it, EL Education decided to become experts in it. It had a relationship with one of the heads leading the ELA Common Core effort and also with Jason Zimba, the premier author of the math Common Core. So EL Education started working with them as soon as the Common Core was written. It became experts in the Common Core, and when EL Education teachers created a curriculum for New York State that won them the grant, it resulted in half of the students in New York State using the curriculum. The curriculum, which is open source, has been downloaded 8 million times as of 2017. EL Education is now considered a leader in instructional practice.

This focus on instructional practice also created new professional development and learning opportunities for teachers. Sydney Chaffee, who had interned at other schools before her time at Codman Academy, noted that while she had learned about the importance of building community and culture in other school networks, EL Education was where she "learned . . . how to teach . . . how to take these cool ideas that we have and how to take these fun games that we want to play with kids and actually translate that into kids learning something." She noted, "I've learned how to design lessons that work."

Berger observed that EL Education has "a whole different credibility" as a result of responding well to policy incentives created by the Common Core. He noted, "As many or more people know us as Common Core experts, as character experts. It's kind of a weird shift [in that] that our background is more building character, citizenship, inner-personal/interpersonal skills. That's how people knew us more. We're the Outward Bound group. Now when I walk into people—situations, people say, 'Oh, you're the Common Core experts.'"

Berger reflected that while the decision to become experts in the Common Core was controversial within the organization, EL Education played a critical role in Washington, DC, during Common Core meetings to "be the voice" that said, "If the Common Core stays as narrow as the way you guys are describing it, it can't endure. Everyone's going to fight it. The Common Core has to embrace arts, it has to embrace character, it has to embrace noncognitive skills, or you're in trouble." Berger reflected, "We actually have more of a voice by having become experts in it than had we not." Berger said that "the curriculum bakes in social and emotional skills right into the curriculum itself. It requires a form of teaching where the teacher isn't talking mode, and where the kids are meeting in small groups and talking and critiquing and working together."

Thus, for the first twenty-two years, EL worked exclusively with schools. Recently, it has begun to implement a credentialing process for schools with three tiers (partner schools, credentialed schools, and mentor schools, the highest tier) to encourage schools to implement the model more deeply and to provide benchmarks for this process. But now, according to Berger, only "half of our work is the schools within our network. The other half of our work is mining the schools within our network to produce open-source materials for everyone else in the country." The new scope of work for EL Education is, according to Berger, taking what it has learned from those sixty schools to create open-source resources with the goal of creating change nationally based on what it has learned in those schools. It has recently doubled staff size to accommodate this second area of work.

The lesson for policy makers here is that what gets prioritized in policy gets put into practice in schools and organizations. The lesson for funders might be that resources and networks directed to help spread an organization's good practice is critical to its survival and relevance. The lesson for practitioners might be that continual reflection and evolution to adapt to changing contexts is vital to an organization's relevance, survival, and flourishing, even as it stays true to its core values, mission, and purpose.

CHAPTER EIGHT

Working in Times of Uncertainty to Prepare for the Future

A Study of Singapore's Leaders in Education Program

Oon-Seng Tan and Ee-Ling Low
National Institute of Education,
Nanyang Technological University, Singapore

In Singapore, three major stakeholders work in tandem to select and prepare potential candidates to become school principals at the primary, secondary, and junior college levels. These include the Ministry of Education (MOE), the National Institute of Education (NIE), which is an autonomous institute of the Nanyang Technological University (NTU), and Singapore schools. An executive program, the Leaders in Education Program (LEP), is a six-month program designed to help potential principals develop the skills to deal with the complex and uncertain twenty-first century, and to equip them with much-needed knowledge, skills, and competencies. It also provides invaluable experience through an authentic project in an attached school that enables them to lead schools so that the teachers may empower students with the competencies needed to thrive in the future. This chapter focuses primarily on the LEP, which is a significant developmental period of a larger career development continuum for participants. This continuum involves the larger process of identifying and developing participants for leadership roles. Singapore believes that these future leaders must be adaptable and flexible while being able to implement national policies in each particular school context and attend to the needs of the school, amid the torrent of other demands. Singapore has put in place various supporting structures to help develop prin-

222 PREPARING TEACHERS TO EDUCATE WHOLE STUDENTS

cipals to meet these uncertainties. The program creates a powerful network where each principal is supported by peers. From the research we conducted on a cohort of LEP participants, four realized outcomes show how the LEP helps potential principals meet the challenges of the uncertain future. The research revealed that the LEP helps future leaders by being a platform to: (1) create a strong fraternity of colleagues, (2) thrive in complex situations, (3) be prepared for change, and (4) be able to effectively work in Singapore's cultural uniqueness. Our findings show how LEP develops people, rather than roles. These people are in a position to lead schools and teachers to meet the future and contribute to the building of the education landscape of Singapore teachers, students, and community. Here, we describe in depth the LEP's effectiveness as a contextualized principalship program and show evidence collected during interviews we conducted with participants.

We also showcase that LEP's uniqueness results in certain outcomes in prospective leaders (1) through a "learning ecosystem" approach that utilizes multiple forms of learning to develop in participants a range of competencies; (2) by placing learning in its context as participants carry out a project in an actual school environment; and (3) by letting participants take charge and direct their own learning through the provision of time and space for reflection.

RESEARCH METHODOLOGY

Why LEP?

Because school leadership and principalship, in particular, are important aspects of a school's development that affect student learning, we selected LEP as the subject of our research study. LEP is the sole milestone leadership program in Singapore that prepares school leaders for principalship.

As the demands on educators become more complex, principals should receive the knowledge and skill base to explore possibilities and to face the challenges of leading schools, allowing them to educate students and equip them with twenty-first-century competencies for a globalized world. LEP presents a viable model of a program that engages principals in collective deep learning to prepare for the uncertainties of the future.

Studying LEP

Our research project studied LEP using qualitative methods. We used a common semistructured interview protocol co-developed and shared with other GEII colleagues and conducted observations of case study sites. We collected and analyzed a variety of documents throughout the project, including curriculum frameworks and existing evaluations and program documentation, including the LEP program handbook and newspaper articles.

We invited the respondents (LEP participants) to participate in the interviews. We selected them from the 2013 batch of LEP participants (this was the most recent batch at the time of researching and writing), as the LEP happens only once a year and the research sought to analyze the difference in participants before and after (i.e., one year) the program. We also interviewed school teachers who had been working with these new principals for a year to ascertain their effectiveness. In all cases, after participants had read and signed the participant consent forms, we conducted and recorded face-to-face interviews. Thereafter, the interviews were coded using the coding scheme developed by the GEII Research Consortium and analyzed.

Sample Size

Participants

There were twenty-two interviewees involved in the study: fifteen LEP participants, three teachers from the respective schools of LEP participants, two LEP facilitators, the LEP associate dean, and the MOE adviser of the LEP. This wide range of participants allowed for better synthesis and triangulation of views. Being qualitative in nature, the project's sample size sought to include sufficient participants to understand, explain, or describe principal preparation in depth, and to cover the complexity of principal preparation in Singapore.

The data analysis of the project was an iterative and reflexive process. Content analysis techniques were employed to examine the interview transcripts.

Coding scheme

The coding scheme, developed collaboratively by the GEII Research Consortium, went through several iterations with some codes added and removed based on input from partner researchers. The Singapore research team carried out content analysis and used the coding scheme designed by the GEII team. Data that could not be coded were identified and analyzed later to determine if they represented a new category or a subcategory of an existing code. The findings from a directed content analysis offer supporting and nonsupporting evidence for Singapore's study on LEP. This evidence can be presented by showing codes with exemplars and by offering descriptive evidence. The coding and analysis from the interviews, together with other information sources such as the program handbook, framework, and journal papers, guided the discussion of findings.

CONTEXT OF SINGAPORE PRINCIPALS IN THE TWENTY-FIRST CENTURY

Educational Context of Singapore

About 464,000 students attend 369 primary schools, secondary schools, and junior colleges in Singapore, and are taught by about 33,000 teachers.[1] The majority of teachers are female (about 71 percent), as are the majority of principals and vice principals. In 2004, about 96.5 percent of students who were enrolled in the Primary 1 cohort progressed to postsecondary education in 2014.[2] The literacy rate among Singapore residents was 96.8 percent in 2015, and the average years of schooling was 10.7.[3] In the international assessments of student knowledge and skills, Singaporean students score, on average, at the top of the world distribution of participating countries in reading, mathematics, and science.[4]

Of all the schools in Singapore, 277 are government schools, 76 are government-aided, 8 are independent, 4 are specialized independent, and 4 are specialized schools. MOE plays a direct administrative role in the government and government-aided schools, while it plays a strong supervisory role for the other schools. Therefore, government-aided schools are still regarded as public schools and receive about 95 percent of their funding from the government. In these schools, the principal, vice principals, and teachers are all MOE staff members. Independent and specialized schools are able to employ their own teachers who may not necessarily be MOE staff.

The strength of the Singapore education system lies in its systemic coherence and goal alignment across different institutions, educational process, and education stakeholders. MOE sets the overall direction and ensures consistent alignment of policies and practices between the initiatives that it develops, while NIE ensures alignment in its preparation of teachers and schools, and in turn, ensure alignment in the implementation of policies. This collective collaboration establishes a long-term and sustained cooperation and aims to provide the necessary collaborative framework of shared values and goals for a coherent system that produces consistent and unified outcomes.[5] This collaboration also produces an alignment between the curriculum, teacher preparation and support, management of teachers' careers, and evaluation and supervision functions. There is considerable consistency and alignment in the norms, expectations, and practices of various actors in the education system: ministry officials, teacher educators, school leaders, and teachers.

Twenty-First Century in Singapore

It was clear by the start of the twenty-first century that holistic education was essential for participation in the workplace and society; this was in response to the changing demands of an increasingly global economy. In particular, for a multiracial, multicultural society like Singapore, the inculcation of shared values and the focus on academic skills allow its citizens to appreciate the rich diversity of the nation, while maintaining cohesion and harmony. The government's vision for education in the twenty-first century is "Thinking Schools, Learning Nation"; it aims to improve the education system to prepare the young for future challenges.

In line with these aims, the 21st Century Competencies (21CC) framework was developed as a reference document with the goal of producing students who are confident persons, self-directed learners, concerned citizens, and active contributors—competencies deemed critical for the future.[6] Values are at the core of the framework, as they shape the character, beliefs, and attitudes of individuals and provide the foundation for the remaining competencies. Social and emotional competencies, such as self-management and social awareness, have been included in the framework as well. The specific competencies that are considered necessary for the twenty-first century and articulated in the framework are civic literacy; global awareness; cross-cultural skills; critical and inventive thinking; and communication, collaboration, and information skills.[7] The framework is in place so that schools will strike a better balance between the teaching of content knowledge and the acquisition of the necessary competencies and values for effective functioning in a future environment. From this framework, MOE hopes to nurture in students the desired outcomes of education (DOEs), which include the values, skills, and attitudes that students should attain upon completion of specific milestones in their education journey. The MOE considers that a student needs to achieve the following DOEs to survive in the working world:[8]

- a *confident person* who has a strong sense of right and wrong, is adaptable and resilient, knows himself, is discerning in judgment, thinks independently and critically, and communicates effectively
- a *self-directed learner* who takes responsibility for his own learning, who questions, reflects and perseveres in the pursuit of learning
- an *active contributor* who is able to work effectively in teams, exercises initiative, takes calculated risks, is innovative, and strives for excellence
- a *concerned citizen* who is rooted to Singapore, has a strong civic consciousness, is informed, and takes an active role in bettering the lives of others around him

Role of the Principal in Singapore Schools

The mission of education in Singapore is simple: to develop citizens who are able survive in the future and will be significant contributors to the nation. This clear and ambitious purpose places a weighty responsibility on schools. The work of school principals is complex; they must be able to lead a school toward that mission. They must have also the conviction to shoulder and sustain that responsibility.

New principals are appointed in a formal ceremony with all fellow principals in attendance. In his speech at the 2014 Appointment and Appreciation Ceremony for Principals, then-minister for education Heng Swee Keat highlighted five roles of principals that they are expected to fulfill: leading learning, leading culture, leading change, leading people, and leading nationally.[9] To lead learning is to be responsible for the holistic development of each child, including cognitive and character development. To lead culture is to inspire colleagues in their schools to greater heights. To lead change is to translate policy into results and to be able to communicate effectively the need for change to all key stakeholders. To lead people is to develop teachers.

And to lead nationally is to work together with other principals to co-build the national school system (e.g., through the sharing of ideas and resources) and to instill in every child the skills and character to succeed in the global economy.

At the 2015 ceremony, Ng Chee Meng, then education minister, gave the new principals a reminder of their heavy responsibility: "Through your hands passes the future of the nation."[10] He reminded them of the important role that principals play in shaping the next generation and how their work affects not only individual students, but also their families, the community, and the entire nation.

Twenty-First-Century Skills and Competencies for Principals

Singapore's national vision for the role of a principal highlights five necessary key aspects for a school leader that align with experts' perspective in the international education leadership literature:[11]

1. Mission- and vision-oriented. Principals should be able to formulate, communicate, and disseminate a clear mission and vision in order to bring about the desired learning outcomes for all students. Principals should be clear in the purpose of education for the present and for the future, and be clear about their own personal purpose for being in education. Setting a clear direction helps the school develop a shared understanding of the task at hand. This also allows teachers, and perhaps students and all stakeholders, to be motivated in reaching the milestones or goals set.
2. Strategic leadership. Principals should be able to manipulate different types of strategies (e.g., transformational, distributed, inspiring, ethical and inquiry-based leadership) in order to develop the school.
3. Contextual awareness. Principals should be able to fully acknowledge the school's context as they make informed decisions, provide for the consequences of decisions, and actualize them in well-thought-out plans to improve student learning.
4. Organization awareness. Principals should be able to steer the school's structure and culture, pedagogical climate, personnel, and the facilities to meet the mission and vision of a school. The importance of the quality of personnel has become increasingly significant. Schools have one driving force: their teachers. Developing teachers as education professionals is

as important as building a good professional relationship with them, and communication is pivotal in the twenty-first century to enable this.

5. Higher-order thinking. Principals should be able to harmonize the different factors of the school's mission and vision (including their own beliefs, experiences, and personality characteristics and desired student outcomes), the school's community, the institutional context, and organizational and cultural characteristics. Principals should possess good judgment and be able to make sound decisions.

These broad categories show the competencies and skills principals need to lead schools effectively.

Meeting School Needs of the Twenty-First Century through School Leadership

Leading learning and leading people

Many studies have shown that school leadership, especially that of principals, affects student learning, albeit in indirect ways.[12] They suggest that "successful leadership can play a highly—and frequently—significant role in improving student learning."[13] In their research, Kenneth Leithwood, Alma Harris, and David Hopkins reached seven important conclusions about leadership:[14]

- School leadership is second only to classroom teaching as an influence on pupil learning.
- Almost all successful leaders draw on the same repertoire of basic leadership practices.
- The ways in which leaders apply these basic leadership practices—not the practices themselves—demonstrate responsiveness to, rather than dictation by, the contexts in which they work.
- School leaders improve teaching and learning indirectly and most powerfully through their influence on staff motivation, commitment, and working conditions.
- School leadership has a greater influence on schools and students when it is widely distributed.
- Some patterns of distribution are more effective than others.
- A small handful of personal traits explain a high proportion of the variation in leadership effectiveness.

Leading culture and leading change

As school leaders, principals are integral to implementing change for improvement. One area that principals should engage in is facilitation. Sharing or distributing leadership with other school leaders (vice principals, heads of department, teacher leaders, etc.) is an important facet of effective leadership. Not only does it allow principals to focus on what is truly required of them, but it also develops other school leaders and equips them with the proper experience for future responsibilities. This allows for the empowerment of other leaders in the school and a tighter working team.[15]

The school culture must also change for the distribution of leadership to work. The principal is able to create this environment and allow for this mind-set shift since he or she has great impact on the direction of the school, the quality of the school organization, and the quality of the school culture.[16] Creating a school culture is the direct responsibility of principals and has an impact on other school leaders' and teachers' perceptions of the school and their behaviors within the school. Singapore recognizes that schools are complex organizations. Therefore, principals empower teachers to take the lead in various aspects of a school's work. Distributing leadership is a good way to develop leadership skills in teachers.

Principals in Singapore support teachers' continuous learning and development. These are important attributes in which twenty-first-century educators need to remain relevant with the changing landscape. Principals should participate in the learning as a leader and/or a learner themselves.[17] The principal can exactly model the proper way of learning to teachers, and this modeling signals the importance of continuous development. Leithwood et al. also found in their study that "while school leaders made modest direct contributions to staff capacities, they had quite strong and positive influences on staff members' motivations, commitments and beliefs concerning the supportiveness of their working conditions."[18]

Leading the nation, for now and the future

Yin Cheong Cheng pushed for the need to consider the kind of "'future leadership' that aims at leading and ensuring the direction and practice of school education effective and relevant to the future of new generations in an era of globalization, transformation and intelligence-based economy."[19] Cheng sees education leadership as not only affecting a school as an individual entity in society, but being a part of a bigger body. Cheng further stated that "principals need to expand their dimensions of leadership from the structural and social leadership to the political and cultural leadership to deal with the complexity and uncertainties during the process of localization in education."[20] As schools cultivate the next generation of citizens, who are not only national citizens but also global citizens, principals need to be aware of the significance of the school's work and the important implications of what schools do for the future of the nation and the world.

Principals must bear in mind what the present economic and social landscape of the world is and what it is becoming. Having this forward-looking attitude is important for the school that each principal leads and for the overall national education system. The importance of developing effective school leaders for the future, not just for the present, seems to be where academics and policy makers are leaning. But using traditional or even current approaches are insufficient.[21] To prepare principals for the future, innovative approaches must be used to expand the roles, responsibilities, and accountability of principals.[22] Principals play a key role in "integrating external and internal accountability systems by supporting their teaching staff in aligning instruction with agreed learning goals and performance standards."[23] The Organisation for Economic Co-operation and Development stated that principals must use core technologies to achieve their intended goals for the school and students. The principals must realize they work in student-centered schools and must see their work from a systemwide perspective where the pedagogy and curriculum employed by the school must align to national needs and individual requirements.

Career Path: From Teacher to Principal

Principals in Singapore generally begin their careers as teachers. The MOE provides a wide range of professional development opportunities to teachers, which includes differentiated career tracks for career progression aligned to the strengths and interests of each. These differentiated tracks develop teachers to their fullest for the benefit of the school and education system. The multiple pathways also help to create a meaningful lifelong vocation as teachers are provided with different avenues to develop skills, deepen knowledge,

FIGURE 8.1   Career tracks for teachers

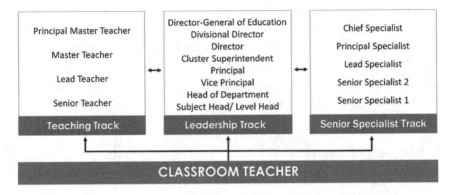

Source: "Career Information," Ministry of Education (MOE), https://www.moe.gov.sg/careers/teach/career-information. Used with permission.

and progress in their careers. The three career pathways are the teaching track, the leadership track, and the senior specialist track (see figure 8.1).[24]

Advancing in each career track means that teachers are deepening their level of expertise, accomplishment, and experience. Those aspiring to advance must meet the criteria spelled out for each track. There is also flexibility for lateral movements across the different tracks, as long as the teachers also satisfy those standards and criteria of the position. The leadership track is for those particularly focused on school leadership and administration. Leaders are identified early as part of the annual performance reviews that all teachers undergo and are specifically groomed from among teachers who demonstrate leadership potential.

At annual performance reviews, every teacher is given a current estimated potential (CEP) that indicates how far the individual might progress in his or her career. The CEP is also used to groom potential leaders for the system through professional development activities, all geared toward helping them to realize their CEP.[25] CEP helps the MOE gauge a teacher's readiness for new challenges, allowing the MOE to regularly provide additional tasks and learning opportunities. When the panel of appraisers deems them suitable, the MOE sends them to leadership preparation programs at the NIE, with the LEP as the principal preparation program.[26]

The MOE carefully and purposely chooses candidates for the LEP every year; candidates cannot nominate themselves. These candidates have a proven track record, have successfully passed a situational test, and have interviewed for the program.[27] Once selected, candidates become full-time participants in the program and are fully sponsored while still receiving their employment salaries and benefits, as they are still employed by the MOE. They receive new school postings upon graduation from the program.

THE LEP IN THE TWENTY-FIRST-CENTURY COMPETENCIES

Next, we briefly explain (1) the history and development of the LEP and the need for such a program in Singapore, (2) the capacity and competencies that a Singapore principal needs for the future, and (3) the continual development of the LEP and its alignment to the national context and requirements.

The Need for the LEP and Expected Outcomes

Singapore saw the need for strong and autonomous leadership in each school, based on the premise that it is achieving the DOEs and enacting school transformation. Then-education minister Ng Eng Hen commented on the role of the LEP: "Our cardinal belief is that principals play a pivotal role in achieving our desired outcomes of education. Principals set the tone and are held accountable for their schools . . . Our philosophy is that principals are like CEOs; because schools are complex, so we have to prepare them. This course [LEP] combines the rigor of academic inquiry with insights from practitioners."[28]

Singapore has committed itself to nurturing school leaders and has sought to update the LEP accordingly: it was initially formed as the Diploma in Educational Administration (DEA) in 1984.

Building Principals' Competencies in Times of Uncertainty

In the knowledge-based economy, every organization needs to address increasing complexities, advancements in technology, and nonlinear socio-economic dynamics.[29] Organizations need to grow into highly flexible and adaptable entities that are able to deal with the tensions specific to the complex and uncertain world.[30] While many would shy away from dealing with the unknown, there is a need to admit that there are no simple and straightforward resolutions.[31]

Leaders must confront the dynamics of complexity when governing and implementing policies. They must rise to the challenges posed by implementing education reforms or implementation of new structures that comes with opposing demands from different sources in different directions.[32] This is especially necessary when values are considered. Rushworth Kidder stated, "[L]eaders, especially those in education organizations, cannot dwell on issues too long and have to make difficult choices that might pit one right value against other values."[33] Michael Fullan further observed, "Reform is not just putting into place the latest policy. It means changing the cultures of the classrooms, the schools, the districts, the universities, and so on."[34] Singapore was cognizant of this as it looked to equipping principals with not only twenty-first-century competencies and skills but also with mind-sets for the future.

With the MOE launching its 21CC framework, principals also have to remember to model and demonstrate these significant values and competencies for teachers and students alike. Not only must teachers teach these competencies and skills, but principals and teachers must also "model the knowledge, skills and disposition their students are to acquire."[35]

Continual Development of the LEP: Alignment to National Context and Requirements

Programs are only as good as they are relevant to the specific time and context. The LEP associate dean commented in an interview, "To ensure the effectiveness over the years, a program must be reviewed at regular intervals to ensure its responsiveness to new realities." These regular and systematic reviews allow any program to be robust and relevant for the present and the future.

In an interview, the MOE adviser commented on how the DEA was redesigned into its present LEP form, "with the intent of producing strong executive leaders within a shorter time frame . . . We needed school leaders able to operate independently, to be innovative, and to raise the quality of the schooling experience . . . Within the broader national context, there was a push to develop an innovative and enterprising mind-set."

The impetus to designing the LEP in 2001 was motivated by the desire to strike a good balance between developing visionary principals who were innovative and enterprising, and supporting grounded principals who understood the realities and the various dimensions of their role. In this iteration of the program, developing the innovative spirit of school leaders was emphasized more—something the LEP continues to emphasize today. For example, the NIE and the MOE reviewed the LEP and implemented the 5 Leadership Roles and 5 Minds (5R5M) framework in 2011. The 5R5M framework is a model of action and reflection that allows principals to adopt the right mindset in fulfilling their roles. It shows how the LEP stays relevant and current. It also shows the continuous learning process in the program's evolution that is pertinent to the twenty-first century.

The MOE adviser we interviewed explained that there is now a greater emphasis on making "school leaders understand not just education policies, but also to understand national policies. School leaders can better design learning experiences when they have a more in-depth understanding of the present and future realities of Singapore."

The present LEP aims to develop "principalship capability in an increasing complex world."[36] With the ever-changing landscape of education and the twenty-first-century learner profiles, principals have to:

> deal with the uncertainties and multiple contingencies in a complex world, while maintaining his/her clear focus on the educational needs of children and youth under his or her care. The principal must be prepared to deal with unexpected contingencies and "intractable problems" that are not easy to define or mutate over time, and engage in problem-solving complex negotiations with stakeholder with differing and at times conflicting perspectives.[37]

LEP's objectives are in line with the nation's values and educational philosophy. It develops a pool of school leaders from which the MOE is able to post to either schools or the MOE headquarters to spearhead important initiatives.

LEP is expected to help to build potential principals with a strong conviction about their values, knowledge of advanced theories of leadership, and the ability to translate their knowledge into practice anchored in good values. The LEP associate dean explained that at the individual level, LEP develops the person; at the national level, LEP develops "a fraternity of capable and committed school leaders, ready to be deployed in various leadership positions in the education system."

ANALYZING LEP

Theory of Change: Reflection and Application Loop

LEP's theory of change is based on the belief that principals must have the ability to hold an education philosophy and a model of practice with sufficient conviction to inspire and motivate themselves and others to action. (We further explain how LEP exemplifies the theory of change in a program in the "Program Realized Outcomes" section later in this chapter.) At the same time, principals must be open-minded enough to refine, revise, or refute the philosophy and model when new information is presented. To better operationalize this, the 5R5M framework (see figure 8.2) becomes a helpful platform for the reflection and application loop.

The framework is based on and integrates Thomas Sergiovanni's "five forces of leadership" (with associated leadership roles) and Howard Gardner's "five minds."[38] LEP describes this combination as a useful lens that "frame[s] the roles and minds of school leaders in our contexts."[39] Contextualized to Singapore's education system and school leadership context, 5R5M is an innovative approach to school leadership development that helps shape principals for the future work ahead:

> How leaders think (their "minds") affects how they act (the actions associated with their roles). That is how leaders apply their "minds" to their "roles." But leaders also need to reflect on their actions in the various "roles" to refine their "minds." This is a continuous and virtuous application–reflection spiral in the journey of school leaders, which helps them to appreciate different pathways, generate multiple solutions and manage dynamic relationships in leading a school in an increasingly complex environment.[40]

Sergiovanni's five leadership forces or roles are: educational (E), technical (T), human (H), symbolic (S), and cultural (C).[41] According to Sergiovanni, the practice of E, T, and H allows principals to achieve effectiveness but does not guarantee excellence. To achieve school excellence, principals need to practice S and C. In line with the MOE's philosophy for educational leadership, S and C roles are core to the identity of principals.[42] MOE's philosophy

FIGURE 8.2   5R5M framework

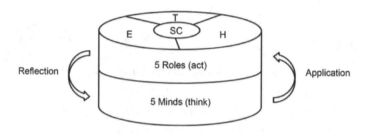

Note: educational (E), technical (T), human (H), symbolic (S), and cultural (C).

Source: National Institute of Education (NIE), *LEP Handbook* (NIE, Singapore: 2016), 6. Used with permission.

is made up of guiding principles that state educational leadership is anchored in values and purpose, inspires all toward a shared vision, is committed to growing people, and leads and manages change. The identity of principals permeates the other three roles of E, T, and H because Singapore school leadership is anchored in the values and purpose of education.

Gardner's five minds are ethical, respectful, creative, synthesizing, and disciplined. These mind-sets are essential for principals to function effectively now and in the future. With them as a foundation, principals can prepare to meet current and future challenges. Gardner explained: "With these 'Minds' . . . a person will be well equipped to deal with what is expected, as well as what cannot be anticipated; without these minds, a person will be at the mercy of forces that he or she can't understand, let alone control."[43]

The "forces" are the uncertainties or complexities of the twenty-first century. Principals are challenged to ensure that their schools are adaptable enough to survive.[44] They must deal with high levels of complexity in governance and policy implementation.[45]

Coupled with the 5R5M framework in undergirding the LEP is complexity theory, which provides a way for the LEP participants to tackle the complexities of their role as principal. Complexity theory is a theory of social change, development, and evolution that emphasizes the features of nonlinearity, dynamism, and unpredictability, and allows for the generation of interesting insights for educational governance and leadership. It highlights the need to focus on people, relationships, and learning rather than structures and compliance, which is much of what LEP attempts to do.[46]

LEP Faculty

LEP is facilitated by academic members at NIE. Those include various NIE academics, seconded principals with years of invaluable experience, and current, as well as recently retired, senior policy makers and administrators. These academics are invited to give talks. Each of them is an expert with academic rigor and practical experience.

LEP Curriculum and Activities

The LEP was developed with a key principle in mind: using a social constructivism paradigm for knowledge construction, sharing, and application.[47] The LEP sees learning as an active process of construction rather than the acquisition of knowledge. Jean Piaget commented that the information that flows into an individual's mind must be constructed by that individual via knowledge discovery.[48] Commonly linked to Lev Semyonovich Vygotsky, social orientations of constructivism emphasize the cultural and social context in which learning takes place.[49] This is extended in the social orientation for the LEP participants as they learn as a cohort group and small learning groups, called syndicates.

Knowledge is something that people construct together, rather than a possession in people's heads.[50] From the perspective of the social constructivism paradigm, knowledge is a social, consensual interpretation of what is reality; the group co-constructs knowledge through interaction and complex response processes.[51] The LEP places self-organizing interaction with its intrinsic capability to produce emergent coherence at the center of knowledge co-creation.

While various leadership programs prepare their participants to become competent individuals who can deal with problem-solving models and advanced technology, these programs do not focus on the human dimensions of management, which is often shifted to the background.[52] The LEP, on the other hand, is firmly established in these human dimensions through its social constructivism philosophy. The syndicates create conditions where relating to other people is a pivotal factor to learning. Participants interact and learn more about themselves and other participants. They also constructively scrutinize their own perspective on education with their supportive peers, lecturers, and mentor principals. This engagement is crucial to their active learning and co-construction of knowledge. According to the *LEP Handbook*, the learning vehicles are geared to encourage engagement:[53]

LEP participants are expected to learn beyond the inputs of the courses by engaging in deep and meaningful social generation of knowledge. The various learning vehicles in LEP are designed to provide the platform for interactions among participants to construct, share and apply new knowledge. In particular, some of the learning vehicles of the program facilitate the internalization of values, and promote self-awareness as well as personal mastery among participants.

There are eleven learning vehicles in the LEP, but we focus only on those related to the LEP's development of future leaders by being the platform to: (1) create a strong fraternity of colleagues, (2) thrive in complex situations, (3) be prepared for change, and (4) be able to effectively work in Singapore's cultural uniqueness. These sessions are conducted at the NIE campus, schools, respective visit locations, and various sites. (Table 8.1 lists and gives a brief description of each selected learning vehicle.)

Realized Outcomes of the Program

Having all potential principals go through a single executive leadership program co-developed by Singapore's education ministry and the country's only teacher preparation institute might seem to produce only one type of leader. This, however, is not the case. Singapore's MOE and NIE were mindful that to have good leaders, the leaders need to be adaptable, flexible, and cognizant of the country's present and future needs. The co-developers used the theory of social constructivism along with the 5R5M framework to surface the possible skills and competencies that potential principals need to address.

The program encourages the LEP participants to grow into the principals they think that the Singapore education system needs, and in doing so, they have to find their place as individuals in the system. Lessons are taught in the form of modules and explored in each individual's professional experiences, whether from lecturers or fellow participants. Many participants reported that they entered the program with their own values and perceptions of the kind of principal they aspired to be; the LEP setting gave them a clearer idea of their values and concepts. Here, we describe how these expected outcomes have been realized as the LEP helps participants to build a strong fraternity, thrive in complex situations, be prepared for change, and engage in Singapore's cultural uniqueness.

TABLE 8.1   List and description of selected learning vehicles

Learning vehicle	Description
Learning syndicate	The main driving vehicle for learning and knowledge generation in LEP; comprises five to six participants. It is led and facilitated by an NIE faculty member who acts as the syndicate leader. They regularly meet to escalate their learning and support one another during visits and projects, to discuss and internalize ideas, and to debate current issues of concern.
Learning journals	All participants are required to reflect on their beliefs, values, and purposes about leadership, management, teaching, and learning by writing in learning journals throughout the program. Journaling and reflecting encourages them to adopt a reflection and application process (as seen in the 5R5M framework) and track their learning progress.
Management dialogue sessions	Management dialogue sessions allow participants to interact with MOE senior management and help them focus on these principles and values that drive education policy formulation. Participants develop an appreciation for how their future actions and decisions should align with the direction of Singapore's education system.
LEP courses	The courses differ from traditional forms of lecture. Courses are meant to spark critical thinking and professional dialogue, and are conducted in interactive classroom-based sessions, facilitated by NIE faculty members and visiting professors.
Mentoring	Experience can never be underestimated; what good and veteran principals know is tacit and not documented. LEP participants are assigned to an experienced principal, which allows for the transmission of values and ways of thinking. These experienced principals are called principal mentors and also host the LEP participants in the Creative Action Project (CAP) in their schools.
Creative Action Project (CAP)	CAP helps the LEP participants strike a balance between theory and practice. They are assigned to a school to propose and carry out an innovative project that adds value to a school. The project is student-centered and designed to improve student learning in a holistic way.
International visits and industrial learning	LEP participants are sent for a two-week overseas study visit and also for local industrial learning. These expose them to different ways of thinking about leadership-related issues and generate an understanding of how value is added to other education systems and industries. They also give participants an understanding of the local and global contexts that they are preparing students for.

A strong fraternity

LEP participants are prepared to be principals for the future and to be part of a fraternity that has the culture to support and help others. They form a cohort (or class) and a syndicate. As the participants study alongside and collaborate with each other, especially during the international visits and industry learning, they naturally form a bond. This grouping allows them to interact with different types of people and behaviors, which is especially useful as these future principals need to manage others to achieve school and national goals. The fraternity of principals forms a strong support system.

Participants reported two outcomes: forming friendships and resolving conflicts. Many formed strong friendships and supported one another during the course. Even before joining the larger fraternity of current principals, one participant, a month before graduation, commented: "We are a fraternity, we share a lot of knowledge and experience, we bounce off ideas . . . so the fraternity gets closer and we are not talking about competition anymore . . . it's more really about the touching base with each other on the regular basis, not just on professional matters but also on a personal basis." (Participant #6)

After graduating from the LEP, participants truly appreciated the fraternity that they started building during the program: "Some people say that leadership is a very lonely journey. Sometimes I sit in this room, I grapple with the problems and I can't share them with others. But they [the LEP participants] have shown me . . . that leadership can be shared. It need not be a journey alone . . . We all need to be encouraged." (Participant #7)

This encouragement came at both the personal and the professional levels, mostly through instant messaging on a mobile phone app. On the personal level, fellow participants became good friends who gave emotional support and sympathized with each other. After a year, they still messaged each other individually or in a group chat "just for humor and laughter," and regularly met for meals during religious and cultural holidays. They felt that "[n]o matter where we are, we want to consciously make that effort to come together. Because we feel that that kind of support and collegiality is very important." (Participant #6)

At the professional level, they were ready to give advice and opinions, be each other's critical sounding boards, provide encouragement, and share professional experiences. The same participant reported that "we will actually come together once a month to actually share ideas, bounce off ideas," and reflected on the importance of forming relationships in LEP: "It is the relationship that I formed with my fellow classmates and with my Principal Mentor . . . as well as our Syndicate Leader and also the course lecturers. It is the relationship that we built that we will take away with us. It's how you remember the LEP people." (Participant #6)

The 5R5M framework, which emphasizes human interaction, naturally prepares participants to engage with peers, staff members, students, and parents. The already-present supportive culture and close relationship have been so ingrained in them that being supported and supportive have become a professional lifestyle. After a year in school, one participant said, "It's still the friendship that we have forged. We still have a group, we chat with each other. When somebody does well, we celebrate, or we cheer each other up . . . I think the friendship and experiences I had through the trips and through the network are the strongest, biggest takeaway and benefit that LEP has given me." (Participant #7)

These principals, who are just a year into their principalship, are not only shaping their respective schools but also have an impact on the education system in Singapore: "A lot of things that happen in schools impact other schools. If something happens in one school, the public will start asking, 'What about this other school? How come that school leader did not make a similar decision, even though the case was similar?'" (Participant #6)

The fraternity contributes to the overall education system as lasting relationships between school leaders are forged. With like-minded colleagues as friends, the system becomes more unified, as colleagues can understand one another despite the different circumstances in their schools. Participant #6 expressed this coherence and unity: "The leaders' autonomy and different schools have different profiles; that's why they have to make different decisions regarding a similar case. This means we are not working in silos anymore, we are a fraternity."

Thriving in complex situations

LEP aims to prepare participants to thrive in complex situations by emphasizing the need to focus on people, relationships, and learning rather than on structures and conformance.[54] Educational leadership and governance exhibit many features of complexity as schools operate in a dynamic and unpredictable environment. Schools have to both shape and adapt to the community around them, co-evolving in a nonlinear manner. Thus, principals need to have the competency to continuously frame and translate the future into present strategic plans.

LEP applies complexity in knowledge generation and emergence. LEP does not follow a predetermined syllabus but presents broad areas that participants discuss with their syndicate leaders. This allows for knowledge creation in a co-constructed fashion. With a course to introduce the complexity theory, LEP has a curriculum that is dynamic, emergent, relational, autocatalytic, self-organized, and open.[55] The lecturer moves from the role of an expert and teacher to a facilitator, co-learner, and co-constructer of meaning, enabling learners to connect new knowledge to existing knowledge. Learners have to be prepared to exercise autonomy, responsibility, ownership, self-direction, and reflection, which were practiced in some of the learning vehicles, as previously stated. The course on complexity theory includes complex challenges in the topics of educational leadership, the complexity paradigm, nonlinear dynamics, quantum paradoxes, and the uncertainty principle, and the edge of chaos.

In the learning vehicle the Creative Action Project (CAP), we found that participants learned important skills. One such skill, "futuring," is about scanning environmental trends, exploiting possible opportunities, and riding shock waves.[56] Principals need to navigate nonlinear paths of change and manage their complexities to prepare for the challenges of the twenty-first century.[57] CAP requires participants to envision their attachment school ten to fifteen years in the future by critically examining trends in education, looking beyond the immediate vision of the project school, and developing the foresight to strategically move the school into the future.[58] As one participant observed, "You see a lot of our policies and initiatives are really based on 'futuring.' We always keep preparing the children for the future." (Participant #15).

In futuring, participants have to consider the goals of the project and figure out how to achieve these future goals from their present position. The LEP participants learned how to handle complex human dynamics while working toward a common goal, and they realized the importance of understanding the context and the need for sensitivity to their colleagues in the attachment school. They commented:

CAP was an excellent way for me to join a new school environment, to assimilate myself into a new school culture, to work with a new set of people, to see how I can energize them, how I can excite them on a new project that has been placed on the table even though you know they have other things to manage in school. (Participant #7)

It's about how we manage people's expectations such that we are able to have a common understanding while doing our project . . . it takes a lot of negotiation, explaining or even buying in from the people to work with you so that the project will do something good for the students. (Participant #12)

Participants develop the key skills of adaptability and flexibility to deal with an uncertain future. They do this through CAP, as seen in a facilitator's comment: "What LEP seeks to do is to build a kind of leader who is able to adapt to a new environment. So it's not just for building specific competencies. It's about allowing them to think through the relevance of these competencies in their own context in today's world." (Facilitator #2)

The CAP experience offers a deeper appreciation of the ever-changing environment in which schools find themselves. Participants have said they have changed the way they have thought about issues. The LEP provides the appropriate conditions and environment to practice being adaptable and flexible.

LEP has helped me to find myself and find that calling again, it was there but to see myself touch that and see it come alive in CAP . . . I think LEP has helped me to become more situational because there are a lot of other scenarios that can emerge . . . I found myself learning to just slow down and sometimes recognizing that things are so complex. Sometimes, it is good to let the outcome emerge than to immediately jump in and say I have an answer. (Participant #7)

Prepared for change at a national level

Principalship is not only limited to the length (i.e., time) of a principal's tenure or to the complexity of context, but also deals with the breadth, which pertains to how schools translate education policies into teaching and learning that affect the country at a national level. The LEP associate dean noted the impact that LEP and its participants can create is one that affects the entire nation, since LEP is the only program in Singapore that prepares school leaders.

Principals have to discern which policies to focus on based on their students' needs, the teachers' capabilities, the school's facilities, and the gaps in the system. But one can never be fully prepared for the uncertain future because, as one participant describes after one year in the role: "School leadership is such a dynamic work that you can never be prepared for. However hard you prepare, it will not prepare you wholeheartedly for a school leadership because you can't anticipate and that there are certain challenges or certain moments that might happen." (Participant #14)

LEP works with this dynamic and inculcates in participants the necessary skills and competencies to understand that no one knows all the answers. In this regard, LEP strives to prepare potential principals to work effectively in a dynamic landscape as the leader of a school and the go-between of schools and the government. LEP achieves this through a combination of formal and informal preparation; one facilitator commented: "It is LEP that systematically and structurally prepares our aspiring principals and they are the ones who are out there leading the schools. This is a formal preparation but a lot of things happen informally during the time when they come together at LEP. Different people from different schools take their shared experiences to a much higher level." (Facilitator #1)

This deliberate intention can also be seen in the LEP participants who knew they needed to learn from LEP and gain experience and practice. LEP's 5R5M framework and other learning vehicles provide a preparation structure (table 8.2 provides participants' views of the various facets of LEP).

LEP offers participants a myriad of different learning experiences. Preparation allows LEP participants to view situations from various perspectives that give them examples of how to react according to the situation. One participant commented:

> All these are useful in preparation for leadership because you see the different leadership styles. You can come up with your own mishmash of what you think would be the style that suits you the most. And the other important thing is contextualization, knowing which type of school are you going to take over and what should you do: what are some of the key issues if you are having a sinking school, a struggling school versus you are having a high performing school. It is going to be very different. So that kind of exposure to how differ-

TABLE 8.2   Participants' views of LEP's framework and learning vehicles

Item	Participants' views
5R5M framework	"It maps out what that whole body of leadership is." (Participant #4) "The 5R5M Framework actually helps us to think through more carefully about a certain dimension or issue, we are more careful in thinking, really understanding the cause of the issue rather than coming up with solutions that actually may cause another kind of problem." (Participant #12)
International visits	"Simply because it's really an opportunity to go beyond what is in our national context and look at practices, whether it's educational or noneducational issues. Not necessarily copying these practices but trying to understand different cultures, different contexts, and how leadership is practiced in foreign context." (Participant #14) "International visits are a different catalyst for you to get inspired . . . The international trip was great and I think that . . . it is great because it allowed me to work with my syndicate. Very different personalities and it helped me to find my space with a group of leaders, all of us are leaders. We complemented each other in our own areas." (Participant #7)
Industrial learning	"We went to visit different organizations. It gives you a different perspective, so if it's possible within the same society, something to think about whether we can do, like [a well-known technology innovator and service provider], we hear about what a great place it is to work in. Their vision, mission statements were not about what they wanted but was about what they can give . . . There was something to think about, because if we look at schools now, we always set standards and goals but maybe this is an approach to think about: we start off with this is, what can I give to you first." (Participant #1)
Course modules	"The modules, thematically speaking, are all good and all made sense because they pertain to what a principal should be considering thematically." (Participant #8) "We can look at the whole purpose of leadership first in abstract terms before we funnel down to leadership in different elements of a principal's job. I think LEP is good in that sense that it helps provide that big picture and then strengthens your thinking in different aspects throughout the program. It really forces you to distill and crystalize for yourself what you would really do." (Participant #8)
Management dialogue sessions	"I thought principalship is a very straightforward job, I thought it's all about charting direction, monitoring, implementing, reviewing, and encouraging people and all that. But having gone through the MDS sessions, I've realized that the job of the principal is not just about the actions but more of who you are as a person who is able to carry out this role." (Participant #8)

ent leaders have dealt with schools at different stages has helped prepare us very much for school leadership. (Participant #11)

Cultural uniqueness

Each organization functions within its unique cultural context. In Singapore, there are unique characteristics of the education system. A further exploration of the LEP brings out Singapore's cultural traits and the LEP's role in developing and passing on this cultural know-how to principals.

Working in a "centralized decentralization" system. Andy Hargreaves and Dennis Shirley have said that a government should not drive and deliver education but steer and support schools instead, so as to achieve an equal partnership between the government and the people.[59] The paradox in Singapore, however, is that the government both drives and steers the system, a situation described as a "paradoxical form of centralized decentralization."[60] On one hand, the government has decentralized decision making to schools to encourage diversity and innovation, and to promote creativity and a holistic education. Then-minister for education Tharman Shanmugaratnam, for example, said, "Quality will be driven by teachers and leaders in schools, with ideas bubbling up through the system rather than being pushed down from the top."[61]

On the other hand, the government is still largely responsible for achieving national outcomes and accountable for the spending of public money.[62] Hence, the government exercises a certain level of control in order to ensure that the country's goals are achieved, even if schools are empowered to have some degree of flexibility to cater to the needs of their students.

Being accountable and taking responsibility. The accountability culture and structure are strong and well established in Singapore.[63] Quality assurance is achieved through excellence models and external validation.[64] On the one hand, principals are meticulous in fulfilling all the demands the MOE requires of them and adhering to the policies and guidelines the ministry sets out; on the other hand, they are also driven by their inner sense of responsibility for the children in their schools.[65] Some participants expressed that they felt burdened by this responsibility and were concerned that they would not do well enough, while others said they wanted to perform well so as not to let their country down.

LEP helped participants reconcile both accountability toward the powers that be and responsibility toward each child. For accountability, LEP provided tools and frameworks for reporting and strategic planning, and fostered a better understanding of the policy-making process and the reasons behind some of the policy decisions. One participant reflected:

> [The LEP] has exposed me to wide range of tools and frameworks and it has clarified some of the practices I have seen in the past and has given me a handle on how those decisions were made. Because now there is a framework or tool or theory behind it, it is easier for me to look at the issues more comprehensively and look at various ways of approaching the issue in future. (Participant #2)

At the same time, the LEP helped participants come to terms with the huge responsibility by providing numerous opportunities for interactions with experienced principals. Participants realized that accountability and responsibility need not be at odds but should coexist to allow the school leader to make better decisions for the good of the students. One participant stated: "I used to think that [principalship] would be manageable, I know about the risk involved now. The interactions with the veteran principals and also my Principal Mentor have helped me to appreciate the role of school leadership and to bear the great weight of accountability and responsibilities on my shoulders." (Participant #7)

Shared values within the fraternity. The MOE ensures that the teaching profession adheres to the following guidelines to ensure education quality for the system:

- philosophy of education that points to the core beliefs of the teaching profession
- desired outcomes of education that set the common purpose for schools and guides programs and practices
- teachers' vision that lays out the aspirations and roles of teachers
- teachers' pledge that every teacher makes to uphold the highest standards in professional practice
- teachers' creed that collects the practices of past and present educators that serves as a guide for all teachers[66]

Participants started with certain values that were personal or learned at work. The LEP not only helped to reinforce these values, but it also helped surface other values that principals would need in their role:

> The whole process [the LEP] has been enriching. I would say it was a recap of our leadership journey as well as affirmation and reinforcing some of our values and beliefs . . . I think [the LEP] helped me to be more explicit about my beliefs and values because some of the beliefs and values I assume that everybody share but may not be true. (Participant #12)

> LEP helps to build up a sense of values or aspired values that a school principal should have. So, guided by these values, we should all be able to lead our school in the same way. (Participant #8)

It has also helped participants review their teaching philosophy through reflection and renew the initial calling that brought them to the vocation of teaching:

> For me, the importance of self-awareness about knowing why I do certain things and why it is compelling for me to say I want to do it first. LEP has helped me to see that part most clearly and I'm glad that this journey has helped me to find myself again to remember why I chose education as a vocation and a calling. At the heart and the core of it is what education means to me and what is it going to stand for in future. (Participant #7)

Involving the community. For policies to continue improving and remaining relevant in this fast-changing twenty-first century, the MOE realizes that it needs to consult school leaders, teachers, parents, and industry partners in formulating policies. The MOE emphasized forging closer ties with stakeholders and, especially, parents. At a work plan seminar in 2015, then-minister for education Heng Swee Keat announced that MOE would spare no effort to ensure that every parent would be a supportive partner.[67] He mentioned parent support groups as a key platform to bring schools and parents closer together. A few of the LEP participants also mentioned working with parents. One remarked:

> The parent support group—we actually had quite a strong group—we get them to come in during Chinese New Year. The parents in the support group are the ones that teach the scholars how to wrap dumplings, and then they prepare

dumplings for the whole festival celebration. Whenever we have post-exam activities, there's actually this healthy living segment that the parent support group does. They teach the students how to make things. (Participant #11)

Heng also mentioned that partnership with industry was an essential factor for future success as it provides opportunities for students to learn outside of schools. LEP also does this through industry learnings so that principals themselves are not left behind in the push for relevance in the fast-changing twenty-first century. One participant observed, "[Industry visits are] good because it gave us exposure to views held by industry players outside of education and it gives me, it helps me check what are things I need to bear in mind as I lead school, as I shape my students development." (Participant #14)

A closely knit system only works if all its relationships are healthy and strong. Therefore, not only does the MOE have to ensure that schools establish close ties with parents and community, but it also has to work hard to ensure that strong links are forged internally between school leaders and policy makers, and among the fraternity of school leaders.

THE PRINCIPAL IN COMPLEX TIMES

Benefits of LEP

Participants, in general, saw the LEP as beneficial. It has given them a better sense of who they are in the education system and their role. Knowing with certainty where one is positioned has allowed one participant to work more effectively and be more confident:

> [The LEP] is designed whereby it helps the participants to be more emotionally and mentally prepared for the next phase of their career . . . From that angle, it was lot of a reflection and self-thought and questioning to get a better understanding of myself and to have a clearer idea of what I stand for. Because I think ultimately when we talk about the leadership journey, it is very much about what do I bring forth in terms of my belief to the job, that process of clarifying, the process of sharpening my ideals, my core belief is important. It is something I find important. (Participant #9)

Although the LEP participants were already effective vice principals or education policy makers, principalship requires a different way of thinking. In this aspect, the LEP course and activities, and simply the time at the LEP to interact with each other, lecturers, principal mentors, and MOE colleagues, have given participants the knowledge and opportunity to make this shift and focus on their purpose in education:

> Firstly, it is the revisiting the purpose of education. I think a lot of times in our daily work when we get busy with firefighting and doing all sorts of things to help our students, sometimes we forget why we are here, the purpose of teachers and purpose of education itself. At least LEP has given us time and space to actually reflect on some of these very fundamental issues and I think a lot of the speakers and a lot of the lecturers also place emphasis on this aspect: revisiting the very purpose of why we are doing what we are doing. (Participant #2)

Challenges Ahead

Challenges for the LEP

The LEP is lauded for creating a strong fraternity, but how long will that fraternity remain strong? Can it remain as robust as it grows? How like-minded can a large group be? What can Singapore do to maintain a tight fraternity that is always focused on national needs?

As in any organization, there are possible conflicts. In the research cohort, there were disagreements, and some participants could not see eye-to-eye on certain issues. For example, some suggested that the LEP scaffolds a reality-based learning experience through its CAP. But other participants suggested that it is an artificial setting, as the CAP is unable to fully mirror real life, despite being a project in a real school. For example, the luxury of time to carry out a project in the CAP may not exist in real life. Furthermore, day-to-day tasks often prevent principals from seeing an entire project through from conceptualization to implementation. The more precise question, however, is how the LEP ensures that each participant has the right mind-set and sees the CAP in the way it was meant to be, as helping expose them to the role of principals.

Challenges in adopting the LEP model

For international systems that find some usefulness in how the LEP is structured and would like to adopt it or components of it, the challenge is to build an environment where the participants will be able to grow into the roles in the context of a specific system. The LEP is specially designed for the principals in Singapore, starting from the full sponsorship by the MOE to the support structure the education system has built since the start of the DEA. Although LEP is tailor-made for Singapore, the components, the philosophy behind the program, and the motivation may be learning points for interested systems looking for ways to tackle the future of complexity and uncertainty, and adapt them.

Developing People, Not Roles

The challenges of the future are the impetus for the MOE and NIE to develop people, not roles. Developing a broad mind-set is what LEP hopes to inculcate in its participants and was the initial purpose of the program. Participants were found to have broadened their mind-sets and have developed good competencies. LEP has changed the person, rather than defined the role of principals. For some LEP participants, this broad mind-set was not only good for their schools but also for their own families.

> One particular aspect that we need to do as our Creative Action Project is about futuring. So when we do our futuring we need to envision ourselves in the future, what kind of a school, what kind of a world we will have. I really thought that is very powerful especially for my children who are in Primary 1, 3, and 6. While I have always been inculcating values in my family, this provides me an added incentive to emphasize the importance of positive mind-set and developing an inquiry mind. This is something I'm developing in my children now based on what I have learned [from LEP]. (Participant #3)

Having good school leadership in the twenty-first century is imperative. But when we think of the leaders we want to lead our schools, we must ask what kind of people do we have in mind? It is people who make and build a school, who are part of a community, and who form a nation. Educational leadership needs people with the right values and twenty-first-century skills and competencies who can empower our teachers to help children succeed in the complex and uncertain challenges they face in their lives.

CHAPTER NINE

Conclusions

Fernando M. Reimers and Connie K. Chung

I n this book we examined programs that support teachers and principals to effectively prepare their students with the diverse range of competencies that will equip them to meet the demands of the twenty-first century. We studied programs in Chile, China, Colombia, India, Mexico, Singapore, and the United States that supported education for students' socio-emotional as well as cognitive development. We had little difficulty identifying a number of programs with those aims, which had reached a significant scale and were reputed to be achieving success. Most of the programs work in public schools, serving low-income students.

The first finding of this study is that twenty-first-century education is already happening in several school systems around the world, supported by programs that build the capacities of teachers and school leaders to help students develop those competencies. Such programs do not need to be invented, but identified and studied. Many of the programs found a point of entry into schools when countries included in this study broadened the curricular aims over the last several years. Broadening curricula with a focus on cognitive as well as socio-emotional competencies created the demand for professional development that could help translate such aspirations into instructional practice.

Though they share the similar aim of supporting teachers and school leaders to teach socio-emotional and cognitive competencies, the programs we studied are diverse. While each of the various programs prioritizes several domains of competency, they differ in the specific competencies and skills within these categories that they target. Most focus on helping teachers develop instructional capacities that support whole-child education; one focuses on helping school principals lead schools that can support whole-child education. By whole-child education, we mean broad goals that include the development of cognitive, social, and emotional competencies of students, and that do not prioritize a subset of those three categories over the others.

Such programs are capacious not only in the vision they have for the goals of instruction, but also in the approaches they use to support teachers in teaching a broad range of instructional practices. They tend to be multidimensional in their approach, including the kind of curriculum, teacher professional development, instructional resources, and assessment they provide. They also reach beyond building individual teacher capacities to support organizational and cultural change at the school level. Essentially, these are not just programs to help individual teachers develop new skills, but human resource development programs that help schools and districts achieve their instructional goals by advancing an ambitious, multiyear strategy of development of all human resources. All are school based and involve multiple staff in each school, including teachers, principals, and other staff.

The programs that we studied include the Escuela Activa Urbana (EAU) program in Colombia; the Programa de Educación en Ciencias Basada en la Indagación (ECBI) in Chile; the UNETE program in Mexico; the district-based professional development program in Qingyang District, China; Dream-a-Dream program in India; and EL Education in the United States. They have seemingly different curricular foci, including inquiry-based science education, citizenship education, technology literacy, core academic subjects, and character development. Underneath such variation in curricular focus, however, are commonalities in overarching goals. In addition, two of the programs we studied focus on the development of individual teachers and principals, and are not directly aligned with instructional activities to support student competencies; they include the Dream-a-Dream program in India, and the Leaders in Education Program (LEP) in Singapore.

In this chapter we examine seven characteristics of these various programs, including the specific student competencies that they focus on, how a broad vision and a compelling narrative create space to teach such an ambitious set of competencies, what professional development looks like for them, how they approach organizational and cultural change as a mind-set shift, how they use assessment to support continuous learning and improvement, how they align with and are supported by the policy environment, and the role partnerships play in their success.

WHICH PARTICULAR COMPETENCIES DO THESE PROGRAMS DEVELOP?

Amid a diversity of forms, twenty-first-century global education efforts share recognizable common features. Based on our prior research about national curricular frameworks and the competencies necessary for education in the twenty-first century, we looked for programs that taught a broad range of competencies to students in school, addressing multiple domains (cognitive, social, and emotional) and competencies that traditional schools rarely acknowledge as important, such as creativity, innovation, collaboration, self-awareness, and life skills.[1]

That we were able to find such programs in public schools in the seven countries we studied illustrates that it is a false dichotomy to assume that teachers have to choose between teaching basic academic subjects and developing competencies such as creativity, collaboration, or character. The existence of these programs in schools serving low-income children also challenges the notion that schools serving the most marginalized should prioritize core academic skills and that an expanded curriculum is relevant only for more privileged children. For example, the systemwide program of improvement implemented in Chengdu's Qingyang District in China focuses on teaching core academic and twenty-first-century competencies, while also working on closing equity gaps in the district and improving education quality. The result of such an ambitious vision in a district where 30 percent of the students come from migrant worker families is that all students graduate to junior high school, and 97 percent proceed to senior high school, with remarkable achievements on a wide range of academic and socio-emotional outcomes.

However, there are variations in the programs we studied in terms of the competencies they emphasize and in the overarching focus of the curriculum. The main difference across programs is that while some focus on a small (but nevertheless broad) range of competencies, others focus on a more extensive set of competencies. In different ways, they all emphasize a mix of some cognitive, social, and emotional competencies.

For example, the EAU program in Colombia focuses on the development of comprehensive academic, socio-emotional, and citizenship competencies among students. These include cognitive skills, such as decision making, problem solving, and creativity; relational competencies, such as leadership, teamwork, communication, conflict resolution, and environmental responsibility; organizational skills including general management, administration, and information management; and socio-emotional skills such as empathy, appreciation for diversity, and inclusion.

The program is aligned with the country's National Standards of Citizenship, which emphasize performance domains in the area of living together and peace; these include generating multiple ways to address conflicts and thinking through consequences of each alternative. Another domain of the citizenship competencies includes participation and democratic responsibility. A third domain emphasizes identity, plurality, and respect for differences, which includes the capacity to value diversity and stand against discrimination. These competencies encompass emotional, cognitive, communicative, integrative, and knowledge-based domains. EAU also offers an early college program, where students can participate in college-level courses offered by university faculty while enrolled in high school.

In contrast to the rich array of competencies that are the focus of the EAU program, the Dream-a-Dream program in India focuses on helping children in poverty develop a more limited, but still diverse, set of life skills such as thinking creatively, managing conflict, responding with empathy, working in teams, taking initiative, and being adaptable. The opportunities to develop these skills are offered directly to students through afterschool programs in sports and in the arts as well as in career programs focused on the development of job-related skills. In addition, Dream-a-Dream provides professional development programs to teachers so they themselves develop these skills in the belief that this will develop their capacity to cultivate those same skills in their students.

The focus of UNETE, in Mexico, has evolved from helping students develop technological literacy, in the early stages of the organization, to currently focusing on activating student motivation to develop technological literacy, as well as problem-solving skills, critical thinking, communication, conflict resolution, and self-direction.

ECBI in Chile focuses on science education to support the development of curiosity, scientific inquiry, critical thinking, and an understanding of the natural and material world, with the goal of preparing students for lifelong learning. Some of these higher-order skills are intrinsic to the use of inquiry-based teaching, such as engaging learners in making observations; asking questions; studying other sources of knowledge; collecting, analyzing, and interpreting evidence; generating explanations and predictions; and communicating the results of such processes. Learners are encouraged to monitor their own learning and to develop critical thinking. Students also learn to communicate what they have learned, practicing scientific writing as well as communicating with authentic audiences as they lead public lessons in which they recreate their learning process for parents and other members of the community.

In the United States, EL Education develops the capacities of teachers and supports the transformation of school cultures to help students achieve mastery of knowledge and skills, develop character, and create authentic high-quality work. Mastery of knowledge and skills includes the development of critical thinking skills, application of knowledge, and core competencies in the disciplines, while character includes working to become effective learners, ethical people, and taking active positive roles in school and in their communities. The LEP in Singapore prepares future school leaders to lead people and influence school culture in ways that are responsive to changing societal trends and opportunities. In China, Chengdu's Qingyang District adopted a districtwide program of educational transformation focused on the development of meta-learning skills (including a positive attitude to learning, asking questions in class, synthesizing material, preparing for tests, and critical reading skills), creativity, citizenship, and emotional regulation.

The diverse contexts and purposes of these programs contribute to the different range of competencies that they emphasize, but ultimately, they all address both traditional core academic cognitive skills as well as additional social and emotional competencies.

OPENING SPACE FOR TEACHING A BROAD RANGE OF COMPETENCIES

Why and how did these programs take on such a wide range of goals for learning? We found that the programs shared the ability to communicate a clear, broad vision that included a compelling narrative about the need to teach and learn a wider set of competencies in the twenty-first century. In the case of EL Education, for example, a clearly articulated and high-level vision for education created the demand to change school practices and norms. In the case of EAU, the input from a range of stakeholders and viewpoints in the creation of the program broadened the aims and vision as well. Across the programs, we found that a clearly articulated organizational vision encourages the building of additional organizational and human resource capacities, and the alignment of different institutions and actors within the education ecosystem toward a common purpose and direction.

At the same time, however, organizations work within systems with many factors at play that influence the decisions of education leaders and schools. Thus, while curriculum goals may have broadened in the context of reforming national standards or curricula, narrower high-stakes assessments that gate the entrance to middle schools, high schools, or colleges may remain as additional motivators in charting the work of teachers and school leaders. In fact, schools may only be held accountable by their governments for their students' performance in traditional literacies like reading and math.

This tension between curriculum frameworks that have been broadened to encompass multidimensional and dynamic competencies, and assessment and accountability systems that remain two-dimensional and flat may explain why most of the examples of effective teaching and learning for the twenty-first century within public school systems that we studied involved the support of nongovernmental organizations (NGOs). These NGOs may help schools resolve that tension. Singapore and China remain the exception, with education systems centrally run by the district or national government, but in Chile, Colombia, Mexico, India, and the United States—even as curriculum frameworks broadened—schools, for the most part, remained captive to an emphasis on traditional literacies. In such contexts, we found that NGOs were able to step into the gap created between the aspirations stated in curriculum frameworks and the implementation not yet taking place in the majority of public school classrooms. Thus we argue in this book that where national curricula communicated a clear, broad vision for the goals of education, the independently run programs we studied emerged as important partners to traditional schools.

We also found that involving multiple stakeholders helped broaden the curricular goals. For example, as part of the process of updating the national curriculum in Mexico, policy makers initiated a national consultation to capture the perspectives of different stakeholders in education, including leaders of NGOs, parents, academics, teachers, and students enrolled in public schools. Thus, even as the UNETE foundation evolved from delivering computers to delivering curriculum material and pedagogical content to teach teamwork and collaboration, the fact that there was a broader curriculum framework already articulated at the national level helped UNETE more easily partner with local and state governments and schools.

Similarly, in Colombia, the Ministry of Education also promoted discussions among a range of stakeholders to identify the minimum citizenship competencies all students should develop. This process resulted in a set of national standards that shifted the content of the curricula from knowing facts alone, to knowing how to do and how to be, placing emphasis on the acquisition of skills and attitudes as well as knowledge, and in the formation of healthy relationships between and among teachers and students in schools. This relatively simple initiative enabled the development of many education programs that went beyond teaching basic skills, and the Ministry of Education itself compiled the best national and international programs and practices for schools to implement, including the program described in this book, EAU. Even in the United States, known for its local control of education systems and curricula, EL Education took advantage of a rare opportunity when the Common Core was introduced to the majority of states in the country. With Common Core's articulation of a common, broader set of educational goals, EL Education was able to construct an English language arts curriculum that was used by the state of New York and then downloaded by millions of users all over the country.

Similarly, the Indian 2005 curriculum reform involved inputs from hundreds of stakeholders. The country's broad aims for education as articulated in its curriculum framework reflected the interests of this broad consultation. Following the identification of these aims, the Indian NGO Dream-a-Dream explicitly saw itself as part of a larger vision to "build a society that models" well-being and in which people "respond to challenges with empathy and self-awareness" rather than with apathy, "violence, retribution, and anger."

Thus, the program explicitly focuses on building resilience in children from vulnerable backgrounds. As the staff of Dream-a-Dream began to build this vision, they realized that they needed teachers who could be expert problem solvers, be able to manage conflict, and exercise self-awareness, empathy, and creativity.

Singapore calls its teachers "nation builders" so the tight bond between the work of schools and the work of building a nation is already articulated in its learning framework. These broader learning needs also guide the leaders of LEP to emphasize teaching principals about "how to thrive in complex situations" and "to face and lead during times of change." Singapore's broader learning framework also aligns with the principals' job description to "formulate, communicate, and disseminate a clear mission and vision in order to bring about the desired learning outcomes for all students, including being clear in the purpose of education for the present and for the future." These principals recognize that "setting a clear direction helps the school develop a shared understanding of the task at hand," and the alignment between the framework, the work of teachers, and the leadership capacity of the principals produces an education system that is coherent in its purposes and practice.

In Chile, curriculum reform that took place in the late 1990s, 2003, and 2009 defined learning objectives that were transversal to different subjects, including citizenship, ethics, the relationship between people and their environments, and self-evaluation. In the domain of science education in particular, reforms emphasize critical, abstract, and hypothetical thinking, problem solving, and analysis, yet the failures in communication and lack of pedagogical knowledge resulted in limited impact. Programs like ECBI found their initial entrance into schools in this gap between aspirations and implementation. With government support, they were even successful in influencing the Ministry of Education to include an inquiry-based approach in science education. Under this broader set of curriculum guidelines that helped Chile transition from a dictatorship to a democracy, ECBI understands that inquiry-based learning is a critical pathway for students to become better citizens.

Much as these programs fit the content of their offering to a broader context, China's Qingyang District did the same in Chengdu, the economic hub of southwestern China. In its context, the school district appears to have a broader framework of prioritizing equity and creativity along with high academic performance. The district has a clear vision, mission, and values about equity and creativity, with a districtwide, systems-level infrastructure of processes and institutions aligned to these goals. For example, the schools within the district share ideas, information, and human resources with the goal of delivering equity and excellence in all of the schools. The district's Teacher Talent Center also encourages teachers to move among schools, particularly having effective teachers move from high-performing to low-performing schools. The authors of the chapter explain that the district officials, in this context, encourage innovation and support their school leaders with funding, policies, and mentorship.

Thus, a broader vision in curricular frameworks enables the NGOs in Chile, Colombia, India, Mexico, and the United States to identify gaps between aspirations and practice, and the school district in China and LEP in Singapore to align their programs to meet a wider range of aspirations. These high-level perspectives also propel government entities to collaborate with NGOs toward a common purpose, and they encourage different components and players within the education ecosystem to align themselves in a common direction and to work together. We suggest that further aligning the other components of the education system—such as high school exit examinations, university entrance requirements, and accountability measures for schools—may encourage schools to make the needed adjustments, so that they no longer have to deal with the multiple demands placed on them.

WHAT DOES PROFESSIONAL DEVELOPMENT LOOK LIKE IN THESE PROGRAMS?

Programs to develop the instructional capacities of teachers and the leadership capacities of school principals are key to effectively advancing such balanced or whole-child education for students. There are many similarities in how the various programs studied in this book go about this, which is surprising given the variation in the goals of each program.

To a large extent, the programs we studied are programs of professional development, but the activities the term "professional development" encompasses are much broader than what is conventionally understood. They support institutional, school, or system transformation, while also helping individual teachers develop skills. While they also aim to do the latter, this is as part of and on behalf of serving the former. All these programs support significant amounts of time for teachers and leaders in the schools to learn new knowledge and skills. None depend exclusively on short courses, but on extended opportunities for learning that span months and even years. The opportunities to support such adult learning include multiple approaches, such as exposure to visible routines, protocols, and instructional practices, where teachers see new forms of instruction or assessment in action, as well as coaching, and the study and discussion of concepts and theories that provide a foundation for the new practices.

Most of the programs engage multiple teachers in the same school in many of these various approaches, creating a "learning ecosystem" in schools that affords multiple teachers and staff opportunities for ongoing development over extended periods. The programs are also often supported by instructional resources for teachers and students, such as protocols, lesson plans, toolkits, frameworks, videos with demonstration lessons, or videos of sample pedagogies that help scale these programs with fidelity across a range of contexts. The LEP in Singapore, for example, relies on eleven different forms of development (called "learning vehicles"), which include a small learning community of peers (a syndicate), ongoing journaling, dialogue sessions with senior management in the Ministry of Education, interactive courses, mentoring, an action project, and visits to other countries and to business firms and organizations to study leadership in those settings.

Stemming from the goal of supporting institutional transformation, rather than individual development of teachers, in most of the programs, the target for professional development is not individuals but teams and groups in schools. The exceptions are the Dream-a-Dream program in India, which supports individual teachers in their personal development, and the LEP in Singapore. In the remaining programs, multiple people in the same school participate simultaneously in programs designed to help them learn together how to advance holistic education. Their learning takes place over extended periods of time, relying on multiple methodologies of learning, with much of it taking place in the school itself.

Holding the professional development in schools where it is directly related to the work of teachers recognizes professional learning as socially situated and responding to current needs of teachers and school leaders. There is a strong direct emphasis on supporting change in instructional practice. Even the LEP in Singapore, which pulls participants from their regular school contexts, creates a learning context that reflects a view of knowledge as socially constructed and situated. Participants work in small groups that become their learning communities during the program, and are also assigned to work in a host school, in which they must develop and implement a school transformation program.

In part, the comprehensive nature of the programs stems from the deep transformation they aim to support in teacher practice. For instance, the goal of the professional development offered by the inquiry-based science education program in Chile is to help teachers plan, adjust, and lead science lessons that are student centered, allowing students to participate in the scientific process of generating knowledge, a stark departure from traditional science education classes focused on teachers delivering knowledge of facts. To support the development of such capacities, the program brings advisers to schools who are themselves scientists (typically science graduate students), who work with teachers in planning and implementing the science program. The program is a systemic intervention encompassing curriculum, professional development, teaching resources, community support, and evaluation. The organization managing the program has learned from the teachers it has worked with, modifying the instructional units that the US National Science Resources Center developed into units aligned with the Chilean curriculum. The lesson plans support specific instructional routines designed to emulate the cycle of scientific experimentation, engaging students in team-based learning through the stages of developing a focus for inquiry, exploring, experimenting, analyzing, extrapolating, and applying. Facilitators in the program collaborate with teachers in planning lessons and leading them in the classroom. The collaboration between facilitators who have deep expertise in the sciences serves as a job-embedded source of professional development for the teachers, who tend to have a weak background in that subject.

The most all-encompassing program we studied, in terms of addressing entire teams, is the district-based initiative in the Qingyang District that targets the entire teaching staff of the district through a program delivered by the Qingyang Institute of Education Sciences. A four-stage career ladder, with clear guidelines and standards for each stage, defines the trajectory of professional development for each teacher. The stages are qualified, core, elite, and expert. Professional development is incentivized by promotions and pay increases. Novice teachers are assigned a mentor teacher whom they shadow for six months. Once assigned to a school, they are paired with an experienced teacher who serves as a mentor, and they participate in school-based training for the first three years of practice. An independent evaluation of the teacher determines whether he or she needs additional training at the Institute of Education Sciences. The Teacher Talent Center rotates teachers from high-performing schools to low-performing schools. Teachers are expected to rotate every six years. Such rotation achieves multiple goals; it is an opportunity for professional development for the teachers, while also bringing new ideas and practices from high- to low-performing schools. Intentional and frequent flow of people, ideas, and practices throughout the district are core elements to their capacity-building approach.

Reflecting the comprehensive approach of most of the Qingyang program, school principals also receive professional development. They are invited to form a school mission and receive mentorship and support. Principals participate in multiple districtwide networks for the discussion of school improvement efforts with peers. Young principals have the assignment of turning around failing schools and starting new schools in a context that encourages risk taking, experimentation, and distributed responsibility with teachers for improvement efforts.

One focus of the programs we studied is supporting teams, rather than individuals, in building their capacity for whole-child education. The focus is to help develop a shared vision of whole-child education among school staff and other stakeholders with influence in instruction and in the life of the school, so that there are synergies and alignment in the work that various teachers perform in their classrooms as well as with other activities that take place in the school. For example, in Colombia, the EAU follows a whole-school reform approach with professional development that includes school-based communities of learning, with the support of a local university in the partnership that operates the program. The program targets schools with a significant percentage of low-income children. Over 80 percent of the teachers must agree with the basic tenets to participate. All teachers must learn the principles and practices and adopt them in their classrooms. The program promotes student-centered learning by transforming the roles of teachers and students and fostering peer collaboration in small groups of students. The training and ongoing coaching is offered by a support team comprising master teachers from across the network of schools who also exchange good practices and discuss solutions to problems so they can be adopted as new practices within the network. In addition, teachers also visit schools that are further along in the adoption of the EAU model to observe instruction.

The various programs aim to build a new mind-set and a new way of thinking among school teams about what teaching and learning are, about what students can and should learn, and about what kinds of teaching and learning are desirable and possible. Following those new mind-sets about education are operational definitions of the intended goals that provide more tangible ways to understand and teach them. The mind-sets include a bias to taking action, taking risks, and learning from mistakes. For example, the LEP in Singapore helps future school principals cultivate the capacities to shape such mind-sets and school culture by emphasizing the development of visioning capacities and the capacity to lead collective learning as a social construction. Qinyang's district-based program of professional development encourages school leaders to experiment to provide all school staff opportunities for learning from experience.

While these programs use protocols, routines, and other tools to support enhanced pedagogical practices, they do not rely on scripts, but instead aim to build the professional expertise and judgment of teachers to deploy the most effective pedagogies in different contexts for particular purposes, sometimes adapting lessons and other resources developed outside the school to their students and their school context.

This emphasis on professionalism and development of teacher expertise is striking given that the countries we have studied differ in terms of the initial conditions of teaching quality. Some face high teacher shortages and have low levels of entry into the profession (India, Mexico, and United States), whereas others do not face shortages and have very high academic levels of entry (Singapore). Despite these differences, all the programs are aligned with a vision of teachers as professionals and experts who must decide how best to support their particular students and contexts, and aim to contribute to advancing that vision.

The programs also focus on helping teachers and leaders develop a range of capacities, which include conceptual and procedural knowledge of new domains of teaching or approaches to teaching, but also target emotional domains in ways that activate intrinsic motivation to learn new approaches and to persevere in pursuing new ways to teach. In EAU, for example, the purpose of professional development is to support teachers in gaining meta-cognitive and socio-emotional skills to shift their role from lecturers to facilitators who can support student-centered learning. The professional development program offered by Dream-a-Dream helps teachers cultivate life skills, on the assumption that this will equip them to help their students cultivate the same skills.

Most of the programs rely on a model of adult learning that involves a cycle of reflection and action that covers examination of new ideas, application, evaluation, and then reexamination of those ideas. To support the development of such reflective capacities, the programs depend on coaches who provide personalized feedback to teachers as they adopt new practices. They aim to institutionalize the practices that support these cycles in schools in ways that transform the culture of schools, turning them into learning organizations that foster continuous learning among staff. In Singapore, for instance, the LEP uses journaling and participation in a small learning community (the syndicate) as key learning vehicles to help future school principals develop reflective skills. In India, Dream-a-Dream delivers programs in which an important component is the creation of opportunities for reflection in which teachers are given information on their students' life skills as measured by a scale developed for the program.

To transform the culture of the school, the programs rely on a mix of opportunities for learning situated in the context of the schools where teachers work, through coaching and professional development communities within those schools, along with opportunities that engage teachers in conversations with colleagues in different schools and with colleagues who have different roles, in addition to classroom teaching.

These programs demonstrate a capacity to learn and adjust their content as a result of what they learn from working with teachers in schools. For example, UNETE, in Mexico, evolved from distributing computers to students to include a professional development program for teachers, assisted by technology. Central to this evolution of its core theory of change was a capacity to learn from the teachers the organization was working with. In this way, UNETE shifted its intervention to creating a learning ecosystem for schools, which includes the design and dissemination of curated pedagogical content, the organization of teacher networks online, and coaching in schools, in addition to providing technology and Internet access to schools. The goal of this ecosystem is to support the development of more effective instructional practices that engage students and help them develop twenty-first-century skills. UNETE's model involves embedding a facilitator in each school who oversees the creation of professional development systems. The facilitator works with education supervisors from the local education authority to develop a strategy of school improvement that uses technology. Facilitators are part of networks of other facilitators who communicate online, sharing challenges and exchanging support and resources. Facilitators instruct and coach teachers in using computers and educational applications, in developing instructional practices related to using technology to implement the curriculum, and in working with students in activities that support the development of competencies such as arts appreciation and other noncore curriculum. In addition to facilitators' support, participation in an online community gives teachers an opportunity for professional development. Here, teachers can access digital education resources, tools to develop lesson plans, lesson plans developed by other teachers, and curated websites.

Some of the programs help teachers develop specific capacities to personalize instruction. To the extent that all give teachers capacities to decide how best to teach their own students, they aim for a form of contextualization that allows for personalization, in the sense that they aim to cultivate teachers' capacities to meet the unique needs of their students, as members of a class who may have unique needs, if not as individuals in a class who may learn at different rates, in different ways and with different interests. For instance, the inquiry-based science education program in Chile, while drawing initially on lessons developed by scientists, recognizes the importance of engaging teachers in adapting such lessons to their students and classrooms. In addition, the reliance on student-led, peer-based experiments inherently allows for personalization in that smaller groups are more likely to be able to accommodate personal interests and learning rhythms than whole-class teacher-centered instruction.

Some programs afford teachers opportunities to personalize to specific students within their classrooms. For example, EAU organizes instruction in small groups that work with self-study guides, allowing each student to progress at her or his own pace and, to some extent, pursue her or his own interests. Similarly, UNETE helps teachers develop the capacities to motivate individual students, engaging them in student-centered learning activities. The professional development and modeling offered by the facilitators embedded in the schools and the access to the curated digital learning objects, lesson plans, and professional communities provided by the online platforms are two specific ways in which the program seeks to support personalized instruction. Even the Dream-a-Dream program, with its focus on personal transformation and development of capacities among teachers, supports teachers' skills to help students develop the same skills, an inherently personalized activity. Similarly, extensive feedback and coaching in the Qingyang program develops the capacities of teachers to personalize instruction.

All the programs examined in this book give the teachers they are supporting a voice in shaping such development programs. In this way, they tap the tacit knowledge of teachers as practitioners to make their knowledge visible to others. The programs are also grounded in the teachers' needs and in their views about their students' needs, and cultivate teacher professionalism in ways that activate intrinsic motivation and habits of lifelong learning. In many of the programs, teachers themselves serve as facilitators of the professional communities in their schools or participate in networks of teachers within and across schools in ways that allow them to be learners as well as teachers.

EL Education, ECBI, and EAU systemically distinguish between different skill levels of teachers, giving mentor teachers the responsibility to introduce other teachers to pedagogical models and curricula. ECBI, for example, distinguishes among participants' three different levels: beginner, intermediate, and competent. Within each school, EAU recognizes one outstanding teacher as a leader with credibility within the institution; the teacher becomes a member of the support team, together with similar teachers from other EAU schools. Dream-a-Dream supports the personal development of teachers so that it helps them reframe their role. This process is highly attuned to the personal needs and stage of development of each teacher. By developing part of the professional development around the needs teachers identify, and by creating online learning communities in which teachers select the resources that interest them and discuss those resources with their peers, UNETE similarly provides opportunities for teacher voice in professional development efforts.

CHANGING SCHOOL AND ORGANIZATIONAL CULTURES FOR TEACHING AND LEARNING IN THE TWENTY-FIRST CENTURY

In order to prepare teachers to lead twenty-first-century instruction, the programs support them in developing twenty-first-century competencies themselves. These competencies are distinctly different from those that focus solely on cognition in that they also embrace social and emotional competencies. To this end, many of the skills encompass learning how to relate to one another, including how to give and receive honest feedback, take risks, and create new projects. As the school coordinator of one EAU school notes, "We have mental structures that are historically and culturally constructed, rooted and ingrained . . . [and] historically teachers are a community that comes from those processes and so we teach students to repeat and to memorize." Similarly, the authors of the chapter on Dream-a-Dream note that in India, teachers and school principals reflect an existing "hierarchical and authoritarian mind-set that is antithetical to twenty-first-century learning," and that working in such a context requires the organization to adopt the explicit goal of "preparing a completely new set of teachers and school leaders with different mind-sets." Similarly, staff members of EL Education in the United States note that they want to teach students to not just fit into the existing society but build a better world. Chile's ECBI sees itself not just as an organization that teaches science, but one that produces better citizens through its practice of inquiry-based learning and lens of scientific thinking. Thus, for these organizations, learning and teaching need to encompass transforming systems of beliefs and behaviors, and many of the programs focus explicitly on promoting a school and organizational culture in which the broader range of twenty-first-century competencies can be both taught and captured.

Capacity building for many of the programs is not about quick fixes or checking off the acquisition of a list of competencies. Rather, capacity building is rooted in deliberately co-created structures, processes, and relationships that facilitate the development of twenty-first-century competencies in students and in teachers. Thus, fostering particular organizational cultures that ask people to develop a mind-set as well as mechanistic shifts is part and parcel of helping individuals engage in the kind of long-term engagement needed for transformation.

Dream-a-Dream in India, for example, notes that it operates on the "values of accountability, trust, and dignity to create empowered individuals within the organization and in the community as positive role models," and not just people who are competent at transferring discrete skills to young people. Dream-a-Dream aims to develop "new visions and new frameworks for learning."

Many of the organizations we studied note that there is a need to "focus on people, relationships, and learning, rather than on structures and conformance," as our colleagues in Singapore observe in their chapter. They observe that the leaders of the LEP believe in equipping their principals with not only twenty-first-century competencies but also twenty-first-century mind-sets. They recognize that "not only [must] teachers teach these competencies and skills, but principals and teachers also must model the 'knowledge, skills, and disposition their students are to acquire.'"[2] Thus, all the programs we studied ask teachers to model the same set of competencies they encourage them to teach to their students.

With the emphasis on cultures and modeling behavior, it makes sense that many of the programs see schools as the hub of their practice and see themselves as rooted in schools. At UNETE, EL Education, EAU, and the Qingyang District program, professional development, coaching, model lessons, and feedback are all delivered at the school level. While these programs ground themselves in key principles, they also remain flexible, and school communities are encouraged to own the programs and adapt them to the local context and needs. As the CEO of UNETE observed, the organization learned quickly, early in its pilot stage, that "if you arrive [in] schools with an inflexible model, where teachers have to follow exactly what you say in order to get some results, the implementation will fail . . . [and] instead of being helpful, you become a burden; it won't work." Thus, while programs have a core series of activities, they allow for variation and customization in different schools. And the authors of the various chapters note that these decisions are at variance with traditional school reform efforts, where school communities are often not consulted or included in decisions.

Further, with the schools being central to their practice, many of the programs—UNETE, Singapore's LEP, the Qingyang District, ECBI, and EL Education—see the commitment of school principals as critical to their programs' success, given that principals can set the vision for the school, lead the staff, establish expectations, and influence the school culture. Singapore's preparation program for aspiring principals focuses on giving the time and means for participants to build good relationships and to be adaptable, flexible, and fluid in their practice, rather than being rigid or programmatic. Further, the Singapore LEP sees itself as developing people, not just roles, and explicitly states that one of the principals' roles is to steer the school's "culture, pedagogical climate . . . to meet the mission and vision of a school."[3] They see teachers and principals as facilitators, coaches, and guardians of school culture.

While principals may be key in changing and influencing school culture, it appears that for Mexico's UNETE, the introduction of new technology and equipment may also lead to openness in trying new pedagogical models and tools. UNETE offers a suite of not just hardware and software, but also pedagogical content, opportunities for teachers to receive training, and a virtual network of like-minded peers to help teachers learn new practices.

At the same time, UNETE and other programs recognize the fine balance between helping schools make changes deemed significant enough to be cultural changes and respecting schools' and teachers' autonomy and self-direction. The programs recognize that meaningful change occurs only when actors are able to own and direct the change themselves, even as the organizations provide the necessary guidance to make the changes when school leaders, teachers, and staff want it. Thus, UNETE, EL Education, and EAU have a selection process that asks the schools to consent to participating in the program; they have learned from experience that they cannot effectively impose or force change.

For EAU, democratic and participatory structures and processes of interaction among their community members are at the core of its work, which create not only a sense of ownership for program participants but also "a culture of engagement and leadership," as the authors of the chapter note. For EAU, the whole-school approach necessarily engenders the result in which every teacher in every grade and classroom uses pedagogy, curriculum, and assessments designed to promote students' learning, participation, and autonomy. EAU requires that more than 80 percent of teachers in a particular school agree with the principles and foundation of EAU before EAU's partners agree to fund the program at a school. It believes that "every member of the school community needs to actively take part in the implementation of the model." Teachers meet with experts weekly to study theories about how people learn, share best practices, and brainstorm solutions to problems together. EAU also seeks a fundamental change in the teachers' roles in how they relate to their students, from lecturers to consultants who promote students' active learning, participation, and autonomy. EAU explicitly asks teachers to "share power and to support and trust students in the process of coordinating, planning, executing, and evaluating their own learning activities," which indicates a profound change in the culture of the classroom and the school. EAU staff members know that in a country and context that has been affected by war, exclusion, and inequality, teachers need to support students in developing constructive values and ways of living together and that school culture plays a powerful role in cultivating attitudes and competencies. Its programs include children who have disabilities and other differences as part of the curriculum.

Dream-a-Dream's organizational cultural shift includes a change from a founder-driven organization to a more empowering people-driven learning organization. The staff reorganized their program to make empowerment a greater focus in its organizational culture. Meanwhile, Qingyang District emphasizes a "culture of collaboration," with "democratic governance" that invites teachers and parents into school decisions.

In ECBI (Chile), teachers learn to interact differently with their students, as children play "the leading role in the learning process." The program wants to transfer the knowledge and the experience of science as "a result of social processes, subject to continuous revision and change." Thus, a culture of embracing change often develops that emphasizes continual reflection and revision, with the aid of engaging in regular assessment practices, such as in EL Education and the Qingyang District, and that process is emphasized over content in many cases.

In these organizations, collaboration is part of the operational culture; they recognize practitioners as having expert knowledge that others simply do not have. Principals play a key role, as do mentor teachers and coaches in ECBI, EL Education, Qingyang District, and UNETE. Specifically, UNETE recognized the need for technical support and specialized knowledge that is separate from but also linked to pedagogical knowledge, as did ECBI and EL Education. Singapore also knows that a high level of complexity is involved in leading schools in the present to prepare for the future. Thus it grounds its principal development program in complexity theory, "a theory of change, development and evolution that emphasizes . . . features of nonlinearity, dynamism, and unpredictability." In addition, it recognizes that "knowledge is . . . something that people perform together, rather than a possession in people's heads," and note that "from the perspective of the social constructivism paradigm, knowledge is social, consensual interpretation of . . . reality" and knowledge itself is a co-construction by the group, through interaction and complex response processes.[4]

ASSESSING PEOPLE, ORGANIZATIONS, AND PRACTICES FOR CONTINUOUS LEARNING AND IMPROVEMENT

Many countries and education systems are emerging from an era in which summative assessments have dominated as accountability measures for teachers, schools, and education systems. For the organizations we studied, these more traditional measures of student achievement remain part of the work. Singapore's principals know, for example, that encouraging their staff and students to excel in traditional academic measures is part of their job, even as they are encouraging them to learn a broader set of competencies.

However, even as they live in this tension, most of the organizations we studied have a practitioners' understanding of the role of assessment in helping them improve the quality of their programs. Rather than using only summative assessments for the purposes of accountability, they regularly incorporate initial and formative assessments at the individual and organizational levels to improve their practice. Assessments, to them, are more often the means to an end, rather than the end. For example, in holding to their hypothesis that life-skills training enables children from vulnerable backgrounds to overcome adversity, Dream-a-Dream in India invested in tools and data systems to provide a continual stream of evidence that this theory translates into good practice and to help guide better practice. Similarly, the Qingyang District not only gathers data from its schools but also contracts with third-party evaluators to assess the district's performance. It also encourages teachers and parents in the district to give more qualitative feedback to school principals. Based on this continual stream of formative feedback, if a school does not meet the district's expectations, it will receive more resources to help it improve. Similarly, for ECBI, UNETE, EL Education, and EAU, a key role of the advisers, facilitators, and coaches who work in and with schools is to give teachers feedback to improve their practice, based on personal trust and respect.

Several of the programs also assess the competencies of their personnel and their participants to determine whether candidates have the requisite skills and to help their staff and participants in their professional development. Dream-a-Dream, for example, developed a special assessment tool. UNETE facilitators in the schools are usually graduates of a teachers' college, and the selection process includes interviews and observations of candidates' social and interpersonal skills. Qingyang District involves third-party evaluators to conduct surveys on parent and teacher satisfaction, along with teacher evaluations and measures each school's performance on various criteria.

From the beginning, the organizations assess the readiness of schools to take part in their programs, gauging organizations in terms of the level of interest, motivation of teachers and school leaders to participate, and whether the mechanisms of management would allow the schools to participate with a degree of freedom and autonomy. UNETE, for example, asks schools to opt in rather than have the government mandate its programs. ECBI program coordinators and monitors also negotiate with the authorities and school principals some conditions to implement the program at the school level, such as teachers' time to participate in weekly planning and training sessions.

Assessments are also inextricably linked to these organizations' efforts to learn and improve their own practice. UNETE facilitators conduct an assessment of the schools' condition, before designing a plan and organizing activities for the academic year. It determines learning objectives based on these school reports. For many, including EAU, assessment is part of an effective mechanism for feedback and innovation, and there is a great emphasis on conducting and gathering formative assessments. In many cases, rather than a special endeavor, the assessments are part of the organizational culture and are important tools in learning and strategizing. Indeed, in Qingyang District, ECBI, EL Education, UNETE, and Dream-a-Dream, assessment plays a role in giving and receiving feedback. While they are not yet part of a systemic effort to evaluate the organization's performance, assessment is regularly practiced.

Organizations combine different evaluations, including existing assessments of traditional competencies, along with other kinds of assessments. UNETE, for example, took part not only in assessing academic competencies in a national examination administered by the federal government, but also in different evaluations, including surveys of student perception and assessment of digital skills, motivation, and noncognitive skills. In addition, pilot studies helped it to improve its intervention activities and organizational model. Monitoring at the school level is very important in all the programs, including ECBI, EL Education, Qingyang District, and UNETE. UNETE routinely listens to the qualitative feedback offered by facilitators and the schools themselves on how its program is received and perceived. EL Education has articulated its aims in multiple rubrics and documents that help schools to assess themselves and commissioned several independent studies to study the impact of its work on measures of student performance.

Self-assessment and self-reflection are key components of EAU, LEP, EL Education, Dream-a-Dream, and UNETE, where individuals have time to reflect and set goals. In Singapore, the LEP directly makes space for principals to become "clear about their own personal purpose of being in education" and opportunities to clarify their values and vision. EAU programs include self- and peer-assessment charts. EAU also uses a system of evaluation that corresponds to the policies of the National Ministry of Education but gives more weight to the part that asks students to evaluate themselves and where they can monitor their own progress, accomplishments, and behaviors. It encourages teachers to get to know their students as part of the evaluation process, with their different strengths and weaknesses. For example, Dream-a-Dream notes that "if learning is to persist, learners have to be systematically supported to look inward," reflecting "critically on their own current state-of-mind and behavior, [and] identify the ways they often inadvertently contribute to the education problem, and then see how their behavior can be change." Many EL Education schools, in their practice of student discipline, encourage students to engage in self-reflection to articulate why they had misbehaved and how they might do better in the future. EL Education schools also create advisories in schools that help students engage in reflection exercises in small groups, with an adult adviser to guide them.

RELATIONSHIP WITH THE POLICY ENVIRONMENT

All the programs negotiate their role and support to the school with the larger policy environment, especially in how it supports and makes demands of schools and it how it enables institution building and the continuity of the programs. Only in China and Singapore is there very good alignment and support from the larger policy environment over extended periods. Qing-yang District, for example, illustrates an approach to whole-district human resource development, which is itself the policy of the district. In this case, there is seamless alignment between the expectations of policy and the work of the organization supporting professional development, with occasional adjustments to the policy as the implementation of the policy creates opportunities for learning. Singapore's LEP for future principals is another case of good fit between policy and professional development.

One way in which the larger policy environment supports the type of deep professional development discussed in this book is through the continuity in leadership and institutional life that enables continuous improvement and refinement of the underlying program theory of how to best support teachers. In China and Singapore, such support for long-term sustainability results from the state's commitment to education institutions. In Chengdu, continuous support for an experimental school established in 1918 by followers of John Dewey has made it an incubator for pedagogical innovation and for talent to work in the district. In Singapore, support for the National Institute of Education, the sole institution that prepares teachers and school leaders, and stability in its staff and leadership, provides this organization the room to take risks, experiment, and learn from experience.

In the remaining countries, in contrast, the short-term policy cycles undermine the continuity of the programs' efforts. In those cases, the NGOs and private stakeholders provide the necessary support to stay the course over time, serving as a buffer to the disruptions caused by policy discontinuities to school-based efforts.

The remaining programs all involve NGOs and thus represent more loosely coupled systems with government policy, which is enacted in short cycles. Among these, Colombia is an exception in that there has been considerable continuity in government's focus on citizenship education expressed in the national curriculum standards. The work of EAU benefits greatly from this government's emphasis on whole-child education, particularly on the development of citizenship skills, and their inclusion in the national standards, the development of approaches to measure them, and the many efforts to identify and disseminate programs and practices in this area. This, in addition to the long history of Escuela Nueva, the predecessor program of EAU, contributes to a very stable policy environment and great coherence in the program approaches.

In contrast to the policy alignment and continuity observed in China, Singapore, and Colombia, programs in Chile, India, Mexico, and the United States had to reconcile the demands that policy and accountability frameworks make in schools with their own focus for improvement. In Chile, the inquiry-based science education program is to some extent at odds with the focus of the national assessment systems that stresses knowledge, rather than on the competencies developed by this program. UNETE and EL Education faced similar challenges. In all these cases, the organizations developed coordinating mechanisms with government policy, not only to receive authorization to work in schools, but also to access public resources and to support the schools in meeting accountability requirements, even as they also sought to advance their own program goals.

THE ROLE OF PARTNERSHIPS AND RELATIONSHIPS IN THE LARGER EDUCATION ECOSYSTEM

We found that the programs studied depend on funds, people, and resources beyond those typically available to public schools. They also require additional expertise to implement a transformation in teaching and learning, including knowledge gleaned from universities. There are economies of scale in developing approaches and supports for instructional improvement, as well as benefits to working on a scale greater than a single school, such as across networks of schools and organizations to identify best practices from a range of teachers and schools, rather than from within a single school. All these initiatives require multiple partners and the resources to coordinate and direct their efforts.

In addition to their relationship with government and with the policy environment, a critical feature of the programs is that they all deployed resources external to the school to support efforts of school transformation. In Chile, for instance, a university and the scientific community were mobilized to support teacher development. In Colombia, the government and a foundation provided the financial resources to support professional development, and a university provided the human resources to guide the program. In India,

Mexico, and the United States, independent organizations supported teachers and schools.

Thus, we found that effective curricular change is difficult for schools to incorporate by themselves. Simply put, partnerships allow the organizations to address challenges that they cannot overcome by themselves. Because the demands of creating and sustaining an effective curriculum, pedagogical practice, and professional development relevant to the twenty-first century are so taxing, often collaborative partners have to provide support. For example, all the organizations used knowledge produced in universities to inform their practice: Singapore's program is run by the National Institute of Education at the Nanyang Technological University. ECBI's partnership with the Chilean university system was instrumental in building its credibility and knowledge base. EAU's partnership with universities occurs on several fronts, including extending the years of learning for its program participants through technical programs offered by several universities, and in the academic partnership with CINDE. EL Education was started with input from the Harvard Graduate School of Education, and it continues to draw on the best research about education to inform its work. Dream-a-Dream partnered with university-based researchers to develop new assessment tools. UNETE commissioned research evaluations from universities.

In many of the programs, close collaboration across different sectors appears to be part of the design of the program. For example, ECBI began in collaboration with national and international networks of scientists and science academies, including institutions from the United States, France, Mexico, Brazil, and Colombia. High-quality materials, training for the leadership team, collaboration in strategic planning workshops, and participation in international conferences helped start the program. For Singapore's LEP, the program designers drew on leading global thinkers of the education community such as Thomas J. Sergiovanni and Howard Gardner. Similarly, for Dream-a-Dream in India, international, national, organizational, and personal networks informed its program design and strategies for scaling. EL Education also takes the findings from the best education research literature and translates them into language and format more easily digestible for practitioners; it also identifies "mentor" schools that other schools in the network are encouraged to visit and hosts regular workshops and an annual national conference where network members share best practices and build community.

For many of the programs, even the content of the curriculum and pedagogy came from collaboration. UNETE has worked with academic and public institutions to develop teacher training programs, reaching about twenty-five thousand thus far, either in person or remotely. Similarly, in Colombia, a public-private-academic partnership is core to the operation and success of EAU in how they provide teachers, principals, and schools with the ongoing curricular, pedagogical, and relational supports they need to teach twenty-first-century competencies to students. For Chile's ECBI, curriculum, professional development, teaching material, community support, and evaluation all became critical components of the program, and like UNETE, they organically created an ecosystem to support positive changes in classroom practice. Experts in science education, a scientist, a teacher, and his or her class design the lesson plan, before being adopted. They understood from research that solely relying on teacher training programs or the distribution of new teaching materials does little to change pedagogical practice, so they deliberately created a more holistic, classroom- and school-based partnership approach. The authors of the ECBI chapter also emphasize that, while ECBI borrowed critical knowledge from other countries to ground its program, it adjusted the curriculum to fit the local context.

Partnerships are particularly critical to the sustainability of the programs. In Colombia, partnership was critical in developing EAU, as the Ministry of Education at the city level cofunds the program with the Luker Foundation and sustains the implementation of the program in the schools. Such partnerships inoculate the program against corruption and even the vagaries of politics and politicians, and provide additional resources that these schools otherwise would not be able to obtain. These cross-institution or cross-sector partnerships enable the programs studied to reach beyond the usual short funding and policy cycles that dominate the public sector, such as five changes in administration over the course of twelve years.

The authors of the chapter about Mexico's UNETE note that program sustainability is inextricably tied to external stakeholders' support. The authors go as far to argue that "any initiative aimed to insert the development of twenty-first-century skills in public schools as one of its educational goals may benefit from designing a plan to create a network of external supporters." The writers of the chapter on ECBI argue that the collaborative partnership between scientists and educators, and particularly the prestigious status of the scientists leading ECBI, helped the program obtain the necessary political and financial support from the Ministry of Education.

Personal interactions are critical to the transfer of knowledge within networks. For example, one goal of ECBI is to close the distance between scientists and teachers, engaging "scientists and science graduates in regular collaboration with science teachers." It also wants to close the "tremendous social distance between students—especially in low-income communities—and scientists." Thus, its program design was built on partnership from the beginning. In Singapore, prospective principals are connected with their peers during their program, becoming part of a "strong fraternity of other emerging school leaders." Meanwhile, in the Qingyang District, schools use clusters to share pedagogy and teacher training; partnerships encourage high-performing schools to share their teachers and administrators to help improve a lower-performing school, and friendship alliances encourage schools to share resources and expertise.

Collaboration with ministries of education can assist in scaling good practice and in providing necessary structural support to programs. For example, in Mexico, the collaboration with the Ministry of Education began when UNETE started distributing computers to the poorest public schools and then built a broad network of supporters to achieve its goals, including industry leaders like Dell, PepsiCo, Ford, Nissan, Hewlett-Packard, Microsoft, Sempra Energy, Deutsche Bank, foundations in the United States and in Mexico, and local governments, signing agreements with thirteen out of thirty-two state governments. Similarly, EL Education owes its existence and first attempts at scale to a federal government–initiated grant application process that it won; similarly, the Common Core endeavor assisted it in funding the effort to codify its pedagogical practice and develop a curriculum that has since been downloaded millions of times. For ECBI, as a result of the collaboration with the Ministry of Education, the program was able to scale nationally. The collaboration led to the creation of a network of universities that implemented the program across the country, and "scientific thinking skills" were incorporated as an axis of the national science curriculum for grades 1 through 8.

Notes

Chapter 1

1. Erik Brynjolfsson and Andrew McAfee, *Race Against the Machine* (Lexington, MA: Digital Frontier Press, 2011).
2. Fernando M. Reimers and Connie K. Chung, *Teaching and Learning for the Twenty-First Century: Educational Goals, Policies, and Curricula from Six Nations* (Cambridge, MA: Harvard Education Press, 2016).
3. J. Hilton and M. Hilton, eds., *Education for Life and Work: Developing Transferable Knowledge and Skills in the 21st Century* (Washington, DC: National Research Council, 2012).
4. World Economic Forum, *New Vision for Education: Unlocking the Potential of Technology* (British Columbia Teachers' Federation, 2015).
5. David Deming, "The Growing Importance of Social Skills in the Labor Market," National Bureau of Economic Research, Working Paper 21473 (2017).
6. Michael Fullan, Joanne Quinn, and Joanne McEachen, *Deep Learning: Engage the World Change the World* (Thousand Oaks, CA: Corwin Press, 2017), viii.
7. Dennis Shirley, *The New Imperatives of Educational Change. Achievement with Integrity* (New York: Routledge, 2016), 5.
8. John B. Carroll, "A model of school learning," *Teachers College Record* 64 (1963): 723–33; John B. Carroll, "The Carroll Model: A 25-Year Retrospective and Prospective View," *Educational Researcher* 18, no. 1 (1989): 26–31.
9. Jaap Scheerens, *Improving school effectiveness* (Paris: UNESCO, International Institute for Educational Planning, 2000).
10. Michael Barber and Mona Mourshed, *How the world's best-performing schools systems come out on top* (London: McKinsey & Company, 2007).
11. Andy Hargreaves and Dennis L. Shirley, *The Global Fourth Way: The Quest for Educational Excellence* (Thousand Oaks, CA: Corwin Press, 2012), xiv.
12. National Conference of State Legislatures, *No Time to Lose: How to Build a World-Class Education System State by State* (2016).
13. Ibid., 10.
14. Marc Tucker, "9 Building Blocks for a World-Class Education System" (Washington, DC: National Center on Education and the Economy, 2016).
15. Ibid., 7–13.
16. Linda Darling-Hammond and Peter Youngs, "Defining 'highly qualified teachers': What does 'scientifically-based research' tell us?," *Educational Researcher* 31, no. 9 (2002): 13–25.
17. Andy Hargreaves and Michael Fullan, *Professional Capital: Transforming Teaching in Every School* (New York: Teachers College Press, 2012).
18. Williamson Evers and Herbert J. Walberg, eds., *Testing Student Learning, Evaluating Teaching Effectiveness* (Stanford, CA: Hoover Institution Press, Stanford University, 2004);

Daniel Muijs, "Measuring teacher effectiveness: Some methodological reflections," *Educational Research & Evaluation* 12, no. 1 (2006): 53–74.

19. Hari Krzywacki, Jari Lavonen, and Kalle Juuti, "There are No Effective Teachers in Finland—Only Effective Systems and Professional Teachers," in *Teacher Effectiveness: Capacity Building in a Complex Learning Era*, ed. Tan Oon-Seng and Woon-Chia Liu (Singapore: Centage Learning, 2014).

20. Hannele Niemi, Auli Toom, and Arto Kallioniemi, eds., *Miracle of Education: The Principles and Practices of Teaching and Learning in Finnish schools* (Rotterdam: Sense Publishers, 2012); Jari Lavonen, "Building Blocks for High Quality Science Education: Reflections based on Finnish Experiences," *LUMAT* 1, no. 3 (2013): 299–313.

21. Lee S. Shulman, "Toward a pedagogy of cases," *Case methods in teacher education* 1 (1992): 33.

22. Eleonora Villegas-Reimers, *Teacher professional development: an international review of the literature* (Paris: International Institute for Educational Planning, 2003).

23. Ibid., 39–40.

24. Fernando M. Reimers et al., "Connecting the dots to build the future teaching and learning" (Varkey Foundation, 2016).

25. Andy Jacob and Kate McGovern, "The Mirage: Confronting the Hard Truth about Our Quest for Teacher Development," The New Teacher Project, 2015.

26. P. Cordingley, S. Higgins, T. Greany, N. Buckler, D. Coles-Jordan, B. Crisp, L. Saunders, and R. Coe, "Developing great teaching: lessons from the international reviews into effective professional development," Project Report. Teacher Development Trust, London, 2015, http://dro.dur.ac.uk/15834/.

27. Villegas-Reimers, *Teacher professional development: an international review of the literature*; John Schwille, Martial Dembélé, and Jane Schubert, "Global Perspectives on Teacher Learning: Improving Policy and Practice," International Institute for Educational Planning (IIEP) UNESCO, 2007.

28. Linda Darling-Hammond et al., *Empowered Educators: How High-Performing Systems Shape Teaching Quality Around the World* (San Francisco: Jossey-Bass, 2017), 3.

29. Ibid., 13.

30. Carol Campbell et al., *The State of Educators' Professional Learning in Canada: Final Research Report* (Oxford, OH: Learning Forward, 2017).

31. Ibid., 8.

32. Ibid., 11.

33. Organisation for Economic Co-operation and Development, *TALIS 2013 results: An international perspective on teaching and learning* (Paris: OECD, 2014).

34. Christopher Day and Qing Gu, "Variations in the conditions for teachers' professional learning and development: sustaining commitment and effectiveness over a career," *Oxford Review of Education* 33, no. 4 (2007): 423–43.

35. Jonathan Supovitz, "Can high stakes testing leverage educational improvement? Prospects from the last decade of testing and accountability reform," *Journal of Educational Change* 10, no. 2-3 (2009): 211–27.

36. Kirabo Jackson and Elias Bruegmann, "Teaching students and teaching each other: The importance of peer learning for teachers," *American Economic Journal: Applied Economics* 1, no. 4 (2009): 85–108; Matthew A. Kraft and John P. Papay, "Can Professional

Environments in Schools Promote Teacher Development? Explaining Heterogeneity in Returns to Teaching Experience," *Educational Evaluation and Policy Analysis* 36, no. 4 (2014): 476–500.

37. Matthew Ronfeldt, "Where should student teachers learn to teach? Effects of field placement school characteristics on teacher retention and effectiveness," *Educational Evaluation and Policy Analysis* 34, no. 1 (2012): 3–26.

38. Susana Loeb, Demetra Kalogrides, and Tara Béteille, "Effective schools: Teacher hiring, assignment, development, and retention," *Education Finance and Policy* 7, no. 3 (2012): 269–304.

39. Etienne Wenger, *Communities of Practice: Learning, Meaning and Identity* (New York: Cambridge University Press, 1998); Marilyn Cochran-Smith and Susan Lytle, "Communities for teacher research: Fringe or Forefront?," *American Journal of Education* 100, no. 3 (1992): 298–324; Rebecca B. DuFour, Richard DuFour, and Robert E. Eaker, *Professional Learning Communities at Work: Plan Book* (Bloomington, IN: Solution Tree, 2006); Ann Lieberman and Diane Wood, *Inside the National Writing Project: Connecting Network Learning and Classroom Teaching* (New York: Teachers College Press, 2003); Milbrey W. McLaughlin and Joan E. Talbert, *Contexts that Matter for Teaching and Learning* (Stanford, CA: Context Center for Teaching and Learning in Secondary Schools, 1993).

40. Andy Hargreaves and Michael T. O'Connor, *Collaborative Professionalism*, World Innovation Summit for Education, 2017, vi.

41. Organisation for Economic Co-operation and Development (OECD), "PISA 2015 results in focus," 2016; Organisation for Economic Co-operation and Development (OECD), "PISA Results in focus," 2012.

Chapter 2

Funding from PIA-CONICYT Basal Funds for Centers of Excellence Project FB0003 is gratefully acknowledged.

1. ECBI is the Spanish acronym for *Educación en Ciencias Basada en la Indagación*, the program's name. Throughout this chapter, ECBI refers to the program's name, while IBSE is the inquiry-based pedagogical approach to science education.

2. Cristián Bellei and Liliana Morawietz, "Strong Content, Weak Tools. Twenty-First-Century Competencies in the Chilean Educational Reform," in *Teaching and Learning for the Twenty-First Century: Educational Goals, Policies, and Curricula from Six Nations*, eds. Fernando M. Reimers and Connie Chung (Cambridge, MA: Harvard Education Press, 2016), 93–126.

3. Cristián Bellei and Xavier Vanni, "Chile: The Evolution of Educational Policy, 1980-2014," in *Education in South America*, ed. Simon Schwartzman (London: Bloomsbury, 2015), 179–200.

4. National Research Council, *Education for Life and Work: Developing Transferable Knowledge and Skills in the 21st Century*, eds. James W. Pellegrino and Margaret L. Hilton (Washington, DC: National Academies Press Research Council, 2012).

5. Bellei and Morawietz, "Strong Content."

6. Loreto Egaña et al., *Reforma Educativa y Objetivos Fundamentales Transversales. Los Dilemas de la Innovación* (Santiago: Programa Interdisciplinario de Investigación en Educación, 2003); Cristián Bellei, "¿Ha tenido impacto la Reforma Educativa Chilena?," in

Políticas Educacionales en el Cambio de Siglo, ed. Cristian Cox (Santiago: Editorial Universitaria, 2003), 125–209.

7. Michael O. Martin, *TIMSS 1999 International Science Report. Findings from IEA's Repeat of the Third International Mathematics and Science Study at the Eighth Grade* (Chestnut Hill, MA: Boston College, 2000).

8. Bellei and Morawietz, "Strong Content."

9. Ibid.

10. Hernán Cofré et al, "La Educación Científica en Chile: Debilidades de la Enseñanza y Futuros Desafíos de la Educación de Profesores de Ciencia," en *Estudios Pedagógicos* 36, no. 2 (2019): 279–93; Hernán Cofre, ed., *Cómo Mejorar la Enseñanza de las Ciencias en Chile. Perspectivas Internacionales y Desafíos Nacionales* (Santiago: Ediciones Universidad Católica Raúl Silva Henríquez, 2010); Egaña, *Reforma Educativa*.

11. Cofre, ed., *Cómo Mejorar*.

12. OECD, *PISA 2015 Results (Volume II): Policies and Practices for Successful Schools* (Paris: OECD Publishing, 2012); Michael O. Martin et al., *TIMSS 2011 International Results in Science* (Chestnut Hill, MA: Boston College, and International Association for the Evaluation of Educational Achievement, IEA, Amsterdam, 2012). The evidence regarding longitudinal trends in students' science performance in Chile is somewhat inconsistent. According to SIMCE, on average, fourth-grade students' performance has remained constant since the early 2000s, while eighth graders slightly increased test scores, but only after 2011; in turn, PISA showed a significant increase in science performance for fifteen-year-old students between 2000 and 2006, and then no increase between 2006 and 2015; finally, TIMMS showed no increase in science performance for eighth graders between 1999 and 2003, but then a large increase between 2003 and 2011, and then no increase by 2015.

13. Rosa Devés and Patricia López, "Inquiry-Based Science Education and Its Impact on School Improvement: The ECBI Program in Chile," in *International Handbook of School Effectiveness and Improvement,* ed. Tony Townsend (The Netherlands: Springer, 2007), 887–902.

14. OECD, *Definition and Selection of Key Competencies* (Paris: OECD, 2005); National Research Council, *Education for Life*; Pacific Policy Research Center, *21st Century Skills for Students and Teachers* (Honolulu: Kamehameha Schools, Research & Evaluation Division, 2010); Partnership for 21st Century Skills, *The Intellectual and Policy Foundations of the 21st Century Skills Framework* (P21, 2007).

15. National Research Council, *Education for Life*.

16. Wynne Harlen and Jorge Allende, *Teacher Professional Development in Pre-Secondary School Inquiry-Based Science Education (IBSE)* (Santiago: Inter Academy Panel, 2009).

17. Ibid., 12; National Research Council, *National Science Education Standards* (Washington, DC: National Academy Press, 1996).

18. Daphne D. Minner, Abigail Jurist Levy, and Jeanne Century, "Inquiry-Based Science Instruction—What Is It and Does It Matter? Results from a Research Synthesis Years 1984 To 2002," *Journal of Research in Science Teaching* 47, no 4 (2010): 474–96.

19. In 2012, representatives from fifty countries participated in a conference devoted to emergent issues in IBSE held in Helsinki. Wynne Harlen, *Assessment & Inquiry-Based Science Education: Issues in Policy and Practice* (Trieste, Italy: Global Network of Science Academies, 2013).

20. National Research Council, *National Science Education Standards*, 23.
21. John D. Bransford, Ann L. Brown, and Rodney R. Cocking, eds., *How People Learn Brain, Mind, Experience, and School* (Washington, DC: The National Academies Press, 2000); and Steve Olson and Susan Loucks-Horsley, eds., *Inquiry and the National Science Education Standards: A Guide for Teaching and Learning* (Washington, DC: The National Academies Press, 2000).
22. Wynne Harlen, ed. *Principles and Big Ideas of Science Education* (Hatfield, UK: Association for Science Education, 2010).
23. Steve Olson and Susan Loucks-Horsley, *Inquiry and the National Science Education Standards: A Guide for Teaching and Learning* (Washington, DC: The National Academies Press, 2000); Wynne Harlen and the IAP Working Group, *Inquiry-Based Science Education: An overview for Educationalists* (Paris: IAP, 2009), Devés and López, *Inquiry-Based Science Education*; Devés and Reyes, *Principios y Estrategias*; Minner, Levy, and Century, "Inquiry-Based Science Instruction."
24. Programa de Educación en Ciencias Basado en la Indagación (ECBI), Universidad de Chile, *Evolución del Programa ECBI 2002—2012*, http://www.ecbichile.clECBI 2013; Minner, Levy, and Century, "Inquiry-Based Science Instruction."
25. Susan Loucks-Horsley et al, *Developing and Supporting Teachers for Elementary School Science Education* (Washington, DC: The National Center for Improving Science Education, 1989).
26. National Staff Development Council, 1999, in Devés and López, 2007, 895.
27. Programa de Educación en Ciencias Basado en la Indagación (ECBI), Universidad de Chile, *Generando comunidades profesionales de aprendizaje en el contexto de las ciencias basada en la Indagación* (PowerPoint slides), retrieved from www.ecbi.cl, n.d.
28. ECBI, *Generando comunidades profesionales.*
29. Alejandra Osses, Cristián Bellei, and Juan Pablo Valenzuela, "External Technical Support for School Improvement: Critical Issues from the Chilean Experience," *Journal of Educational Administration and History* 47, no. 3 (2015): 272–93.
30. Devés and López, "Inquiry-Based Science Education."
31. Devés and López, "Inquiry-Based Science Education."
32. Wyne Harlen and Jorge Allende, *Report of the Working Group on Teacher Professional Development in Pre-Secondary IBSE* (Fundacion para Estudios Biomedicos Avanzados, Facultad de Medicina, University of Chile, 2009).
33. The strategy is based on a model implemented in Seattle, Washington, public schools.
34. Rosa Devés y Pilar Reyes, "Principios y Estrategias del Programa de Educación en Ciencias Basada en la Indagación (ECBI)," *Revista Pensamiento Educativo* 41 (2007): 115–32.
35. Richard Elmore, *School Reform from the Inside Out: Policy, Practice, and Performance* (Cambridge, MA: Harvard Education Press, 2004).
36. Devés and López, "Inquiry-Based Science Education."
37. Devés and Reyes, *Principios y Estrategias.*
38. Harlen, *Assessment & Inquiry-Based Science Education.*
39. Australian Council for Educational Research, ACER, *Evaluation of the Processes and Products Related to the Production of Instruments, Field Operations and Data Management of National SIMCE Tests* (Santiago de Chile: ACER and Agency for Quality in Education, 2013).

40. Carmen Montecinos et al., *Evaluación Formativa de la Implementación del Programa ECBI* (Pontificia Universidad Católica de Valparaíso, 2008); Soledad Concha et al., Evaluación de Estrategias de Desarrollo Profesional LEM Y ECBI (Santiago: Centro de Políticas Comparadas en Educación, Universidad Diego Portales, para MINEDUC, 2010).

41. Montecinos et al., *Evaluación Formativa.*

42. Montecinos et al., *Evaluación Formativa*; Concha et al., 2010).

43. This last finding is consistent with recent evidence that showed a "negative association" between inquiry-based practices (reported by students) and science performance as measured by the PISA test (OECD, 2016). Certainly, the issue of whether this kind of evidence is a valid evaluation of the effects of inquiry-based education on student learning is a matter of controversy, not only because those studies do not allow for causal inference, but also—and even more importantly—because it is not clear that those type of tests are a valid measure of the learning goals of inquiry-based science education (see Wynne Harlen, *Assessment & Inquiry-Based Science Education: Issues in Policy and Practice* [Trieste, Italy: Global Network of Science Academies, 2013] for a detailed discussion). Mariana Huepe, "Evaluación del Programa de Educación en Ciencias Basado en la Indagación Sobre el Aprendizaje y Desempeño de Alumnos y Profesores" (BA thesis, Universidad de Chile, 2008).

44. Programa ECBI, *Generando comunidades profesionales de aprendizaje en el contexto de las ciencias basada en la Indagación*, PowerPoint presentation (Santiago, Universidad de Chile, 2014).

45. Bellei and Morawietz, "Strong Content."

46. Richard Elmore, "Getting to scale with good educational practice," *Harvard Educational Review* 66, no. 1 (1996): 1–27; David Tyack and Larry Cuban, *Tinkering Toward Utopia: A Century of Public School Reform* (Cambridge, MA: Harvard University Press, 1995).

47. Cristián Bellei et al., "School improvement trajectories: an empirical typology," *School Effectiveness and School Improvement* 27, no. 3 (2016): 275–92.

Chapter 3

The authors would like to thank the Kaifeng Foundation for providing the generous financial support to research and write this chapter.

1. "Best-Performing China Cities Report," Milken Institute, http://www.best-cities-china.org/.

2. This list of core competencies is from Qingyang's 2014 districtwide assessment, "Diversify Assessment, Deepen Equity."

3. Carol Dweck, *Mindset: The Psychology of Success* (New York: Ballantine Books, 2006).

4. Ibid.

5. "Work Report on Development of Qingyang Education Experimental Zone (2009–2013)," NIES, 2014.

6. Michael Fullan and Alan Boyle, *Big-City School Reforms: Lessons from New York, Toronto, and London* (New York: Teachers College Press, 2014).

7. Dweck, *Mindset: The Psychology of Success.*

8. Chengdu Experimental Primary School provided us with a list of its alumni and their current positions.

9. David K. Cohen and Heather C. Hill, *Learning Policy: When State Education Reform Works* (New Haven, CT: Yale University Press, 2001).

10. Richard Elmore and Deanna Burney, "Investing in Teacher Learning," in *Teaching as a Learning Profession*, ed. Linda Darling-Hammond and Gary Sykes (San Francisco: Jossey-Bass, 1999), 236–91; Willis Hawley and Linda Valli, "The Essentials of Effective Professional Development," in *Teaching as a Learning Profession*, ed. Linda Darling-Hammond and Gary Sykes (San Francisco: Jossey-Bass, 1999), 127–50; Michael S. Garet et al., "What Makes Professional Development Effective? Results from a National Sample of Teachers," *American Educational Research Journal* (2001): 915–45.

11. Sara Ray Stoelinga and Melinda M. Mangin, *Examining Effective Teacher Leadership: A Case Study Approach* (New York: Teachers College Press, 2010); Lyle Kirtman, *Leadership and Teams: The Missing Piece of the Education Reform Puzzle* (London: Pearson, 2013).

12. Interview with Li Yong, June 2016.

13. David McKenzie and Serena Dong, "China to migrant workers: Take your kids with you," CNN, February 16, 2012, http://www.cnn.com/2016/02/16/asia/china-migrant-children/.

Chapter 4

1. Translates as Active Urban School.

2. Among others, in 2015, the government of Dubai and ONU Habitat recognized EAU for being one of the most significant experiences contributing to positive life environments worldwide. In 2015, the Wharton School and the University of Pennsylvania awarded EAU first place in the Reimagine Award at the Latin-American Level, and the second place for presence learning worldwide.

3. Mariela Narváez and Luis Trujillo, "Evaluación de impacto del proyecto Escuela Activa Urbana en cuatro colegios de Manizales" (Centro de Estudios Regionales Cafeteros y Empresariales [CRECE], Manizales, Colombia, 2006); María Matijasevic, Carolina Villada, and Mónica Ramírez, "Una experiencia exitosa. Sistematización del proyecto Escuela Activa Urbana" (Centro de Estudios Regionales Cafeteros y Empresariales [CRECE], Manizales, Colombia, 2006); María Matijasevic, Beatriz Cárdenas, Gladys Buitrago, and Luis Trujillo, "Evaluación de impactos parciales del programa Escuela Activa Urbana en la Escuela Normal Superior de Manizales: Informe Final" (Centros de Estudios Regionales cafeteros y empresariales [CRECE], Manizales, Colombia, 2007).

4. Secretaría de Educación de Manizales & Fundación Luker, "Una experiencia exitosa: Sistematización de la Escuela Activa Urbana" (Manizales, Colombia, 2012).

5. Cristian Cox, Rosario Jaramillo, and Fernando Reimers, "Education and Democratic Citizenship in Latin America and the Caribbean: An Agenda for Action" (Inter-American Development Bank, Washington, DC, 2005).

6. Ministerio de Educación Nacional, "Estándares Básicos de Competencias Ciudadanas. Formar para la Ciudadanía Sí es Posible. Lo que Necesitamos Saber y Saber Hacer" (Colombia: Espantapájaros Taller, 2003).

7. In Colombia, the primary and secondary education system has eleven grades.

8. Secretaría de Educación de Manizales & Fundación Luker, "Evaluación para seres humanos activos: Una perspectiva desde la Escuela Activa Urbana" (Manizales, Colombia, 2014).

9. Ibid.

10. Juan Castellanos, *Tramas de la deserción escolar en Manizales* (Colombia: Centro Editorial de la Universidad de Caldas, 2003).

11. This theory of change has been developed by the authors of this chapter, based on documents and interviews with key stakeholders.

Chapter 5

1. Low-cost private schools (LCPSs)—sometimes referred to as low-fee private schools—include any market-oriented (nominally, for-profit) schools that depend on user fees for some or all of their operation.

2. Aditya Natraj, Monal Jayaram, Jahnavi Contractor, and Payal Agrawal, "Twenty-First-Century Competencies, the Indian National Curriculum Framework, and the History of Education in India," in Teaching and Learning for the Twenty-first Century, eds. Fernando M. Reimers and Connie K. Chung (Cambridge, MA: Harvard Education Press, 2016), 155–86.

3. http://mhrd.gov.in/sites/upload_files/mhrd/files/document-reports/AR2008-09.pdf.

4. https://www.dasra.org/cause/enhancing-youth-employability.

5. There are various professional courses available for student teachers, for example, two two-year courses like bachelor's in education and diploma in education. There are also courses that develop student teachers into para-teachers who can later become full-time teachers after serving for five years. For secondary and higher secondary, the teachers are offered different courses by different states.

6. The Education Commission (1964–1966) recommended professionalization of teacher education, development of integrated programs, comprehensive colleges of education, and internship. The National Commission on Teachers (1983–1985) recommended five-year integrated courses and internship. The National Policy on Education (NPE) (1986) recommended that the reform bring in professional orientation to the field of teaching. It recommended the launch of a Centrally Sponsored Scheme of Teacher Education. This led to the establishment of District Institutes of Education and Training (DIETs), Colleges of Teacher Education (CTEs), and Institutes of Advanced Studies in Education (IASEs)

7. The MHRD report on teacher education 2012 states that "there is an urgent need to upgrade pre-service elementary teacher education by enhancing the duration of training; making it equivalent to an integrated degree programme and locating the management and control of elementary teacher education within Universities."

8. Ibid., 14–16.

9. Ibid.

10. Natraj et al., "Twenty-First-Century Competencies, the Indian National Curriculum Framework, and the History of Education in India."

11. A recent study conducted by Young Lives and the UNICEF's Multicountry Study on the Drivers of Violence Affecting Children, "Undermining Learning: Multi Country Longitudinal Evidence on Corporal Punishment in Schools" by Hayley Jones and Kirrily Pells (2016), mentions that about 26 percent of interviewed children from India showed waning interest in schools due to physical and verbal abuse from teachers and peers. The report also analyzes how structural factors including the social, cultural, economic, legal, organizational, or policy responses interact to affect everyday violence in children's homes, schools, and communities.

12. Sharon Feiman Nemser, "From Preparation to Practice: Designing a continuum to strengthen and sustain teaching," *Teachers College Record* 103 (2001): 1013–55, www.geocities.ws/cne_magisterio/4/curricfomdocente.pdf.

13. Before post-liberalization, there had been numerous changes in the education sector, including focus on access to education for all children through government-run, large-scale projects like Sarva Siksha Abhiyan (SSA). As more schools were built, the government focused on increasing the number of teachers in schools by ensuring the student-teacher ratio. Schemes were introduced to encourage more people to become teachers. The government also introduced innovative campaigns like the enrollment drive to reach government schools for each child and ensure no child is left behind. As SSA's primary goals of access, enrollment, and retention were being addressed, during the post-liberalization period, the challenge of quality education grew. In its effort to address this challenge, the government initiated a participatory curricular debate that resulted in the articulation of the National Curriculum Framework 2005.

14. Dr. Kennedy is a consultant clinical psychologist. She is a specialist in adult mental health and learning disability. She was with the UK NHS National Health Service, where she developed and headed psychology services. She is a trainer and coach for mental health professionals. Dr. David Pearson is a consultant clinical psychologist. He is a specialist in child and adolescence services, based in the UK. He worked in NHS hospitals and is involved into research and publication of wide range of areas in child development.

15. Pages 3 and 4 of the UNICEF report on Corporal Punishment show conclusive evidence of the chilling effects of corporal punishment on children's lives.

Chapter 6

1. Sergio Cárdenas, "Curriculum Reform and Twenty-First-Century Skills in Mexico: Are Standards and Teacher Training Materials Aligned?," in *Teaching and Learning for the Twenty-First Century: Educational Goals, Policies, and Curricula from Six Nations*, eds. Fernando M. Reimers and Connie K. Chung (Cambridge, MA: Harvard Education Press, 2016), 150.

2. National Institute for Educational Evaluation, *Educational Outlook of Mexico 2014. National Education System Indicators. Basic and High School Education* (México: INEE, 2015).

3. Union of Entrepreneurs for Technology in Education, Annual Report 2014. Fifteen years for education (Mexico: UNETE, 2014).

4. Robert Yin, *Case Study Research. Design and Methods* (Thousand Oaks, CA: SAGE Publications, 2012).

5. National Institute of Statistics and Geography, "Average grade of schooling of the population of 15 years and above by the state," 2010, http://www.beta.inegi.org.mx/app/tabulados/pxweb/inicio.html?rxid=85f6c251-5765-4ec7-9e7d-9a2993a42594&db=Educacion&px=Educaci%C3%B3n_05.

6. Ministry of Education, *National Survey Report of Truancy in School Education* (Mexico: SEP, 2012).

7. National Institute for Educational Evaluation, *Educational Outlook of Mexico 2014. National Education System Indicators. Basic and High School Education* (México: INEE, 2015).

8. Cárdenas, "Curriculum Reform and Twenty-First-Century Skills in Mexico."

9. Union of Entrepreneurs for Technology in Education, Annual Report 2014.

10. Union of Entrepreneurs for Technology in Education, http://www.unete.org/, accessed June 18, 2015.

11. Concern was shared by members of the staff. As an interviewee stated, "[O]ur main actions cannot be guided exclusively by technology . . . it has to be guided by educational issues." Lluvia Martinez (manager of training and educational services, UNETE) in discussion with the authors, July 23, 2015.

12. Union of Entrepreneurs for Technology in Education, Annual Report 2014.

13. As the CEO described, "There are some basic questions that I love to ask when I visit a school. The first is to ask children what they like the most: is it your lunch break or using computers? So far, one hundred percent of the responses have been using computers! . . . Another aspect that I find helps me see the impact of our program is when I talk to teachers and I ask them about how [their students] were before, after computers arrived at the school. Usually, they link the use of computers to better attitudes from children." Alejandro Almazan (CEO, UNETE) in discussion with the authors, June 19, 2015.

14. The conditions of each locality define different schemes. In the largest urban schools, the connection type is ADSL broadband. In remote places, the service is provided via satellite. For those schools where Internet access is not possible, a server with preloaded content is the main resource used by teachers.

15. Martinez, in discussion with the authors.

16. However, three challenges for the model arise: (a) the lack of experience in the implementation of pedagogical interventions, at least when compared to the delivery and promotion of educational technology; (b) the issue of enhancing school leadership to adapt and adopt an intervention expanding educational goals; and (c) a short timeline for numerous goals, including acceptance and adoption of intervention, developing capacities, and guaranteeing sustainability of the program once facilitators move to another school.

17. See OECD, *New Insights from TALIS 2013: Teaching and Learning in Primary and Upper Secondary Education* (Paris: OECD Publishing, 2014); Eduardo Backhoff and Juan Carlos Perez-Moran, *Second International Study on teaching and learning (TALIS 2013). Results of Mexico* (Mexico: INEE, 2015).

18. Union of Entrepreneurs for Technology in Education, Annual Report 2014.

19. Martinez, in discussion with the authors.

20. Almazan, in discussion with the authors.

21. Principal, parents, and teachers.

22. Cesar Loeza (education director, UNETE), in discussion with the authors, June 19, 2015.

23. Cárdenas, "Curriculum Reform and Twenty-First-Century Skills in Mexico."

24. Union of Entrepreneurs for Technology in Education, Annual Report 2014.

25. For instance, a facilitator explained that during work at the computer lab, he let students conduct free searches through the internet to engage students in the use of technology. The facilitator considered these activities as resulting in a better collaboration among students, developing curiosity, and presenting an opportunity to provide individualized support to students. Israel Vázquez (facilitator, UNETE), in discussion with the authors, November 4, 2015. In addition, an interviewed principal reported that "metacognition is happening among teachers and is a key part of improving their teaching practices. By making their own strategies, [change in practices] will continue to happen. Perhaps the

challenge is mine, as principal, to monitor them." Guadalupe Romero (school principal), in discussion with the authors, November 5, 2015.

26. As a staff member explained, "The main challenge UNETE faces . . . is to find facilitators. We struggle a lot, because teachers graduate from a very limited educational system. The people we send to our schools are young, recently graduated, having taken only two courses on educational technology, although in most normal schools, there is no technology, or media room. They are young, unprepared, so we design manuals, tutorials, and tools that help the facilitator understand our intervention. The main challenge seems to be to find people who go to schools and believe in our project profile. We are looking for people able to convince teachers, who know how to teach, and, a key aspect for us, who have high frustration tolerance." Cesar Loeza (education director, UNETE), in discussion with the authors, June 19, 2015.

27. "Formerly, there was no monitoring program: we delivered [computers], and our goal was focused on coverage; today, we are focused on a topic of impact. We gave computers, and we assumed that the model would work, because we were anchored to the school network model. But when we returned to install the network and understand what was going on, we realized that most schools were not operating correctly due to the teacher's abilities. That was when we rephrased the program and the accompanying program first emerged. We went to 870 schools, and that was when we realized what schools really need: a person to look after them, to support them." Loeza, in discussion with the authors.

28. Haiyan Hua and Conrad Wesley Snyder Jr., "Research, Reform, and Reflection: The Three R´s of Educational Policy Analysis" (Development Discussion Paper, Harvard Institute for International Development, Harvard University, Cambridge, MA., 1999).

29. Loeza, in discussion with the authors.

30. A few facilitators commented that some teachers are not used to incorporating technology into their classes or their everyday activities, making it difficult to guide the first stages of the program, as Uriel Alvarez states: "I think the first year, they participate involuntarily, and it requires a lot of work. The previous cycle, I realized that after four months, teachers are just getting used to [technology]. And after [the intervention cycle], teachers tell me that they notice changes in the way they conduct activities, because it helps them to make informal assessments using applications like Hot Potatoes." Uriel Álvarez (facilitator, UNETE), in discussion with the authors, April 6, 2016.

31. In Mexico, one of three teachers mentioned that they would require training for using educational technology. OECD, *New Insights from TALIS 2013: Teaching and Learning in Primary and Upper Secondary Education* (Paris: OECD Publishing, 2014). In addition, a large proportion of teachers in Mexico, especially in the most remote and deprived schools, have not studied in a normal school, given that according to the TALIS 2013 study, nearly 20 percent of teachers have an educational qualification of less than ISCED level 5 (see Eduardo Backhoff and Juan Carlos Perez-Moran, *Second International Study on teaching and learning (TALIS 2013). Results of Mexico* [Mexico: INEE, 2015]). Meanwhile more than 80 percent of teachers in Mexico did not receive any formal induction to their work, compared with a 50 percent average among teachers from other countries who participated in TALIS 2013. OECD, *New Insights from TALIS 2013.*

32. Miguel Ivan Cruz (facilitator, UNETE), in discussion with the authors, November 5, 2015.

33. Another important obstacle is high teacher turnover rates. In the Mexican educational system, many teachers start their careers in poor and remote schools, moving later to urban schools. Therefore, schools with lower performance (many served by UNETE) each year have at least one or two new teachers, which probably dilutes the school's expertise on the use of educational technology in the classroom, affecting also the dynamics of the community. In fact, school principals must train novice teachers.

34. Fernando Reimers and Sergio Cárdenas, "Who Benefits from School-Based Management in Mexico?," *Prospects: Quarterly Review of Comparative Education* 37, no. 1 (2007): 37–56.

35. For instance, UNETE states that technology allows students to learn at their own pace, reducing their dependency on teachers. In addition, it assumes that when students develop technological skills and metacognition, they will become autonomous learners. However, this did not happen in the schools we visited, as many teachers and students lacked sufficient skills to develop these skills. In fact, what we observed was that different levels of mastery regarding use of technology caused students to learn at different paces, with few teachers adequately responding to this situation.

36. It works as a local network, with one server per school, storing nearly 180 GB of information, with videos, text materials, and applications for different subjects and grades.

37. James Pellegrino and Margaret Hilton, *Education for Life and Work: Developing Transferable Knowledge and Skills in the 21st Century* (Washington, DC: The National Academies Press, 2012).

Chapter 7

1. Scott Hartl, Presentation at EL Education Leadership Institute (Amherst, MA, July 2015).

2. "What is EL Education?," EL Education, https://eleducation.org/resources/what-is-el-1.

3. "Impact: By the Numbers," EL Education, https://eleducation.org/impact/by-the-numbers.

4. Ibid.

5. Ibid.

6. Ibid.

7. Ben Smith, "President Obama Visits Capital City Charter School," EL Education website, July 30, 2010, http://eleducation.org/news/president-obama-visits-capital-city-charter-school; Ben Smith, "Education Secretary Arne Duncan Visits King Middle School," EL Education website, September 7, 2010, http://eleducation.org/news/education-secretary-arne-duncan-visits-king-middle-school/

8. EL Education, "Evidence of Success" EL Education, 2011.

9. Ibid.

10. Fernando M. Reimers and Connie K. Chung, *Teaching and Learning for the Twenty-First Century: Educational Goals, Policies, and Curricula from Six Nations* (Cambridge, MA: Harvard Education Press, 2016).

11. Ron Berger, Interview with author, April 2015.

12. Jal Mehta et al., *From Quicksand to Solid Ground: Building a Foundation to Support Quality Teaching* (Cambridge, MA: Transforming Teaching Project, 2015).

13. EL Education, *Expeditionary Learning Core Practices: A Vision for Improving Schools* (New York: EL Education, 2011).

14. Anthony Bryk and Barbara Schneider, *Trust in Schools: A Core Resource for Improvement* (New York: Russell Sage Foundation, 2004).

15. EL Education, "Austin's Butterfly: Building Excellence in Student Work," 2012, https://vimeo.com/38247060.

16. National Research Council, *Education for Life and Work: Developing Transferable Knowledge and Skills in the 21st Century* (Washington, DC: The National Academies Press, 2012), https://www.nap.edu/catalog/13398/education-for-life-and-work-developing-transferable-knowledge-and-skills.

17. EL Education, *Expeditionary Learning Core Practices: A Vision for Improving Schools* (New York: EL Education, 2011), 1.

18. Ibid., 1.

19. EL Education, "What is Expeditionary Learning?," https://eleducation.org/resources/what-is-el-1.

20. Ibid.

21. Ibid.

22. Noel K. Gallagher, "About 400 Portland Middle School Students Call for Action on Climate Change," *Portland Press Herald*, December 4, 2015. http://www.pressherald.com/2015/12/04/400-portland-middle-school-students-march-for-climate-action/.

23. Ibid.

24. Richard Elmore, *School Reform from the Inside Out: Policy, Practice, and Performance* (Cambridge, MA: Harvard Education Press, 2004), 11.

25. Michael Fullan, *The Six Secrets of Change: What the Best Leaders Do to Help Their Organizations Survive and Thrive* (San Francisco: Jossey-Bass, 2011), 57.

26. Ben Levin, *How to Change 5000 Schools: A Practical and Positive Approach for Leading Change at Every Level* (Cambridge, MA: Harvard Education Press, 2008), 83.

27. Mark Conrad, Interview with author, April 2015.

28. http://www.rand.org/pubs/monograph_reports/MR945.html.

29. http://www.rand.org/pubs/issue_papers/IP175/index2.html.

Chapter 8

We would like to thank the members of the Global Education Innovation Lab of NIE's Office of Strategic Planning and Academic Quality, especially Associate Professor Ng Pak Tee for allowing us to conduct our research on the Leaders in Education Program (LEP) and for his insights into the program. We would also like to thank the LEP participants who took time out of their busy schedules for the project. Special thanks also go to Research Associates Jarrod Tam Chun Peng and Janey Ng Wee Leng for providing the initial drafts of the chapter.

1. "Education Statistics Digest 2015," Ministry of Education, Singapore (MOE), https://www.moe.gov.sg/docs/default-source/document/publications/education-statistics-digest/esd-2015.pdf.

2. Ibid.

3. "Latest Data," Department of Statistics, Singapore, http://www.singstat.gov.sg/statistics/latest-data#1.

4. "TIMSS 2015 International Results in Mathematics," TIMSS & PIRLS International Study Centre, http://timssandpirls.bc.edu/timss2015/international-results/timss-2015/

mathematics/student-achievement; "TIMSS 2015 International Results in Science," TIMSS & PIRLS International Study Centre, http://timssandpirls.bc.edu/timss2015/international-results/timss-2015/science/student-achievement; Organisation for Economic Co-operation and Development (OECD), *PISA 2015 Results (Volume I): Excellence and Equity in Education* (Paris, France: Author, 2016).

5. Sing Kong Lee and Ee Ling Low, "Balancing Between Theory and Practice: Singapore's Teacher Education Partnership Model," *In Tuition* 16, https://set.et-foundation.co.uk/publications/in-tuition/intuition-16-spring-2014/opinion-balancing-between-theory-and-practice-singapore%E2%80%99s-teacher-education-partnership-model.

6. "21st Century Competencies and Student Outcomes Framework," Ministry of Education, Singapore (MOE), https://www.moe.gov.sg/education/education-system/ 21st-century-competencies.

7. Ibid.

8. "The desired outcomes of education," Ministry of Education, Singapore (MOE), https://www.moe.gov.sg/education/education-system/desired-outcomes-of-education.

9. Swee Keat Heng, "Speech by Mr Heng Swee Keat, Minister for Education at the 17th Appointment and Appreciation Ceremony for Principals," https://www.moe.gov.sg/news/speeches/speech-by-mr-heng-swee-keat--minister-for-education-at-the-17th-appointment-and-appreciation-ceremony-for-principals--shangri-la-hotel--30-december-2014--at-310pm.

10. Chee Meng Ng, "Speech by Mr Ng Chee Meng, Acting Minister for Education at the 18th Appointment and Appreciation Ceremony for Principals," https://www.moe.gov.sg/news/speeches/speech-by-mr-ng-chee-meng--acting-minister-for-education-at-the-18th-appointment-and-appreciation-ceremony-for-principals#sthash.jQuY0Xwq.dpuf

11. Meta Krüger, "The Big Five of School Leadership Competences in the Netherlands," *School Leadership & Management* 29, no. 2, (2009): 109–127; Kenneth Leithwood, Karen Seashore Louis, Stephen Anderson, and Kyla Wahlstrom, *How Leadership Influences Student Learning* (Minneapolis, Toronto, New York: University of Minnesota, University of Toronto, and The Wallace Foundation, 2004); Ministry of Education, Singapore (MOE), "21st Century Competencies and Student Outcomes Framework."

12. Philip Hallinger and Ronald H. Heck, "Collaborative Leadership and School Improvement: Understanding the Impact on School Capacity and Student Learning," *School Leadership and Management* 30, no. 2 (2010): 95–110; Leithwood et al., *How Leadership Influences Student Learning*; Kenneth Leithwood and Ben Levin, *Assessing School Leader and Leadership Programme Effects on Pupil Learning: Conceptual and Methodological Challenges* (Nottingham, UK: Department for Education and Skills, 2005); Karen Seashore Louis, Beverly Dretzke, and Kyla Wahlstrom, "How Does Leadership Affect Student Achievement? Results From a National US Survey," *School Effectiveness and School Improvement* 21, no. 3 (2010): 315–336; Viviane M. J. Robinson, Claire A. Lloyd, and Kenneth J. Rowe, "The Impact of Leadership on Student Outcomes: An Analysis of the Differential Effects of Leadership Types," *Educational Administration Quarterly* 44, no. 5 (2008): 635–674.

13. Leithwood et al., *How Leadership Influences Student Learning*, 5.

14. Kenneth Leithwood, Alma Harris, and David Hopkins, "Seven Strong Claims About Successful School Leadership," *School Leadership and Management* 28, no. 1 (2008): 27–42.

15. Tony Bush, Ann R. J. Briggs, and David Middlewood, "The Impact of School Leadership Development: Evidence from the 'New Visions' Programme for Early Headship," *Journal of In-Service Education* 32, no. 2 (2006): 185–200.

16. Meta Krüger, Bob Witziers, and Peter Sleegers, "The Impact of School Leadership on School Level Factors: Validation of a Causal Model," *School Effectiveness and School Improvement* 18, no. 1 (2007): 1–20.

17. Robinson, Lloyd, and Rowe et al., "The Impact of Leadership on Student Outcomes: An Analysis of the Differential Effects of Leadership Types," 635–674.

18. Leithwood et al., "Seven Strong Claims About Successful School Leadership," 32.

19. Yin Cheong Cheng, "New Principalship for Globalization, Localization and Individualization: Paradigm Shift" (keynote address presented at the International Conference on Principalship and School Management Practice in the Era of Globalization: Issues and Challenges, Kuala Lumpur, 22-24 April 2003), 9.

20. Ibid., 20.

21. Organisation for Economic Co-operation and Development (OECD), "Developing Effective School Leaders," *Preparing Teachers and Developing School Leaders for the 21st Century: Lessons From Around the World* (Paris, France: Author, 2012): 14–31.

22. Organisation for Economic Co-operation and Development (OECD), "Developing Effective School Leaders"; Pak Tee Ng, "The Evolution and Nature of School Accountability in the Singapore Education System," *Educational Assessment, Evaluation and Accountability* 22 (2010): 275–292.

23. Organisation for Economic Co-operation and Development (OECD), "Developing Effective School Leaders," 19.

24. "Career Information," Ministry of Education (MOE), https://www.moe.gov.sg/careers/teach/career-information.

25. Lin A. Goodwin, Linda Darling-Hammond, and Ee Ling Low, *Empowered Educators in Singapore: How High-Performing Systems Shape Teaching Quality* (San Francisco: Jossey-Bass, 2017).

26. Ibid.

27. Pak Tee Ng, "Developing Forward-Looking and Innovative School Leaders: The Singapore Leaders in Education Programme," *Professional Development in Education* 34, no. 2 (2008): 237–255.

28. Eng Hen Ng, "Building Blocks for Education: Whole System Reform" (keynote address at the International Education Summit, Toronto, Canada, 14 September 2010).

29. Thow Yick Liang and Pak Tee Ng, "Human Resource Management and Development of Highly Intelligent Interacting Agents: A Paradigm Shift in Singapore," *International Journal of Human Resources Development and Management* 5, no. 2 (2005): 180–89.

30. Patrick Duignan, "Formation of Capable, Influential and Authentic Leaders for Times of Uncertainty" (paper presented at the Australian Primary Principals Association National Conference, Adelaide, Australia, 21-24 September 2003); Charles Handy, *The Empty Raincoat: Making Sense of the Future* (London: Random House, 1994).

31. Handy, *The Empty Raincoat: Making Sense of the Future.*

32. Elizabeth Atkinson, "The Promise of Uncertainty: Education, Postmodernism and the Politics of Possibility," *International Studies in Sociology of Education* 10, no. 1 (2000): 81–99; Michael Fullan, "Leadership for the 21st Century: Breaking the Bonds of Depen-

dency," *Educational Leadership* 55, no. 7 (1998): 6–10; Andy Hargreaves, *Teaching in the Knowledge Society: Education in the Age of Insecurity* (New York: Teachers College Press, 2003).

33. Rushworth M. Kidder, *How Good People Make Tough Choices: Resolving the Dilemmas in Ethical Living* (New York: William Morrow, 1995).

34. Michael Fullan, *The New Meaning of Educational Change*, 4th ed. (New York: Teachers College Press, 2007), 5.

35. Clive Dimmock, Dennis Kwek, and Yancy Toh, "Leadership for 21st Century Learning in Singapore's High-Performing Schools," *Educational Research and Innovation Leadership for 21st Century Learning* (2013): 107–134.

36. National Institute of Education (NIE), *LEP Handbook* (NIE, Singapore: 2016), 5.

37. Ibid., 5.

38. Thomas J. Sergiovanni, *The Principalship: A Reflective Practice Perspective*, 6th ed. (New York: Pearson, 2009); Howard Gardner, *Five Minds for the Future* (Boston: Harvard Business Review Press, 2007).

39. National Institute of Education (NIE), *LEP Handbook*, 5.

40. Ibid., 20.

41. Sergiovanni, *The Principalship: A Reflective Practice Perspective*.

42. National Institute of Education (NIE), *LEP Handbook*

43. Gardner, *Five Minds for the Future*, 2.

44. Pak Tee Ng, "Developing Singapore School Leaders to Handle Complexity in Times of Uncertainty," *Asia Pacific Education Review* 14, no. 1 (2013): 67–73.

45. Elizabeth Atkinson, "The Promise of Uncertainty: Education, Postmodernism and the Politics of Possibility"; Fullan, "Leadership for the 21st Century: Breaking the Bonds of Dependency"; Hargreaves, *Teaching in the Knowledge Society: Education in the Age of Insecurity*; Pak Tee Ng, "How Participants Understand Complexity Theory Through a School Leadership Programme in Singapore," *International Journal of Complexity in Leadership and Management* 1, no. 3 (2011): 301–313.

46. Chris Goldspink, "Rethinking Educational Reform: A Loosely Coupled and Complex Systems Perspective," *Educational Management Administration & Leadership* 35, no. 27 (2007): 27–50; Pak Tee Ng, "The Evolution and Nature of School Accountability in the Singapore Education System."

47. Pak Tee Ng, "Developing Forward-Looking and Innovative School Leaders: The Singapore Leaders in Education Programme."

48. Jean Piaget, *The Psychology of Intelligence* (Littlefield, NJ: Adams & Co, 1960).

49. Lev Semyonovich Vygotsky, *Mind in Society: The Development of Higher Psychological Process* (Cambridge, MA: Harvard University Press, 1978).

50. Kenneth J. Gergen, "The Social Constructionist Movement in Modern Psychology," *American Psychologist* 40, no. 3 (1985): 266–75.

51. Ralph Stacey, *Complex Responsive Processes in Organisations: Learning and Knowledge Creation* (London, UK: Routledge, 2001).

52. Robert L. Dilworth, "Action Learning: Bridging Academic and Workplace Domains." *Employee Counseling Today* 8, no. 6 (1996): 48–56.

53. National Institute of Education (NIE), *LEP Handbook*, 8.

54. Goldspink, "Rethinking Educational Reform: A Loosely Coupled and Complex Systems Perspective"; Pak Tee Ng, "The Evolution and Nature of School Accountability in the Singapore Education System."

55. William E. Doll Jr., *A Postmodern Perspective on Curriculum* (New York: Teachers College Press, 1993).

56. Karl Albrecht, "The Power of Bifocal Vision," *Management Review* 83, no. 4 (1994): 42; Pak Tee Ng, "Developing Singapore School Leaders to Handle Complexity in Times of Uncertainty."

57. Francis M. Duffy, "Dancing on Ice: Navigating Change to Create Whole-District School Improvement," *Organization Development Journal* 21, no. 1 (2003): 36–45.

58. Pak Tee Ng, "Developing Forward-Looking and Innovative School Leaders: The Singapore Leaders in Education Programme"

59. Andy Hargreaves and Dennis L. Shirley, *The Fourth Way: The Inspiring Future for Educational Change* (Thousand Oaks, CA: Corwin Press, 2009).

60. Pak Tee Ng, "The Phases and Paradoxes of Quality Assurance: The Case of the Singapore Education System," *Quality Assurance in Education* 16, no. 2 (2008): 112–125.

61. Shanmugaratnam Tharman, "Achieving quality: Bottom up initiative, top down support" (Speech, the MOE Work Plan Seminar 2005 at the Ngee Ann Polytechnic Convention Centre, Singapore).

62. Pak Tee Ng, "The Evolution and Nature of School Accountability in the Singapore Education System."

63. Ibid.

64. Ka-ho Mok, "Decentralization and Marketization of Education in Singapore: A Case Study of the School Excellence Model," *Journal of Educational Administration* 41, no. 4 (2003): 348–366; Pak Tee Ng, "Developing Forward-Looking and Innovative School Leaders: The Singapore Leaders in Education Programme"; Pak Tee Ng, "The Evolution and Nature of School Accountability in the Singapore Education System."

65. Pak Tee Ng, "An Examination of School Accountability From the Perspective of Singapore School Leaders," *Educational Research for Policy and Practice* 12, no. 2 (2013): 121–131.

66. "Ethos of the Teaching Profession," Academy of Singapore Teachers (AST), http://www.academyofsingaporeteachers.moe.gov.sg/professional-excellence/ethos-of-the-teaching-profession.

67. Swee Keat Heng, "Keynote address by Mr Heng Swee Keat, Minister for Education at the Ministry of Education (MOE) Work Plan Seminar 2015," https://www.moe.gov.sg/news/speeches/keynote-address-by-mr-heng-swee-keat--minister-for-education--at-the-ministry-of-education-work-plan-seminar-2015--on-tuesday--22-september-2015-at-9-15am-at-ngee-ann-polytechnic-convention-centre.

Chapter 9

1. Fernando M. Reimers and Connie K. Chung, *Teaching and Learning for the Twenty-First Century: Educational Goals, Policies, and Curricula from Six Nations* (Cambridge, MA: Harvard Education Press, 2016); James W. Pellegrino and Margaret L. Hilton, "Education for life and work. Developing transferable knowledge and skills in the 21st century," Washington, DC, National Research Council, 2012.

2. Andy Hargreaves, 2003, as cited in Clive Dimmock, Dennis Kwek and Yancy Toh, "Leadership for 21st century learning in Singapore's high-performing schools," in *Educational Research and Innovation Leadership for 21st Century Learning* (Paris: OECD, 2013), 107–34.

3. Meta Krüger, "The big five of school leadership competences in the Netherlands," *School Leadership & Management* 29, no. 2 (2009): 109–127; Keith Leithwood et al., *How leadership influences student learning* (Minneapolis; Toronto; New York: University of Minnesota, University of Toronto, and Wallace Foundation, 2004); Ministry of Education, Singapore, "21st century competencies and student outcomes framework," 2016, https://www.moe.gov.sg/education/education-system/21st-century-competencies.

4. Kenneth J. Gergen, "The social constructionist movement in modern psychology," *American Psychologist* 40, no. 3 (1985): 266–275; Ralph D. Stacey, *Complex Responsive Processes in Organisations: Learning and Knowledge Creation* (London: Routledge, 2001).

Acknowledgments

This book owes much to the generous contributions and support of numerous colleagues. Most immediately, it is the product of the research and writing of my colleagues in the Global Education Innovation Initiative who are the authors of the various chapters included in the book, and of those who supported them in their respective institutions. I appreciate that they accepted my invitation to join this effort. Collaborating with all of them has been a delight from which I have learned much.

The Global Education Innovation Initiative is a research-practice collaboration with the goal of understanding how public education systems support students in gaining the competencies necessary for meaningful civic and economic participation in the twenty-first century. The initiative encompasses work in three domains: conducting applied research that can support policy makers, leaders, and practitioners in making schools more relevant to the needs of our times; organizing informed dialogues among diverse groups of stakeholders so that they can collaborate in the adaptive challenge of transforming public education; and developing protocols and tools that can help translate policy and programmatic innovation into transformed practice in classrooms, schools, and systems.

Many individuals and institutions have generously supported the realization of this vision, from its very start when I traveled around the world looking for institutional collaborators when this project was just an idea, to today. I appreciate the trust, support, and productive fellowship of our research partners in now ten countries, in addition to the numerous partners who have participated in facilitating informed dialogues in those and other countries, contributing in this way to the development of the necessary collective leadership so that schools empower students to become architects of their own lives and committed members of their communities. I am grateful to the many collaborators who have developed curriculum and other resources to help execute the vision of a transformative education for the twenty-first century. I am also appreciative of the many contributions of Connie Chung to the research presented in this book and to other work of the initiative during the first four years of this effort.

I am most grateful to the members of our advisory board: David Barth, Luis Enrique García de Brigard, Jim Champy, Akhil Gupta, Arjun Gupta, Charito Kruvant, Luther Luedtke, Charlie McCormack, Leonard Schlesinger, and David Weinstein for their wise counsel as we advance on the ambitious journey of contributing to the transformation of public education globally. I am also very appreciative of the financial support provided by Akhil Gupta, Charito Kruvant, and Luis Enrique García de Brigard to this project.

A grant from the Jacobs Foundation supported the Initiative during our first four years, including the research reflected in this book. Simon Sommer, our project officer at the Foundation, was a valuable supporter and thought partner, and a delight to work with.

Many colleagues at other institutions have been generous in providing opportunities to disseminate the ideas generated through the initiative. Those conversations have, in turn, educated us and expanded our thinking. I appreciate the support of Oon-Seng Tan and the late Sing Kong Lee of the National Institute of Education of Singapore, Irina Bokova and the late Gwang Jo Kim of UNESCO, Wendy Kopp and her colleagues at Teach for All, Vikas Pota at the Varkey Education Foundation, Stavros Yannouka at the World Innovation Summit for Education, Robert Adams at the National Education Association Foundation, Rebecca Winthrop at the Brookings Institution, Stephanie Hirsch at Learning Forward, and Deborah Delisle at the ASCD.

At home, at the Harvard Graduate School of Education, I am indebted to many colleagues who supported this work in big and small ways: my assistants, Kristin Foster and Lee Marmor; Helen Page in the Office of Sponsored Research; Jim Ryan, who was the Dean of HGSE during the last four years, and his predecessor, Kathleen McCartney, who provided seed funding to get the initiative started. Jack Jennings as Executive Dean for Administration, Keith Collar as Associate Dean for Planning and Outreach, Daphne Layton as Senior Associate Dean for Development, and Steve Hyde and Mitalene Fletcher in Programs in Professional Education have been generous advocates for the Initiative and contributed good ideas and support to expand the reach of this work.

My colleagues on the HGSE faculty from whom I continue to learn and who inspire me provide the collaborative and generative context that makes this work possible. And, of course, my graduate students, from whom I learn every day and who collaborate in just about every aspect of the work covered by the Initiative.

It is always a joy to work with Douglas Clayton and his colleagues at the Harvard Education Publishing Group. Their commitment to producing high-quality publications that advance our understanding of education and its practice is inspiring and helpful. I am grateful to Christopher Leonesio, Laura Cutone Godwin, and Christina DeYoung for their good work in the preparation and distribution of this book.

I am especially grateful to Ana Teresa del Toro, whose intelligent and exact editing has greatly improved the presentation of the ideas in this book.

Finally, I thank those of you, the readers of these pages, who have invited us into conversation with your own thinking and efforts to transform education for a better world. Ultimately, if any of the ideas in this book make a difference, it will be because of how you make them your own.

Fernando M. Reimers
Global Education Innovation Initiative
Harvard Graduate School of Education

About the Editors

Fernando M. Reimers is the Ford Foundation Professor of the Practice of International Education and director of the Global Education Innovation Initiative and of the International Education Policy Masters Program at Harvard University. An expert in the field of global education, his research and teaching focus on understanding how to educate children and youth so they can thrive in the twenty-first century.

Connie K. Chung is a researcher and former high school English teacher who works with education organizations that are focused on ensuring young people can thrive in a rapidly changing world. She received her BA, EdM (Teaching and Curriculum and International Education Policy), and EdD from Harvard University.

About the Contributors

Roberto Arriaga is the head of staff at the Center for Regional Cooperation on Adult Education in Latin America and the Caribbean (CREFAL). He holds a master's degree in public policy and administration from the Centre for Research and Teaching in Economics (CIDE), where he worked as a research assistant.

Cristián Bellei is an associate researcher of the Center for Advanced Research in Education and an associate professor in the Department of Sociology, both at the University of Chile. He previously worked at the Chilean Ministry of Education and for UNICEF in Chile. His main research areas are educational policy, school effectiveness, and school improvement. He has published extensively about quality and equity in Chilean education. Bellei received his doctorate in education from the Harvard Graduate School of Education.

Francisco Cabrera is the director of research at the Center for Regional Cooperation on Adult Education in Latin America and the Caribbean (CREFAL). He was assistant professor at the Centre for Research and Teaching in Economics (CIDE). His main research areas are economics of education, educational policy, and program evaluation. Cabrera received his doctorate in economics from the University of Sussex.

Sergio Cárdenas is the director-general of the Center for Regional Cooperation on Adult Education in Latin America and the Caribbean (CREFAL), and associate professor at the Center for Economics Research and Teaching in Economics (CIDE) (on leave). He holds an EdD from Harvard Graduate School of Education and is the editor of *Reformas y Políticas Educativas*, a journal published by Fondo de Cultura Económica.

Silvia Diazgranados Ferráns is the senior researcher for education at the International Rescue Committee (IRC), an international organization that is the global leader in humanitarian aid and protection of human rights in contexts of emergency. Silvia leads IRC's global research agenda for education as well as an internal team focused on education research, with a focus on identifying the effect of education interventions on the access to safe learning environments and the academic and socio-emotional outcomes of at-risk children in conflict and crisis-affected settings. Silvia holds an EdD in human development and education and a MA in prevention science and practice from the Harvard Graduate School of Education, and BA degrees in psychology and philosophy from the University of Los Andes, Colombia. Silvia is the author of several peer-reviewed articles and book chapters that explore issues related to socio-emotional development, moral decision making, school climate, violence prevention, and citizenship education.

María Figueroa Cahnspeyer is the dean of the education faculty at the Universidad Externado de Colombia. María has participated as adviser on educational and assessment issues to several institutions including ICFES (Colombian Institution for Education Evaluation), the Ministry of Education of Colombia, the Ministry of Education in Dominican Republic, Teach for Colombia, and several educational foundations. She was also part of the team that developed the new teacher evaluation system in Colombia. María previously worked as a professor and a researcher at CIFE (Center of Investigation and Formation in Education) in Universidad de los Andes, working in areas such as learning and assessment of different subjects, teacher evaluation, and evaluation of generic skills. María is a biologist and earned a master's degree in education from Columbia University, and a PhD in education from Stanford University.

Luis Felipe Martínez-Gómez is a teacher at Colegio los Nogales and Universidad Externado in Bogotá, Colombia. He has worked in several research, public policy, and consultancy projects with the World Bank and Universidad Externado. His main research interests are teaching, curriculum, and the development of socio-emotional skills. Felipe holds an EdM in international education policy from the Harvard Graduate School of Education, and is an alumni and founding corps member of Teach for Colombia.

Monal Jayaram is the cofounder of Piramal Foundation for Education Leadership (PFEL) and director of Center of Excellence for Social and Emotional Learning, Assessments, at the foundation. Throughout her professional life, she has been an educator to children, youth, and education leaders. Monal has trained and worked with more than three thousand teachers, school leaders, and district leaders with an aim to improve students' learning and holistic growth. She plays a significant role in policy and curriculum discussions in India and works with national experts from NCSL and NCERT as well as global experts from OECD, HGSE, New York University, and KEDI to build innovative interventions and tools. She has twenty years of experience in the field of education and expertise in creating contextualized and successful solutions for the transformation of education in India. She is also the coauthor of the chapter on India in GEII's first book, *Teaching and Learning for the Twenty-First Century*, edited by Fernando M. Reimers and Connie K. Chung.

Xueqin Jiang is a China-based educator and writer. He advises Chinese schools on how to teach creativity, and writes for a variety of Chinese and global media. He is on the selection committee of the Global Teacher Prize, is a Fellow of the Royal Society of Arts (RSA), and was formerly education editor of the *New York Times* Chinese website. From 2008 to 2012, he built and managed study-abroad programs at two of China's most prestigious public schools—Shenzhen Middle School and Peking University High School—to teach Chinese students creativity, critical thinking, and global citizenship. In April 2014, Jiang published *Creative China*, which discusses his education reform efforts.

Ee-Ling Low is dean of teacher education and professor of education (applied linguistics and teacher learning) at the National Institute of Education (NIE), Nanyang Technological University (NTU). She was previously chief planning officer, Director's Office. She has led a series of international research projects on World English, teacher education, and learning in Singapore. She has also served as an international expert on initial teacher preparation for the OECD Teaching and Learning International Survey (TALIS).

Zhijuan (Charlotte) Ma is the director of education innovation in the 21st Century Education Research Institute based in Beijing. She leads the initiative of the Learners' Innovation Forum on Education (LIFE) that promotes cross-sector research, dialogue, and action. She received her doctorate in politics from Peking University. Her research focuses on innovation policy and management.

Liliana Morawietz is assistant researcher at the Center for Advanced Studies in Education at Universidad de Chile, and doctoral researcher at Leiden University and Diego Portales University. She holds a BA in anthropology from Universidad de Chile, and an MA in oral history from Columbia University. Her research focuses on education quality and effectiveness, and on the nondisciplinary contents of schooling.

Aditya Natraj is the cofounder and director of Piramal Foundation for Education Leadership (PFEL). PFEL is a change management organization that supports leadership development of state leaders, district leaders, and school leaders to improve life chances for all students. Through his organization, Aditya currently works with 1,400 school leaders, 1,400 teachers, 4,200 district leaders, and 1,200 state leaders across fifteen states in India to effect systemic change. He also is the founder of an innovative and grounded social–change-making fellowship program known as the Gandhi Fellowship, a two-year full-time program to train young people in leading social change. His organization impacts education transformation in India through developing leadership, improving processes, and deploying technology in the public education system. With over fifteen years of experience in the domain of education and an expertise in behavior change in youth and education leaders, Aditya has been a recipient of the Ashoka Fellowship, Echoing Green Fellowship, Aspen India Fellowship, and the Times Now Amazing Indian award in the education category. He is associated with many organizations in India as a mentor and is on their boards. He is also the coauthor of the chapter on India in GEII's first book, *Teaching and Learning for the Twenty-First Century*, edited by Fernando M. Reimers and Connie K. Chung.

Oon-Seng Tan is director of the Centre for Research in Child Development (CRCD). He was previously director of the National Institute of Education (NIE), in Singapore, where he played a significant role in enhancing teacher education and revitalizing NIE's preparation programs to raise the image and professionalism of teachers. Prior to his directorship, he was dean of teacher education at NIE where he spearheaded the Teacher Education for the 21st Century (TE21) initiative. He was also one of the first board directors of the National Institute of Early Childhood Development (NIEC). He is editor-in-chief of *Educational Research for Policy & Practice* (ERPP) and lead editor of the *Asia Pacific Journal of Education* (APJE).

Index